THE *Everlasting* ARMS

THE *Everlasting* ARMS

BEVERLY SCELLATO

LitPrime
"Your story is our priority"

LitPrime Solutions
21250 Hawthorne Blvd
Suite 500, Torrance, CA 90503
www.litprime.com
Phone: 1-800-981-9893

Published by LitPrime Solutions   03/28/2022

ISBN: 978-1-955944-72-4(sc)
ISBN: 978-1-955944-73-1(hc)
ISBN: 978-1-955944-74-8(e)

Library of Congress Control Number: 2022906127

CONTENTS

Foreword. vii

Chapter 1. Aggie's World 1

Chapter 2. Marika's World. 37

Chapter 3. Two Worlds Collide .49

Chapter 4. Beginning the Path toward Discovery. 55

Chapter 5. Marika's Secret 73

Chapter 6. An Interpreter. 87

Chapter 7. Pulling it together. 133

Chapter 8. Startling Revelations. 161

Chapter 9. Reunion 185

Chapter 10. At the Altar. 219

Afterword 227

FOREWORD

T he places in this story are places which were important in the author's childhood. Although the events depicted in this work of fiction take place before my birth, I have a heritage of stories and events stored in my memory. This work of fiction incorporates many mountain legends and folk tales my grandparents—primarily my grandmother—told me when I spent the night at her house.

Since the events which are portrayed in this story occur near the end of the Great Depression and most readers had not yet been born, a word of explanation about the setting seems appropriate.

The setting of this novel is Mohegan, located in McDowell County, West Virginia. Mohegan is a real place of which only a skeleton remains today. However, the events and characters in this story are fictitious and contrived based upon the imagination and the memories of the author who grew up in this area. Mohegan in this writing is meant to picture a typical coal mining camp (community) during the Great Depression.

A bit of the history of this region of West Virginia will help you better understand the interaction of the characters portrayed. Southern West Virginia is rich in one thing—coal. As long as the demand for coal continued, southern West Virginia flourished. Coal mining made McDowell County the richest county in America at one point in its history. Today, it is the poorest county in West Virginia, which is one of the poorest states in the country.

Prior to the depression, the coal companies' operations resembled that of a feudal kingdom during the Middle Ages. All the workers lived in a community of company owned houses located within walking distance of the coal processing plant called a tipple. The company store was situated nearby. The miners were paid with company money called script; when sick, they and their families were treated by the company doctor. On payday, their rent and fees for other "company services" were deducted from their pay. The saying,"Coal is King", could be more aptly stated, "The Coal Company is King". Every aspect of life in a coal camp was dictated and controlled by the company.

Because the Great Depression brought the closure of most mining operations, it broke the grip that the coal companies held over their employees and opened the path for the unionization of the industry. Legislation passed under the influence of Roosevelt's New Deal encouraged industrial cooperation on wages and prices and collective bargaining. As a result, the United Mine Workers succeeded in unionizing most of the coal mining operations in McDowell County. Many of the unemployed miners returned to work with higher wages, but the increased labor costs and competition from other energy sources led to increased mechanization of the mines. This presented a revolution in the way that coal was mined and the way that coal miners' families lived. Gradually the grip of the coal companies on their employees diminished. One by one, the company stores, which were a constant reminder of the company's domination, disappeared from the coal camps in McDowell County. Many of the foundations of those buildings still remain as scars of a by-gone era.

West Virginia was one of the states hardest hit by the Great Depression (1929-41). Unemployment exceeded 80% in some counties. The coal mining industry underwent wrenching changes during this time. In the early stages of the Depression, the industry suffered from a virtual collapse as mining companies failed and unemployment grew. Coal camps were idle and thousands of miners and their families were stranded. Those who had the means to do so made their way out of the hills to vie for the few chances of employment in the industrial cities farther north. The escape of thousands of desperate families who rode the empty freight trains on the Norfolk and Western Railroad is well documented. The railroad which was built to take coal to distant mills and markets became the means of miners' departure.

With the election of Franklin Roosevelt, came a measure of optimism and hope that there was relief in store for the country. One of the programs of Roosevelt's New Deal was the Civilian Conservation Corps (CCC) which put young men to work on conservation projects in West Virginia and elsewhere. The State Park System in West Virginia benefited greatly from the CCC projects.

Another government program that benefited unemployed coal miners was the Works Progress Administration (WPA). The WPA offered work for the unemployed and built needed facilities throughout the nation. West Virginia benefited from numerous WPA projects. They built roads, hospitals, schools, bridges and health facilities. Several of the projects were built in McDowell county and the surrounding counties. The workers were paid a wage which was generally less than earned at the mines but it helped put food on their tables.

I wanted to try, in my humble way, to tell the story of a family of my grandparent's generation during the latter part of the Great Depression. It's a story of the faith of one family and God's sustaining grace through the trials of their life. This time period in history represents the prime of life for my grandparents, who stayed in the hills to raise their family in a "coal camp" in southern West Virginia.

Beverly Urps Scellato

The eternal God is thy refuge, and underneath
are the everlasting arms.

Deuteronomy 33:27a

The Everlasting Arms

CHAPTER ONE

Aggie's World

It was Christmas Day 1936. She rose from the chair where she had spent the night at the bedside of Alvin, her eldest son. She pulled back the curtains from the window to reveal the early morning light. The frost on the branches of the trees along the ridge shone like sequined lace as the sun crept over the tops of the mountains. In the dimness of the early morning, she could see her. She was sitting in her usual spot at the community well. It was a cold frosty morning and yet she sat there seemingly unaffected by the cold. No one else had ever seen her—not even John. She wore a dark veil over her face so it was impossible to see her features. She just appeared at the well from time to time. She was there and then she was gone. Agnes did not believe in ghosts but this made her wonder.

A movement on the bed grabbed her attention. She hurried over to check on Alvin, her sick son. She felt his head—he didn't seem as feverish as last night. *Good, she thought, maybe he's made a turn for the better.* She and her husband John had given him an icy bath on Christmas Eve to bring the fever down. The new doctor in the camp had suggested it. Maybe it had worked. Alvin was so desperately ill. The doctor said he had "the throat fever". The best thing to do was to try to get him to drink water which had been boiled and keep him quiet. He said to give him 2 aspirins when his fever went up. His body would have to fight off the illness on its own. The most important thing she could do was to not let his fever go too high—he could go into convulsions.

Making sure he was covered, she pulled the several layers of homemade quilts up to his chin. She made a mental note that she would have to shave him this morning. The Jones family was coming to visit him today. In the few months before he got sick, Alvin had been keeping company with Susan Jones from Roderfield. Susan's mother, Mrs. Jones had sent a letter saying they planned to visit on Christmas Day. She was bringing some of Alvin's favorite foods. She did not know he was too ill to eat.

As she entered the kitchen of the company house which the Wertz family called home, she was pleased to see John in his usual spot at the table. As was his morning custom, he was drinking a cup of "johnny bull" tea, as he called it. She thanked him for stoking the fire in the cook stove and for making the coffee. She poured herself a cup and joined him at the table.

"Alvin's cooler this mornin'. Our ice bath must've worked. His fever never went back up overnight. I thank the Lord for that."

Then she added, "Do you 'member that the Jones' are comin' this afternoon?"

John nodded and took a sip of his tea.

"I'd like to get the ham I put back for Christmas out of the smoke house so I can get it in to bakin' early. Would you git it for me? I need you to fetch in some water too. I don't wanna go out to the well. She's out there agin this mornin'. She's jist a-sittin' on the step. It seems like she's a-waitin' fur me. She's dressed in black with a veil all covered up like she's in mournin'. Reckon she's the death angel comin' to take our Alvin?"

"No, I don't!" John exclaimed. "Honest to Pete, Aggie, I don't reckon what's got in to you! Ain't nobody 'cept you sees the woman. It's your 'magination. Shake it off."

"Can't reckon why I'm the only one who's seen 'er. I first seen 'er about the time Alvin got so sick. It's spooky. She always runs off when I seen her. She skeers me. I reckon she ain't never tried to hurt me or even to touch me fur that matter--but I'm still skeered. It's like she's got somthun' to say but jist can't say it. I can't figure what to make of it all."

After a few minutes of silence, Aggie said, "John, we're gonna make it through this. I just know God will bring us through. I feel like we are being held by the Everlasting Arms. Do you feel like that? I know things looks bad for the mines and for things in this valley. We can't reckon on if the mines'll ever come back. And if'n they don't come back what will we do? I know all that but I ain't one tiny bit afraid, are you?"

Looking at her and studying her face, he smiled and said, "Well, I declare, my Aggie, if y'ain't a-quotin' scripture to me."

Then reaching for his Bible which lay near his elbow, he said, "Let me see if I can find it. I know it's in Deuteronomy. Here it is, Deuteronomy 33:27: *The eternal God is thy refuge, and underneath are the everlasting arms.*"

He continued, "I know that there's a promise made to Israel but I reckon it speaks to us, too, 'cause it talks 'bout God's constant care and providin'. When you think on them everlasting arms, your faith will just grow natural like 'cause you are relyin' on God."

John was a quiet man who did more listening than talking. Aggie had a lot of things to talk to him about today. There was a lot of catching up to do. He had been away for a few months working with the WPA in Beckley. They had two projects going over there. They were building a sanitarium to treat tuberculosis patients and a court house for Raleigh County.

John was a coal miner but the mines had shut down over 2 years ago. They were thankful he found work with the Works Progress Administration. The various government projects designed to provide temporary employment to the unemployed during the economic depression were located all over the United States. Many of them were in the southern part of the state of West Virginia. John enjoyed the work far more than the work in the mines. He could use some of the skills he learned on the farm. The downside was that he was gone from home most of the time.

John Wertz was born and raised on a farm in Smyth County Virginia. When they were first married, he and Agnes had come to this valley because there were jobs in the coal mines. John never forgot his "farm education", as he called it. He and Agnes fed several families in the valley from their garden each summer. Agnes loved the soil and growing things as much as he did. Coal mining became a necessity of his life but he never got used to working in the dark tunnels of the deep mines. In the winter, he would go down into the pits in the darkness of the early morning, work all day in the dark tunnels and come out when the sun was setting. It was a battle of the mind to keep from allowing the circumstances to drag him down. When the mines were going at full capacity, he worked ten hours a day six days a week mostly crawling along on all fours picking the clumps of coal from the shallow seams. Some days he worked as a picker and some days he was a loader, shoveling coal into the car.

Coal mining was one of the most dangerous occupations in the world in the 1930's and 40's. When the women of the valley kissed their men as they left for work each morning, there was a real fear they might not return. Such was the life of the coal miner and his family. When the alarm sounded at the mine, every wife in the valley rushed to mine headquarters praying with each step that it was not her man this time. In many respects, the shadow of death always hung over the valley.

Many of John's fellow miners found solace in the bottle. During the years of prohibition, a lucrative business developed in the hollers of this valley and every valley in the county. "Corn Likker" was easy to find and it was cheap. When prohibition had been lifted, the demand for legal liquor was great and the prices rose too high for the average laborer to afford. This was especially true for the miners. Because they were paid mostly in company script which could be spent only at the company store, a coal miner never had much change in his pocket. If he were of a mind to drink liquor, homemade brew was the practical choice—it was pure and had high alcohol content. Because it was made in secret and the work was done mostly during the night hours, it became known as 'moonshine'.

Aggie was glad John had two days off so he could be home for Christmas. She missed those days when he came home after work caked with coal dust from the mines. She even missed carrying and heating the water for his daily bath. It was hard on them but at least he was close to home.

John and Agnes were both thankful he was able to find work and earn some money. They were better off than most. Since they had hogs they always had bacon and ham in the smoke house for the cold months. Their plentiful garden provided them food all summer. There were home-canned vegetables, potatoes, onions and carrots in the root cellar to feed the family until the next growing season. They were careful to preserve as much as possible either by canning, pickling, preserving or smoking. The forests which surrounded them yielded a bounty of berries in the summer for jams and jellies. Apples wrapped in pages from the Sears Roebuck and Montgomery Ward's catalogs kept well in the coolness of the root cellar. Strawberries from the garden were a spring time delight every member of the family looked forward to. They had a cow and chickens for milk and eggs. But they needed cash money to buy flour, sugar, cornmeal, salt and baking powder and of course, coffee and tea. John's WPA job provided these things.

During the long weeks when Alvin was so sick, she was mostly alone in taking care of him. Her daughter Louanna came and helped when she could. Although she was two younger than Alvin, Louanna was married and lived in Hemphill with her husband, Reginald, and her in laws, the Lovins family.

Their second son, nineteen year old Joseph, had been working with the CCC at Panther. The crew Joe worked with was building a State Park along the Kentucky State Line. She was glad to have him home for Christmas week. He had ridden the train home from Iaegar to Davy and hitched a ride to Mohegan. He had to be back by January 2nd. The two younger boys, Jim and Dan, 18 and 14, respectively, stayed at home. After school, they helped with chopping wood and taking care of the animals. They were a big help but she needed her John with her.

When John had walked in the kitchen door yesterday, he said, "Hey, Aggie, I got good news. After Christmas, the WPA is startin' a work project in Davy. We'll be a-buildin' sidewalks and pavin' streets over there. That's practically in our backyard. And it looks like a project that could last a few months. Since Davy is so close, I'll be able to come home at night. And they run a bus from Welch to Davy ever' day to carry the workers. Ain't God good?"

She had been so excited by the news she jumped up from where she sat and hugged him. "Hallelujah! That there's the best Christmas present I ever did get! God is good, indeedy" she exclaimed.

When the Jones family arrived about two o'clock, the house smelled of baking ham and buttermilk biscuits. Aggie had met the Jones family on only one occasion so the situation was a bit awkward. When they came in, she led them to Alvin's room. She had bathed and shaved him and then propped him up in bed. He looked pale and gaunt. It was obvious he had lost weight—a lot of it. She wondered what Susan thought.

Susan was stunned when she saw him. He had his eyes shut. She thought that he looked like a corpse. Tears were running down her cheeks as she approached the bed. "Hi, Alvin", she said.

He opened his eyes and muttered in a tone so low it was barely audible, "Hi Susan. I didn't know you were coming. I'm sorry you have to see me like this. The doctor says you can catch this so stay back. I don't want you to get sick too."

"Okay, I'll stop here. We just wanted to see you and let you know we're praying for you to get better. I miss you and I'm so sorry you're sick. Mom made the chocolate cake you like so much. I hope you will feel like eating some of it. I think you need to eat something—you've lost a lot of weight."

"I'm going to get better. You wait and see. Thanks for the cake and thanks for coming." He whispered. Then he closed his eyes and seemed to drift off to sleep again.

Susan walked out of the bedroom and nearly collapsed in her father's arms, her body shaking with sobs. "I didn't dream he was so sick, Mrs. Wertz. I just didn't know." She managed to mutter between sobs. "I've been praying for him. Now, I'm going to be praying harder.

I'll ask all the people at our church to pray. I believe God answers our prayers, don't you."

Aggie walked over and put her arms around Susan and said, "I surely do believe in prayers. You keep prayin' honey. I believe God is going to heal him. I know we're doing all we can for him. I believe God is holding us in His everlasting arms."

After Susan had recovered from her shock and the situation had calmed, the Wertz's and the Jones's sat down to Christmas dinner. Since the dining room had been made into a bedroom for Alvin, they all crowded around the table which sat in the middle of the kitchen.

John bowed his head and began to bless the meal. "Thank you, Lord for the food we are about to eat on this blessed Christmas Day. Many of our friends and neighbors are hungry today but You have chosen to favor us and we are thankful. We are glad to have the Jones family with us to share all these good things. And Lord, if it's Your will, please touch Alvin's body and heal him. Amen."

They feasted on ham, green beans with potatoes, pickled beets, buttermilk biscuits and homemade apple butter. Alvin's favorite chocolate cake was served for dessert.

As the last slice of cake was consumed, Mrs. Jones said, "Tell Alvin we ate all his cake. It will be my honor to bake him another when he gets well."

John said, "The sick pigs don't have a chance around here." They all laughed.

When the Jones' had taken their departure, Aggie set about making ham biscuits with the leftover ham and biscuits from dinner. She placed one of her prized bread and butter pickles on the top of each. She stacked them in a metal lunch box with a tight fitting lid and put them on the back porch. She knew the tin box would be empty by morning but she never saw who took the food she put out each night. When she began the practice of putting leftover food on the porch, she assumed it was men from the trains who came and took the food each night. But now the trains were not running as much. She wondered if it was the woman at the well who took the food.

When the New Year dawned, Aggie was beginning to despair of her son's condition. It seemed that he had been sick forever. In reality, it had been almost a month now. She had grown weary of the struggle and worry. Many nights she had paced the floor and prayed. She did not want to lose hope that he would get better. She focused on scriptures that she remembered:

> *Fear thou not; for I am with thee: be not dismayed; for I am thy God: I will strengthen thee; yea, I will help thee; yea, I will uphold thee with the right hand of my righteousness. Isaiah 41:10*

> *Be careful for nothing; but in every thing by prayer and supplication with thanksgiving let your requests be made known unto God. And the peace of God, which passeth all understanding, shall keep your hearts and minds through Christ Jesus. Philippians 4:6-7*

That's what Aggie did—she poured out the desires and longings of her heart to God as she paced the floor night after night. She talked to Him about everything that was on her mind—even the woman at the well. In the process, she received the promised peace that propelled her through the uncertainties of the next day and helped her to focus on the everlasting arms.

Alvin was 25 years old and she was caring for him like a baby— bathing his feverish body and trying to get water down his throat. Although she had done more than her share of nursing in her life, she dreaded the various tasks involved. As she lovingly tended her son, she thought about working in the garden tending to the growing of vegetables and flowers. She anticipated the fragrance of newly turned soil in the spring. How she hoped and prayed he would be better by the time the winter turned to spring. She wanted to put out a bigger garden this spring. There were so many hungry families in Mohegan.

The sun was well up and there was a balmy feel in the air. She opened the window in Alvin's room to give him some fresh air. The soft breeze fluttered the curtains. Alvin stirred and moaned as he felt the breeze reach his bed.

"Good mornin', Alvin and Happy New Year. It's 1937. We got to git you well. The air is a little warmer today so I opened the window. How does that feel? Breathe in deep. The air is stale in here. I'll close the window in a few minutes—I don't want you to get too cold. Tell me if you get cold."

She pulled up a chair close to his bed and leaning close to his ear she whispered:

The Lord is my Shepherd, I shall not want.

He maketh me to lie down in green pastures.

He restoreth my soul.

He leadeth me in the paths of righteousness for His name's sake.

Yea, though I walk through the valley of the shadow of death, I will fear no evil.

For thou art with me.

Thy rod and thy staff, they comfort me.

Thou preparest a table before me in the presence of mine enemies. My cup runneth over.

Surely goodness and mercy shall follow me all the days of my life and I will dwell in the house of the Lord forever.

She hoped she got it right. Since she had never gone to school, she could barely read. She had to learn Bible verses by memorizing what she heard.

Then she said, "Alvin, I miss you reading the Bible to me. I love those precious words."

She got up to close the window. As she pulled the curtains together, her gaze went to the well. Although it was a little later in the morning than usually observed, there she was in her usual place. As Aggie watched, she stood. *She is a small framed woman, she thought, she is much smaller than me. I wish I knew who she is.* And then she was gone—she seemed to evaporate into thin air.

The next day was Thursday. That was the day the doctor came to Mohegan. The doctor worked for the coal company and even though the mines were not working, he kept regular office hours. The fact the doctor still came weekly kept the miners hoping the mines would indeed open again. Aggie walked over to the doctor's office. As she crossed the swinging bridge, she thought about what she would tell the doctor. She desperately wanted him to come to see Alvin.

Dr. R. C. Bondy had grown up in Davy and graduated top of his class at Welch High School in 1927. He had recently graduated top of his class from Medical School in St. Louis. He passed up big city opportunities to come back to the valleys he knew and loved. The R. C. stood for Roy Campbell. Everybody called him R. C. or just Doc. He was brilliant in diagnosis and the practice of medicine but had not always demonstrated common sense. When he was a young teenager, he had lost part of his right leg while trying to jump a train in Davy. Now, as a 28 year old full -fledged doctor, he limped heavily with a wooden leg. Seemingly unhampered and unaffected by the lack of two perfect limbs, he carried out his duties with compassion and a cheerful attitude.

The town of Davy was located about four miles from Mohegan as the crow flies. Its main street was built on a narrow strip of land between the Tug River and the Norfolk and Western Railroad. It was a commercial center for the cluster of mining camps which surrounded it, nestled in the hollers of northern McDowell County. Along its single street were situated grocery stores, a dry goods store, a filling station and garage with mechanic on duty, taverns and a movie theater to provide supplies and entertainment for the residents of Davy and Asco, Twin Branch, Marytown and Mohegan. Additionally, there were several churches which were each filled to near capacity on Sundays. The school building housing Davy Elementary and Junior High School was the largest building in the town and provided education for the children from the surrounding area. Unlike the uniformity of the various coal camps which surrounded it, the homes in Davy reflected the different occupations and economic status of their owners. They were all different and individually owned. Davy was the center of business and entertainment for the area.

Doctor Bondy had his main office in Davy in the back room of the furniture store, which was owned and operated by his brother. In addition to office hours in Davy, he served each of the other communities where he maintained office hours on certain days of the week.

When Aggie arrived at the doctor's office, she was surprised to see about 15 patients ahead of her. As she waited, she was aware of the coughs and sniffles of those who were waiting. She did not want to catch whatever they had. She remembered the great flu epidemic of 1918 when her grandfather and grandmother had both died. The memory of the suffering and death in this coal camp still brought her pain and was something she wanted to forget.

When the doctor appeared to call the next patient, he noticed her sitting in the waiting room. He said, "Mrs. Wertz, I guess you are coming about Alvin. I will be over to see him just as soon as I finish with office hours. Okay?"

She replied, "Thank you, doctor. I will tell him."

On her way home, she stopped by the post office to check the mail. The postmaster handed her three letters and a seed catalog. As she glanced at the pictures, she thought, *Spring is coming! John and I will have fun planning the garden. I love getting the seed catalog it makes winter bearable.* As she made her way back to the house there was a little skip in her step. She had a lot of trust in this young doctor and for some unknown reason she was feeling optimistic today. Maybe it was the seed catalog which contributed to her state of mind—it was the harbinger of better days.

She laid the mail on the table for John to read and went about her duties of getting ready to feed her family the evening meal. Earlier, she had put on a pot of dried beans to cook. She quickly checked to see if she needed to add water. Then she went to the smoke house and pulled down a string of smoked sausage. *She thought, this will go good with the beans and some corn bread.*

When she got back to the house, Dr. Bondy was driving up in his new car. She walked into the house with him and into Alvin's room.

Alvin roused up slightly when she and the doctor arrived.

Dr. Bondy pulled up a straight backed chair beside the bed. He shook Alvin and said, "Alvin, I need to talk to you about something. I need you to wake up because this is important and I know you will want to hear what I have to say."

He waited a moment for Alvin to rouse and straighten up in the bed. Then he continued, "I've been reading about your condition in the latest medical journals. You have what is called 'Strep throat.' It is a serious infection caused by a germ called Streptococcus. People all over the world are suffering from it and up to now there's not really been any good treatment except salt water gargles and painting the throat with purple tincture. The good news is most patients eventually do recover from it. I've been reading about a scientist in Germany who has developed a medicine called sulfa drugs. This is a new kind of medicine called an anti-biotic. They have tested these drugs and they have been successful in treating strept infections and a lot of other kinds of infections, too. The name of the drug I'm going to give you is the one developed in Germany—it is called Prontosil. As soon as I read about it, I ordered as much as I could get from the distributor. The demand for this medicine is great but I was able to get a two weeks supply for you and two other patients who are about as sick as you are. It just arrived yesterday. I hope it will be enough to get you over this. I've already reordered because I really believe it will be helpful. Even if I don't need it for patients right now, it will be valuable to have on hand for the future—because I know somebody else will get this infection sooner or later. That's just how it is. I want you to take one tablet three times a day for two weeks. Mrs. Wertz, I would like for you to come over to the office next week and let me know how he's doing. If he's doing better, I'll see him in two weeks—hopefully at the office."

As he reached for his bag, he asked, "Do you have any questions?"

As he counted out 42 pills into a small vial, he continued, "I have high hopes for this drug. This is a miserable infection which gives the patient a high fever and terrible sore throat. But the real danger is it can go into rheumatic fever and can damage the joints and heart muscle. Just take these with a prayer."

"One more thing" he said, "these are pretty big pills. You may have to cut them in pieces especially at first till the swelling and soreness of the throat diminishes. If you have to do it, mash them up and dissolve them in water. Do whatever you have to do to get them down his throat. Also continue to boil drinking water. Okay?"

"Now, buddy, let me listen to your heart and lungs. Roll over and take a deep breath. Hmm—lungs sound clear—that's good. Now let's see about the ticker."

He put his stethoscope on Alvin's chest and listened for a few seconds. He repositioned the instrument and listened again. "Well," he said, "I'm not 100% sure, but I think I detect a slight murmur in the aortic valve. It's very slight. I hope we got this medicine soon enough."

As Doc was ready to exit the room, he turned back and said to Alvin, "Get well and I'll give you a ride in my new car. She's a beaut. See you buddy."

Alvin waved and smiled. "You bet, Doc", he whispered. He wondered if he would ever be well again.

Life in the Wertz household had taken on a new routine since John was working on the WPA project in Davy. Aggie found herself singing as she prepared supper for her family. For the first time in months she felt optimistic. She was content with the new routine.

When John came in the back door, he took his muddy boots off at the door. "Hi honey" he said, as he walked over to the stove where Aggie was stirring the beans. He gave her a quick kiss and walked over to look at the mail lying on the table. As he looked through the letters, he said, "One of these is for Alvin. It looks like it's a letter from Susan Jones. I'll take it to him. How's he doing today?"

Aggie said, "Doc came by this afternoon. He give Alvin some new met-sin. He talked like it was some kind'a new miracle met-sin and he 'spects it to really hep Alvin. I hope to goodness he's right. I'm prayin' he's right. I'll tell ya 'bout it after while. Go ahead and give Alvin his letter."

John walked into Alvin's room. He was sleeping. When John felt his son's head, he felt hot. "Aggie" he called "bring a wet rag. Alvin's a-burning up." Aggie put the cool cloth on Alvin's forehead and straightened his bed and pillow. "Alvin, you never took your pill." she scolded. "Do ya need me to mash it up for ya?" Alvin nodded and whispered, "I can't swallow it. It's too big."

John said to Alvin, "Son, there's a letter for you. It's from Susan. It's kinda sticky, must be drippin' with honey." he teased. Alvin stirred, "Just lay it down on the chair, I'll read it after while." He seemed to drift off again.

John remarked, as he turned to leave, "I see ya ain't in no mood fer humor."

When Aggie returned, she had mashed the pill in a spoon and dissolved it in water. "Okay, son, sit up for a minute and open wide." She poured the contents of the spoon into his open mouth. Alvin swallowed hard and gagged but managed to get all of the medicine down. *Okay, she thought, one down 41 to go.*

As they returned to the kitchen, John said, "He's a-feeling bad, he never seemed to care about the letter from Susan." Aggie replied, "Don't cha worry, Dear, he'll read it when he's a- feelin' better."

When Aggie stepped on the back porch to call the boys in for supper, she was aware of movement to her left. She caught just a glimpse of her—the woman at the well again but she was gone in a flash. *Where does she go? Who is she? What is she—is she a person or a ghost? I don't believe in ghosts but this is about to make me believe. I don't know if I'm seeing things or maybe I'm just going crazy!*

When supper was over, the two young men stood up to leave the table. "Wait just a minute, gentlemen." John said. "You know we always read from the Bible after supper."

Aggie smiled. She still thought of them as boys but they were in reality young men. Jim was 18 and would soon finish school. He had wanted to quit school the minute he turned 16 and go to work in the mines just about the time the mines shut down. The youngest of the boys in the family was Daniel who had just turned 14. He was industrious and trustworthy. Aggie could always count on Daniel to keep the wood box full and the cow milked on schedule. She was grateful for Dan. Her second son, Joe, who was almost 20 had been working with the CCC over in Panther for the past two months. He had gone back to his work project after being at home for a week. Aggie was always sorry when he had to leave again. The Wertz family also included two girls. Louanna, who was 23, lived in Hemphill with her husband's family. The baby of the family was 10 year old Louise who lived with Aggie's sister in Tennessee. Aggie's sister, Callie and her husband, Ben Hollings had never been able to have children. So, at a weak moment, Aggie gave into the pleadings of her sister and allowed Louise to go home with them for a visit and there she remained. Aggie missed her little girl and regretted that decision every day. However, she was consoled by the fact that Louise seemed quite content and enjoyed being pampered as the princess in the Hollings household.

Dan helped his mother clear the table and wash the dishes. When the dishes were dried and neatly stacked on the sideboard, Aggie and Dan sat down at the table to join the other family members. John opened his Bible and said. "I want us to look at sumthun' I found the other day. I went lookin' for these verses after I heard last Sunday's sermon. It's in Ephesians 2:8-9. Listen carefully and then tell me what it says about being saved. John read the passage very deliberately emphasizing certain words. *"For by **grace** are ye saved through **faith**"*. He paused for a minute and looked at each of them, then continued. *"and that not of yourselves: it is a **gift of God**: **Not of works**, lest any man should boast."*

Then John asked, "What do those verses say about how to be saved?"

Jim said, "That sounds like a person is saved by grace through faith all by itself. He don't need to do nothin' else. That there is for sure differt from what that preacher said last Sunday. Didn't he say that you have to repent and be baptized?"

John looked at Aggie, who had been sitting quietly and listening, and said, "What do you think, honey?"

She replied, "Well I don't think the Bible says one thing in one place and somthun' else in the th'other. So I am confused. I know that there preacher said it plain as day, repent and be baptized. In fact, I reckon he was a-readin' it right out of the Bible hisself. Repent and be baptized for the remission of sin. And then he said the blood of Jesus Christ that takes away our sin is applied by water when you get baptized. But I don't think that last part was in the Bible. That last part—well, it was his own way of thinkin', I reckon."

John continued, "He was a-readin' from Acts chapter 2. So, which is right? Look what else our verse says, 'not of works, lest any man should boast.' A work is sumthun' a person does to try to gain favor with God. Is baptism a work?"

John continued, "Let's think about this. Ry-chere is two differt ways for a body to get saved. Which is right? Can they both be right? How do you decide which way is right?"

John looked around the table into four puzzled faces. Then he said, "Alright, I'm goin' give ya'll somthun' else to think over. Look at Matthew 19:16-22 and see if we can find the answer about how a body is saved. Dan would you read that—here's my Bible."

John passed his Bible to Dan, who began to read.

> And, behold, one came and said unto him, Good Master,
> what good thing shall I do, that I may have eternal life?
> And he said unto him, why callest thou me good? There
> is none good but one, that is, God: but if thou wilt enter
> into life, keep the commandments. He said unto him,
> which? Jesus said, Thou shalt do no murder, thou shalt
> not commit adultery, thou shalt not steal, thou shalt not

bear false witness, honour thy father and thy mother: and thou shalt love thy neighbor as thyself. The young man saith unto him, all these things have I kept from my youth up: what lack I yet? Jesus saith unto him, if thou wilt be perfect, go and sell that thou hast, and give to the poor, and thou shalt have treasure in heaven: and come and follow me. But when the young man heard that saying, he went away sorrowful: for he had great possessions.

John asked, "What does Jesus say is the way to be saved?"

Dan said, "If that's how a body gets saved, I reckon no body would be saved. Do you reckon any body can keep the Law perfect? That sounds like a body'd have to do some things and not do sumthun' else to be saved, I reckon. So don't that make it all about works? But since the Bible don't lie, how can one thing be true and somthun' differt be true too? What do you think, Dad?"

John, looking at each of them, answered, "Well, I reckon we need to be sure the scriptures we go by are written to us and about us. Jesus hisself said that He came jist to the lost house of Israel. Let me see where that is."

Taking the Bible from Dan, he began flipping through the pages of the gospels. "Here it is" he said.

> *Matthew 15:24: But he (Jesus) answered and said, I am not sent but unto the lost sheep of the house of Israel.*

Jim said, "Daddy, you ought to be a preacher. You help me to understand better than any preacher I ever heard."

John responded to his son, "I don't reckon God called me to be no preacher, Jim. But I do reckon God did call me to be a father and to lead my family so they know the truth. Everythin' in the Bible is for us but everythin' in the Bible is not special to us. It's important to tell the diff- ernce between what God is saying special to us and what He said to somebody else. If we can't tell the diff-ernce, we'll be pulled one di-rection and then th'other. Paul calls that bein' tossed about by ever' wind of doctrine. It's right here in *Ephesians 4:14: That we henceforth be no more children, tossed to and fro, and carried about with every wind of doctrine, by the sleight of men, and cunning craftiness, whereby they lie in wait to deceive.*"

John looked around the table. He was thankful for his family. He was glad that these young men wanted to understand God's Word and to spend time searching it. Then he said, "Let's git back to what we was talkin' 'bout--how to be saved and all. I'm just learnin' this myself. They's a fellow on the crew in Davy was talkin' to me 'bout this. He saw me a-readin' my Bible and started askin' me questions 'bout what I was learnin'. He said he was a "rightly divider". I weren't sure what that meant so he began to show me. He was so excited about studyin' the Bible and the more he talked, the more it made sense. He said that you always need to ask questions: Who? When? Where? Why? What?. He said the Who and When are the more important to ask. So, let's look at each one of the scriptures we talked about and see if we can determine the Who, what, where, why and when of each one."

Let's start with Jesus and the rich young ruler and go backwards, "when Jesus was a talkin' to the rich young ruler, who was he talkin' to? Back in them days, the important thing to ask was: Are you a Jew or a Gentile? So, was he a Jew or a Gentile?"

Dan said, "I reckon he was a Jew. Wudn't the Law for the Jews? Didn't God give the Law to Moses for the Israelites. Ain't the Israelites the same as the Jews?"

John smiled and said, "Good thinkin', Dan. So now let's ask, when was this that Jesus was talkin' to this here man?"

Jim, not wanting to be left out, answered, "It was when Jesus was a-preachin' and a-healin', I reckon."

This is going well, John thought. He said, "You're 'zackly right, son. And 'member that Jesus came to minister to His own people, the Jews. So, we can see that this method of gaining eternal life is not for us—it's for the Jews when Jesus was on earth. Remember if Jesus said it, it is truth. It was truth for that time—for that dispensation. They was under the Law with Messiah living among them but Israel did not accept Jesus as their Messiah."

With a puzzled expression, Dan asked, "Wudn't the disciples Jews? Like Peter and John—they was Jews, wudn't they?"

John replied, "Yes they was Jews, fer a fact, and they believed in Jesus as Messiah (King). But the Jewish nation as a whole did not accept Him. It was the Jewish religious leaders who really wanted Jesus crucified. They worked in cohoots with the Romans to get it done."

Not wanting to overwhelm them with too many details at once, John continued, "I want us each to look up Acts chapter 2, read it and ask the questions. Who is speaking and who is he speakin' to? What's he talkin' about? I want you to answer those questions from Acts chapter 2."

He continued, "We are going to pray and ask God to open our eyes to see the truth. This is the most important thing we need to understand from the Bible—how to be saved and go to heaven. I want us all to think about this and we will talk about it again tomorrow after supper. I have a little hint for you. When you read the verses, in particular look at who's bein' talked to. Now, let's bow our heads."

In hushed tone, John spoke, "Dear Lord, we know we are saved by your grace because we have put our faith in Jesus Christ and what He went and done when He died and rose again. It is so easy to get mixed up by what we hear from other folks and start to figure we's big enough to do sumthun' that would save us for all eternity. We know you are the only One big enough to save us. We trust the Bible is your Word and it cannot lie. Help us to understand why it seems to say two different things. We want to walk in truth—your truth. Please open our eyes to see the truth for us. Amen."

As Aggie went about the business of packing her nighttime box to put on the porch, she commented, "My dear, I wanna say one thing, you don't talk too much but when you do talk, it is worth a-listenin' to. I did notice what that preacher said on Sunday. I wondered why that was differt from what I heared before? Thanks for takin' the time to 'splain it to us."

John watched as she packed leftover corn bread and sausage and tightened the lids on jars of soupy brown beans. Not wanting to spill anything, she carried the tin box carefully to the porch.

Then she went to check on Alvin. He was awake and sitting up in the bed. He looked up and said, "could you give me a light, Mom?" Since there was no electric light in the room, she lit a candle and sat it on the chair beside the bed. Alvin reached for the letter which lay on the chair beside the bed. He carefully opened it. He had a serious look on his face as he read the words:

Dear Alvin,

I hate to write this letter but I know I must. It is the hardest thing I've ever done. I love you but I have to break up with you. After we came to visit you on Christmas, I was so upset because you were so sick I felt ill myself. I hope you are better. That day I thought you looked like you were going to die and I couldn't stand it. My Daddy told me I had to break it off with you. He said you would never be able to support me and a family. You would never be able to go to work in the mines. He said it would be easier to break up now than later when we were more in love. I think he's right and I have to listen to my Daddy. I'm so sorry. I hope you meet someone who will love you in spite of your sickness and will take care of you.

With a breaking heart,

Susan.

Alvin snorted, "I ain't gonna to be sick forever." And threw the letter on the floor and rolled over in the bed toward the wall.

Aggie soon returned with Alvin's second dose of the new medicine. "Okay, mister, it's time for your medicine." It didn't seem quite so hard to get down this time.

Aggie blew out the candle and picked up the letter from the floor and laid it on the chair before she left the room. Since Alvin was not feverish and seemed to want to rest, she decided to sleep in her own bed tonight for a change.

It was just getting dark when Aggie closed the curtains. She could see her at the well from the window. There she was—a small figure draped in black. As Aggie watched, the image in black stood up and walked down the three steps from the well. *Aggie gasped, she ain't got no shoes, she'll get frostbit.*

Aggie remembered a box of Louanna's things, which she left when she got married. *Maybe there are some shoes in that box, she thought.* After finding the box in the corner of her bedroom, she rummaged through dresses, underwear and SHOES. "Hallelujah!" she exclaimed. She took a pair of flat shoes, which Louanna had worn to school, out of the box. Then she found an old handmade quilt atop a stack of unused linens. She hurried downstairs to the porch and placed the folded quilt beside the lunch box and then carefully placed the shoes on top. Her heart was full of joy as she closed the backdoor of her home and gave thanks for a warm place to sleep on a winter night.

As she climbed the stairs to her bedroom, she thought. *I bet my ghost lady takes the food and shoes tonight! Some ghost!* She sort of chuckled at the thought of it. She had no explanation for the woman but she had much fascination. Who was she? Where did she come from? Where does she go? *Oh, Lord, keep that poor woman from freezin' wherever it is she's a-stayin.*

Before Aggie dozed off to sleep that night, she prayed, "Lord, I don't reckon who she is or what she's a-doin' here but I have this feelin' that she really needs hep. Please guide me to hep her. Amen."

The next morning when she went to check on Alvin, Aggie rejoiced to see him propped up in bed. What a change from yesterday. "Hey, mom. Did you oversleep? I've been waitin' for you to git up."

"I'll have ya know, young man, that it is 6 am and I've been up for at least an hour. It's still dark outside. Your dad has already gone up to the road to catch his bus for work." She could hardly hold back the tears of joy at the transformation in her son after one day on the new medicine.

Alvin asked, "Could I get a cup of hot tea with some of Aunt Hattie's honey in it?"

Aggie fairly danced to the kitchen to prepare his tea. While the tea was brewing, she mashed one of the pills in a spoon and put a drop of hot water to dissolve it.

When she returned to the room Alvin was sitting on the side of the bed reading over the letter from Susan Jones.

"Here's your tea. I brought your met-cin too." This time the medicine went down easily.

"The tea smells good" Alvin commented. As he took his first sip, he said, "Mom, did you read what Susan wrote to me?"

"No, course I never read it." She replied, "You know I can't read too good."

Alvin's voice quivered as he spoke, "She said that she had to break up with me because her daddy said I could never make a living because I was so sick. That really makes me mad—what does he know? Well, I'm gonna show him. I may not be able to go into the mines but I'm gonna own my own business—some kind of business that supports the coal mines. I don't know what it is yet but I will and I'll show him. Just as soon as I'm well enough, I'm gonna find me a job and start hepin' out around here. I will not be a taker and I'm sure not gonna be an invalid."

He seemed relieved to get that off his chest and quickly finished his tea. "Boy, some nice warm oatmeal with raisins would taste good right now and feel good on my throat." He said with a grin. Aggie always enjoyed her son's humor. He had a way of getting his way with her and she loved it.

On her way to the kitchen, Aggie said over her shoulder, "Oatmeal on the way. It's been at least a week since you ate."

As she whisked the oatmeal to get all the lumps out, she was remembering to be thankful for all the good things that come from the hand of Almighty God. "Thank you, Lord, thank you." She whispered as tears of joy came pouring down her cheeks.

She filled a bowl with oatmeal and sprinkled some of her home dried raisins on top. Then she finished it off with a generous spoonful of honey and a splash of milk. She carried it on a tray into the bedroom where Alvin was waiting.

While he was eating the oatmeal, Aggie walked to the window and pulled back the curtain. There she was at the well. In the early morning light, Aggie could just make out what appeared to be a heap wrapped in a QUILT. *Aha, Aggie thought, I knew it! I knew it! She **is** the one who takes the food at night and she knows the other things left are for her, too. Why doesn't she just come and knock on the door and ask for help? It's hard times now—lots of people are asking for food and money. She must know that we are aware of her. What could be the reason she runs away? I wonder if she can hear or talk. She may be a deaf mute. I'm going to go out and talk to her.*

"I'll be back in a few minutes" she said as she hurried out of the room. When she opened the back door and looked toward the well, she was gone. *How did she know I was coming? Maybe it is my imagination, Aggie thought. But could my imagination take the quilt from the porch? This is too strange! If she just asked for help, I would help her. Where did she come from? Nobody else I've talked to has ever seen her. Nobody knows anybody like her here in Mohegan. Why does she run away?*

As she looked around hoping to glimpse some sign of her, Aggie noticed something on the ground. When she picked it up, it was a shoe—one of Louanna's shoes that she had left on the porch. *It must be too big for her. When she ran away, she lost her shoe. Just like Cinderella, she thought.*

Now that Alvin was feeling so much better, Aggie felt more comfortable leaving him alone. So, after all her morning chores were done, she walked to the house next door and knocked on McGrady's back door. As she waited for an answer, she looked down the valley. In this coal camp, there were about 40 houses where the coal miners' families had once lived. Many of the houses appeared to be white blocks magically suspended on several levels among the lush forests overlooking the Tug River Valley. The houses in the bottom near the river were laid out in a block with streets. In the midst of the camp sat a four room schoolhouse and a small church.

Today, as on every day for the past two years, the coal tipple across the river sat empty and silent; as did the company store and offices. Mohegan camp was feeling the effects of several years of economic depression. This scene was a constant reminder the nation was going through the direst economic times in its history. President Roosevelt's New Deal was offering some hope to many unemployed coal miners as they found temporary work on various projects throughout the coalfields. Most families that lived in the bottom had left the valley to find work elsewhere or to live with family members in other locations. As her eyes traveled across this section of the valley, she noticed the smoke ascending from the chimneys from a few of the houses below her vantage point. She was glad everyone had not left this valley that she called home. *She made a mental note to visit them and inquire about their food supplies. Maybe she should plan a pot-luck dinner at the church—everybody in the camp would enjoy having a good meal.*

The Wertz's house was the last in a row of three houses on the side of the camp toward the railroad. Besides the superintendent's house, these three were the only two story houses in Mohegan camp. The larger houses were assigned according to seniority with the coal company. John Wertz and Sam McGrady had been among the first to be hired on when the mine opened 25 years ago. The only house larger was the superintendent's brick house located around the bend near the entrance of the camp.

Rising between the two houses was a foot path that led to the black top road which ran above them. It was steep and narrow but it was the quickest way to get to the road by foot. Each morning, John made his way up that path to catch the bus to go to work in Davy. Aggie had often climbed that path on her way to visit John's brother, Jessie and his wife Hattie, who lived above the road. In order for Aggie to reach their house, she must also cross the road and climb a second steep path that rose above the road. Aggie had always liked Jessie and Hattie's house. It was smaller and a perfect size for the childless couple. Aggie especially liked its location as it sat on an open bluff in a clearing just below the tree line. Although their property lay on a slight decline, it provided a wonderful place for a big garden, cows and pigs and bees. From their front porch, one could watch the whole valley. Aggie thought it was a little piece of heaven. Although Jessie and Hattie had come to West Virginia with John and Aggie, Jessie did not work in the mines nor did he want to. Although he could have made a more secure livelihood as a miner, he was quite content with his life as a carpenter. Before the depression fell, he had consistently found work keeping the company-owned houses repaired, painted and habitable in Mohegan and other coal camps that nestled in the hills of McDowell County. Now he and Hattie waited for better times trying to maintain a positive attitude.

On a recent visit with Hattie, Aggie had enquired about the mysterious ghost-like woman at the well. Hattie had not seen her nor heard about her from anyone else. This added to Aggie's own suspicion that she must be having delusions.

Aggie's thoughts were interrupted when Maggie McGrady came to the door, wiping her hands on her apron. "Oh, Aggie, it's so good to see you. How in the world are ya? Come on in here and tell me what's goin' on over at-cher house."

When they were seated at the kitchen table with a cup of coffee, Maggie cut a piece of custard pie for each of them. "I made it yesterdee. I set it out overnight in the cool box, but I reckon it needs to be et up today."

"It's delicious" Aggie said as she took her first bite. Then she asked, "How's things goin' for your bunch?"

"Well, Sam, he's a-gettin' mighty discouraged 'bout the mines. He thinks the unions'll take over if the mines ever do open up agin. Them union men promises lots of good things but Sam don't reckon things'll change much. They say they are gonna do away with the company stores and paying in script. They want the miners to get paid in cash money. I think I like that idea. Whadda y'think?"

Aggie very thoughtfully replied, "Well, you know my John, he don't talk much. This is the first time I've heared a thing 'bout this. Do you mean if we got paid in real cash money a body could go shoppin' in

Davy or Welch? As I think about it, going to town once a month to shop might be fun. Maybe Louanna and me could make it a day to be together. I miss that girl so much. It was nice having another woman around the house. From what I hear, I think I like the idea of unions."

Then Aggie added, "What changes they gonna make inside the mines? I mean, our men they work like mules and it's plum dangerous—what with the explosions, rock slides and the gas pockets and all. It seems like somebody is a-getting' killed ever' month. Are they talkin' 'bout anyways to make the mines safer for the men? They's the ones that bring out the coal! They should be the main thing—they're the most important. Safety first! Hey! That there's a good sayin'! **SAFETY FIRST**! I think I'll have Dan make up some signs and post them around the camp on trees and buildings. That's a good idee, if I have to say so myself."

Maggie just stared at her in unbelief. "Aggie, I can't believe you just said that! Next thing you know you'll be out theres marchin' for miner's rights. Come on, Aggie, we can't do nothun—we're just women. Let's just wait and see what the unions do."

"I reckon you're right. It jest makes a body wanna do sompun to change things." Aggie answered.

Aggie made a mental note to talk to Dan about this. He would surely be on board. He was the next generation of miners.

Then she said, "Okay, let's us change the subject. Alvin he's feelin' a lot better. Doc give him some new met-sin. He called it anti-something or other. Anyway, Alvin perked up overnight and started eatin' agin. That was good news for me. Some bad news though, Alvin got a break up letter from Susan Jones—you know the girl from Rodiefield he was a-callin'on afore he got sick. I never got me a chance to know her too good but I liked her right smart even if she was kinda' uppity. I think she was worried 'bout Alvin bein' able to support her since he got so sick. The whole Jones family came up to visit him on Christmas Day and they seen how he looked. I gotta say Alvin did look awful that day—I reckon he looked like a corpse. Anyway, the letter made him mad enough to get better." Then with a laugh, she said, "That's a good thing, I reckon."

After taking a sip of her coffee, Aggie continued, "Just wonderin', Maggie, have you noticed a strange woman hangin' around the well at evenin' just when it's startin' to get dark or early in the mornin'?"

Maggie answered, "No, I ain't but Sam said he seen a woman run away from the well when he went to get water. I reckon it was day befur yesterdee like you say—early in the mornin'."

Excited at the prospect she might not be considered daft, Aggie continued. "I seen her a few times. She started comin' about the time Alvin got so sick. When I first seen her, I thought it must be the death angel come to take my Alvin. John said that there was a crazy idee. She is small and all dressed in black—you can't see her face. She looks like she's a-mournin', dressed in black with her face all covered and all. She sits all hunched up on the top step at the well. You see 'er and then she's gone. Reckon who she is and where she come from. Got any idee?"

"Well, that there's a puzzle, ain't it?" Maggie replied. "Ever tried talkin' to her?"

Aggie replied, "Can't get that close to her. Just yesterdee I headed out the backdoor to try to talk to her and she was gone. I just seen her from the winder no more than a minute ago but when I got outside she was gone. Poof! Gone! I looked all around but they weren't no sign of her. John thinks it's my magination. I reckon I'm about ready to believe him."

"Another thing, I put food out in a metal lunch box ever' night after supper and it's always gone by mornin'. I used to think the men from the trains come up and took it but now I reckon it's her what takes the food."

"And sompun else, a couple days ago, when I stood watchin' from the winder, I noticed that she was barefooted. And I says to myself, 'Oh Lawdee, she'll get frostbit'. So I put an old pair of Louanna's shoes and a quilt beside the lunch box. Yesterdee mornin' when I seen her at the well, she was all wrapped up in my quilt. That's when I made up my mind to talk to her. She was gone but I found one of the shoes in the yard. Just like old Cinderella, she lost her slipper. I hope she ain't a- waitin' for Prince Charmin'. Huh?" she said with a chuckle.

Then in a very serious tone, Aggie said, "I got this feelin' inside me that she is a-really needin' my hep. She could die if they's a cold snap. Do ya know of any caves or any places where she could be a-hidin'? They's some empty houses in the bottom. But I ain't never seen no smoke comin' out the chimleys. 'Ave you noticed anything?"

Thoughtfully Maggie said, "No, I ain't! I spose I oughta pay more 'ttention to my neighbors. I ain't noticed nothun diff-ert."

Then she added, "Wanna hear sompun funny? Sam came home yesterdee with a story to beat all. He said that Miz Rosievelt is a-wantin' all the coal camps to have new outhouses. Now ain't that a hoot?"

Aggie laughed out loud at the thought. "Go on! You don't mean to tell me the President's wife's a- gonna give us new privies? Well, now, ain't that sompun?"

"Yep! That's what they's a-sayin'. Said they'd be a-havin' the WPA workers build new outhouses for everbody in this here valley-- not just Mohegan but all up and down the whole Tug River Valley. Miz Rosievelt made a speech in Warshington and said they's too many people a-gettin' sick on account of their outhouses. I ain't heared of nobody around here gettin' sick over their outhouses, have you?"

Still chuckling, Aggie stared ahead for a moment, then said, "They's a lot of other valleys like this valley. Now, that there's a mighty big job, ain't it? I mean for a woman to take on and all. I reckon Miz Rosievelt must be bossy as all git out for Mr. President Rosievelt to pay her heed." She laughed and said, "I reckon if she's bossy enough to boss the President of the United States, she won't be havin' no trouble with them WPA men and that's a fact."

Softly laughing, Aggie stood up and took her cup and plate to the sink. "Thank ya fer the coffee and pie." She said as she turned to leave. "I sure did enjoy our talk. You know, it's been quite a while since I had a good laugh. Take care, Maggie." With those words, she opened the door and noticed a black blur disappear into the woods and up the trail. Her eyes followed the path of the trail up the hill but she saw nothing. *Where **does** she go?*

When Aggie went in her back door, she was surprised to see Alvin sitting at the kitchen table. He was drinking a cup of coffee. "Where ya' been?" he asked.

"I was jist a-tryin' to get away from you for a minute" she said with a wink. "Been over to visit with Maggie McGrady next door" she said. "What are you doin' up?"

"I'm feeling so much better, I want to get out and do something or go somewheres." Then holding up his hand, he said, "Now wait! Before you start bickerin' at me, don't'cha worry, I'll be a-waitin' till I see Doc on Thursday."

"Good!" Aggie said. "Can I git ya anythin'? Got some ham in the cool box, do ya want a sammich?"

Alvin said, "I think I'll go lay down for a while. Wake me up for supper."

To celebrate Alvin's recovery, Aggie thought it would be a good idea to have something sort of special for supper. What did she have to fix? She got out her grinder and as she clamped it on the table, she thought, this is last thing my momma ever gave me. When she and John were getting ready to leave for West Virginia, her mother had gone to the cupboard and took out the hand-cranked grinder she had inherited from her own mother. Wrapping it in a feed sack, she handed it to Aggie. The memory brought tears to Aggie's eyes and pain to her heart. She had never seen her mother again.

She ground all the leftover ham from the coolbox into a fine mince. She smiled because it was just about the right amount for a big ham loaf. She went to the root cellar for cabbage, onions, carrots and potatoes and grabbed some freshly churned butter and cream on the way out. She made a mental note that this was the last head of cabbage. Just before closing the door, she returned to retrieve 6 large apples. Then as an afterthought, he picked up a 7th apple and tucked them all into her folded apron. *Baked apples are good with ham, she thought.* Once the root cellar was locked and the key hidden by the back door, she went to the chicken house to check for eggs. *She was blessed today. Her hens had laid 2 dozen eggs. That was enough for her ham loaf and for breakfast tomorrow. Thank you Lord, you are so good to us.*

Once the ham loaf was formed and in the pan, she carefully scrubbed the potatoes and carrots and laid them alongside. *This here is gonna be a delicious change for us, she thought.*

When the family was gathered around the table, Aggie always felt a rush of gratitude for the blessings of her life. She was especially thankful to have Alvin with them at the table for the first time in over a month. When she observed his appetite had returned, she experienced the peace of answered prayer—a peace that passes all understanding. She silently thanked God for the everlasting arms that held them and sustained them in these desperate times.

When they had finished eating, John turned to Aggie and said, "That there was a mighty fine supper if I say so myself. I have a surprise for you. Your birthday's a couple days off but I wanna give ya your birthday present now."

Aggie was overwhelmed. She and John did not usually give each other presents. She said, "John, you should'na done that—with it bein' hard times and all."

John got up and went into the other room and brought a big box. "I did'na have no wrappin' papers. So here it is."

Aggie, enjoying the surprise, laughed and said, "Well, I reckon from the size of that there box, it ain't no nightgown."

Jim said, "Yeah, Maw, I can see Daddy buying you a nightgown." They all laughed.

She peered down into the box and looked at John, "What is it?"

John replied, "It's the latest thing: in-home entertainment. It's a radio. You can hear music that's bein' played in New York City right in your own home. On Sundays you can listen to preaching. You can hear news from all over the world right here in our own house. It's amazin'. So, it's really for the whole family to use."

While Aggie and Dan cleaned up the dishes, John and Jim strung a cord from the ceiling fixture over the table and plugged in the radio. They all were startled when they turned the radio on and music came on full blast.

"Woah!! I 'bout jumped out of my skin! Ain't they no ways to turn that down?" Aggie asked. The whole family laughed. John found the right dial and turned the volume down. "Aah," Aggie said "that there's more like it. I reckon I'm gonna enjoy music like that—that's nice. Ain't that nice, John?"

"It's nice, Aggie." He walked up behind her and put his arms around her. Kissing her on the neck, he said, "I love you, honey. Happy Birthday."

Aggie felt like a queen. She was loved by the most wonderful man in the world.

John said, "We'll listen to the radio after we have our Bible Study. We can't forget 'bout the most important thing ever' time we get a new toy."

John began by bringing Alvin up to date on their previous discussion. He knew Alvin was the most resistant to things of the Lord—like church attendance and reading the Bible. He was eager to create an atmosphere where Alvin would participate amiably. He didn't want any arguments among the brothers.

"Alvin, we've been havin' a discussion about how a person gets saved", he began. "Last night we looked in Matthew and saw where Jesus told a young man to obey the Law and give away his riches to have eternal life. As we discussed it, we decided Jesus was talkin' to Jews and God had give the Jews the Law. In them days, the Jews had to obey the Law."

"We found a scripture from Paul's writing we believe applies to us today. *Ephesians 2:8-9: For by grace are ye saved through faith; it is the gift of God: Not of works, lest any man should boast.*

Looking at Alvin, John continued, "We got started on this here discussion 'cause we heard a preacher say a body had to be baptized to be saved. And he read it out of the Bible."

Taking a deep breath and looking around the table, John continued, "I want y'all to know that what we's a-talkin' 'bout is t'most important thing. Cause Satan's biz-nus is confusin' folks 'bout how to be saved. We know Jesus came to seek and to save the lost. (Luke 19:10) We also know He came to present Himself to His own people as their Messiah-King. When he died on the cross, He died to save us all—Jew and Gentile. But the Jews did not know about the salvation part. For three days, they thought He was a dead King and all his disciples and friends—well, they was crushed. All was lost until Sunday morning when He rose up from the dead. Now they could preach 'bout a resurrected Messiah."

"There's an important verse that applies to us and to everybody who wants to understand what God is sayin' in His Word special for them. *II Timothy 2:15: Study* (that's what we're doin', we's studyin'.) *to shew thyself approved unto God, a workman that needeth not to be ashamed, rightly dividing the Word of Truth.*"

"So that's what we's aimin' to do. We want to really *study* the scriptures so's we can see how to divide 'em right— It means to separate what's for us now and what was for some other people at some other time. I already said too much so Jim, get us goin' on what we talked about before."

Then Jim said, "So Daddy, you asked us to read Acts chapter 2 so as we could talk about it tonight. I read it and I think it was about Peter, Jesus' disciple preachin' a sermon. It was on the day of Penny-cost. And t'was after the Holy Ghost came down on all the Jew men as they was come together in Jer-ussie-lem. I reckon t'was after Jesus had done rose from the grave and gone back to heaven to be on the right hand of God."

"That's some good study, Jim." John said.

"What else did you notice as you read it? What 'bout you Dan?" John asked.

Dan said, "I noticed that they was men from a lotta differt countries and Peter calls them 'men of Judea' and 'men of Israel.' All them visitors must'a been Jew people from other countries. You know the Jews they was spread all over the world."

"Good thinkin', Dan." John said, "We have who's talkin' and who's a-bein' talked to. What is it Peter's talkin' 'bout?"

Aggie said, "You know I can't read much so I had Dan read it to me. When I heard him say, "Repent and be baptized, do you know who I thought 'bout? It was John the Baptist and if my memory serves me right, Mark 1:4 says, *John did baptize in the wilderness and preach baptism for the remission of sins.* It sounds to me like Peter is preaching the same kind of thing in Acts 2. What do you think, John?"

John said, "Well, Aggie, that there's some amazin' dee-ductions. John came preparin' the way of the Lord and he said the kingdom was at hand. When Jesus a-sended up into heaven, He promised he was a-comin' back to set up His kingdom rye-chere on earth. Peter and the A-postles believed what He said and they was thinkin' it would be soon. So, they was wantin' to prepare the men of Israel for when He come back on account of He was comin' back to set up His kingdom. They's lots of folks that calls this the "Kingdom Gospel".

John continued, "So, on the Day of Penny-cost, to be saved a Jew had to have faith in who Jesus is, repent of their sins and be baptized in water. How about you, Alvin, do you understand what we's talking about?"

Alvin just looked at him and said, "I think I'm catchin' on."

To take the attention off Alvin, Aggie said, "They was one thing I paid good 'ttention to when Dan was a-readin' this to me. Peter's accusin' the Jews of crucifying Jesus. And the ways he's a-sayin' it, it looks like he's accusin' 'em of a crime. But when we look at the crucifixion we don't see no crime, we see salvation in the cross. Can ya 'splain why it's differt?"

John replied, "It's 'cause all God was doin' with the cross and resurrection was hid from them. Peter knew Jesus was the Messiah and His death was according to the prophecies in the Old Testament. Jesus hisself had told them—his disciples-- he was going to die and rise again. He told his disciples several times. But they never got a-hold of it. Here Daniel, take my Bible and read Luke 18:31-34:

Dan began to read: *Then Jesus took unto him the twelve, and said unto them, Behold, we go up to Jerusalem, and all things that are written by the prophets concerning the Son of man shall be accomplished. For he shall be delivered unto the Gentiles, and shall be mocked, and spitefully entreated and spitted on: And they shall scourge him, and put him to death: and the third day he shall rise again. And they understood none of these things: and this saying was hid from them, neither knew they the things which were spoken."*

"Paul calls the full accomplishments of the cross a mystery. Let me see if I can find the verse." John leafed through the pages of the New Testament till he came to Ephesians. "Here it is ri-chere in chapter 1. This is what I'm lookin' fer. Verses 6 to 9. Listen.

To the praise of His glory of his grace, wherein he hath made us accepted in the beloved. In whom we have redemption through his blood, the forgiveness of sins according to the riches of his grace. Wherein he that abounded toward us in all wisdom and prudence; having made known unto us the mystery of his will, according to his good pleasure which he hath purposed in himself. Ephesians 1:6-9

Jim, trying to explain what he just heard, said, "Let me see if I get it. The Apostle Peter preached on Penny-cost what he had been told about the gospel. But Paul had a differet message because God revealed more to him about the cross and what it accomplished. Am I close to getting' it?"

Aggie said, "Didn't Paul say he preached Christ crucified?"

John replied, "He shore did. Paul preached that when Christ died, was buried and rose again, it was all that was needed for the salvation of mankind. This is God's final revelation about eternal life. So, if a body was to ask us about how to be saved, we could tell them that it ain't complicated like. It's like Paul wrote in Romans 10:9:

If thou shalt confess with thy mouth the Lord Jesus, and shalt believe in thine heart that God hath raise him from the dead, thou shalt be saved.

So I reckon it is faith in what Christ did and not what we do. They's lots of people try to do lots of things to be right with God but the Bible says that it is faith plus............"

John paused and before he could finish what he was saying, the whole family in unison said, "Nothin'."

John laughed, "I reckon you got it. Faith plus nothin'. That there is how a body gets saved today."

"Well, that was fun," Aggie said, "It's all 'bout what Jesus done not what we can do to help Him. I reckon He meant business when He said 'it's finished'. He done it all."

John looked at his wife with admiration and said, "My dear heart, I reckon that's a good place to close our study for tonight. Let's all pray God will continue to open up our understandin' of His Word. Aggie would you pray for us?"'

Aggie began, "Dear Lord, we are ever so thankful for all the blessins you give us ever'day. I am being blessed by studyin' your Word together as a family. I pray you would plant that Word in our hearts just like we plant seeds in the garden. I pray it would grow and produce a good crop of joy, peace and blessins for this family and others. Amen."

When we seek to know God through His Word, there is a growing awareness of the Everlasting Arms

The Everlasting Arms

CHAPTER TWO

Marika's World

A s she sat by the well wrapped in the quilt she had found, she shivered. *Her mind raced over the details of her existence, she tried to figure out how she got here and how she was going to get back to where she came from. The first problem was she couldn't remember where she came from. Her mind went back to the house near the big coal mine—one that was much bigger than the one here in this place. She remembered she had been happy. She remembered her mother and father and little brother and there was also a baby. She remembered that her mother, her Mama, called her Marika and told her that Marika was a szlachta (noble) name. As she sat there in the semi-light just before dawn, she pondered what it meant to have a noble name. That name was a secret source of pride for her but she didn't know Marika who. She kept repeating her name Marika and pausing as if the last name would come to her—but it never did. Marika ....szlatchta. That would be her name. She would not be just plain Marika anymore. Now she would be Marika Szlatchta—she was somebody.*

As she thought about her situation, she realized she did not know how old she was either. She wondered how many years she had been living. This was the second winter—no, it was the third winter--since she had been taken from her parent's home in the middle of the night. She had been abducted by an unknown man who came into the bedroom where she was sleeping with her little brother. She woke when he put his hand over her mouth and she was being carried out the door. He was a big man and he carried her with ease. She kicked and tried to scream to no avail. He stuffed an awful tasting rag into her mouth and threw her in his truck and drove away. She pulled the rag out of her mouth and began to wail. Her tears knew no limit as she cried for her family. He slapped her and said something she could not understand. When she had the nerve to glance at him, she observed the size of his hands on the steering wheel—he WAS a BIG man. That thought made her even more afraid. She sensed that if she continued to cry, he would make it worse for her. So she just curled her body in a ball and shivered in the darkness.

As he drove, he was talking to her but she understood nothing he said—it sounded like gibberish. He turned to her as if expecting her to answer. Her lack of understanding seemed to frustrate him. With each question or comment, his frustration grew and his voice got louder until she put her hands over her ears. Shrugging her shoulders and gesturing with her hands, she tried to let him know she did not understand what he was saying. But he didn't seem to understand that they were speaking two different languages. How could she ever ask for help if no one understood what she was asking? She pondered that for a few moments. How could she communicate without language?

She wondered what her Mama and Tata did when they found she was gone. Did they look for her? How would they know where to look? She wondered if she would ever see them again. She wept from the heartbreak of separation.

At that moment, she snapped back to reality as she became aware of activity in the house that was nearest to the well. It was the house where she found the quilt. She jumped up and ran for the woods. She had just made it to her nearest hiding place, when the woman came rushing out the door. The woman stood with her hands on her hips and said, "Where **does** she go? Who is she?" Although she did not understand the woman's words, she knew for sure the woman was talking about her. At that moment, she realized she had lost one of the shoes that she had found with the quilt. Her heart sank as she watched the woman pick up the shoe and take it with her. She almost cried because, although she couldn't explain it or even understand it herself, those shoes had been her biggest encouragement. They made her feel hopeful that she could escape. You really needed shoes to go very far and she wanted to go far from this place. As Marika looked at the woman standing with her hands on her hips, she said to herself, *"I don't know who you are but I feel somehow you hold the key for me getting out of here."*

After the woman went into the house, Marika made her way up the path to the road and after walking about a hundred yards, went back down the hill through the woods to the cow barn. She quickly climbed the ladder to the hay loft. She had made a spot to sleep among the hay bales. Being surrounded by the hay bales blocked the wind and offered a hiding place and some protection. The warmth from the animals below made a noticeable difference on a cold night. The barn cats had become her friends and together they kept warm through the cold nights. Because she shared the food, which the woman at the house put out each night with the cats, they had become her friends and they always came around when she arrived. It had been a few weeks since she had escaped—maybe a month. She really had no way to keep track of the days—it was just one struggle after another to find food and stay warm.

She nestled down among the hay bales and curled up in the quilt. *As much as she tried to think ahead and figure out what to do, her mind always took her back. She knew she must keep her wits about her—she must not panic or let fear control her. What was it her Mama said, "God has not given you a spirit of fear, but of power and of love and of a sound mind." She prayed for escape. She prayed God would bring someone to rescue her.*

She didn't know who she was, where she came from or how to speak the language others were speaking. But somehow, she felt she was moving in the right direction although she couldn't say why she felt that way. She could see her escape would be in stages. She would have to be rescued again from this place. She was totally alone in her struggle and yet she felt like she was among friends. The only ones she could talk to were the cats, which she did with regularity. The urgency to keep from starving and to keep from freezing to death was ever before her. She had escaped from him but she could see no way of escape from this life. It was escape from one prison to another prison of sorts. But somehow her freedom from him exhilarated her and gave her a reason to keep trying. As she reflected on the situation, she realized she felt secure here though she couldn't imagine why.

Her situation although it was challenging and desperate, was a dramatic improvement from the prison of the cabin in the woods. That's where he took her that first night. She was a scared child in a cotton nightgown and he was a huge mountain man. When she saw him in the lantern light, he frightened her all over again. Not only was he huge but he was mean. He put her in a cage immediately and padlocked the gate. It was obviously a homemade cage that was just big enough for a small person or animal. She could squat or stand but there was not enough room to lie down or to stretch out her legs. He gave her some old rags to pad the bottom. She felt like an animal in a zoo. Had he made that cage just for her? Had he been watching her waiting for the chance to grab her out of her bed? Those questions haunted her for every little girl who is kidnapped and taken away from their Mama and Tata. She was probably one of the lucky ones—how many didn't survive? These thoughts must keep her going to find her way back.

The cage became her home for the next almost three years. She was locked in her cage at night and anytime he left the cabin. He was usually gone for a few hours at a time but occasionally he would disappear for days. She didn't know what he did or where he went when he left or how he managed to buy the few groceries he brought in. All her thoughts, whether alone or in his presence, were occupied with trying to figure out a way to escape. The key just beyond her reach nearly drove her mad--so close and yet so far away. She shuddered and began to sob as the memories flooded over her. Although she was sure he could never find her, the horror she had experienced every time he came near still haunted her.

He had communicated that his name was Angelo by patting his chest with his flattened hand and repeating, "Angelo! Angelo" Then, with a grin which she did not understand, he shrugged and said "Angel". She pointed to herself and said, "Marika". That was the totality of their introduction. That was enough for her. She had no desire to know him in the first place. Contempt for him was the fuel that kept her going. The primary goal of her life became escaping the prison he had put her in. She watched his routine *and waited for him to slip up and make a mistake with the key or lock. She had waited and waited.*

Within a few days, it had become apparent why she had been brought to this secluded cabin. He wanted her to be his slave and do whatever he wanted. She had to cook his food, wash his clothes, share his bed when he desired and perform as his puppet. No matter what she did for him during the day, she was always locked up in the cage at night.

She remembered the day he came in with a sack full of clothes. When he handed them to her, he had the demeanor of one who was gifting a treasure. She wondered where he found these clothes—they were definitely well used. She had been wearing one of his old shirts, so the feminine clothes were a welcome relief. He watched as she tried on the clothing and insisted she model each piece for him. She hated it when he looked at her that way because she knew what was coming later. Some of the clothes fit but most were too large and most were black—like a widow's garb. She had managed to bring a couple of things with her when she escaped but she left most of them in the cabin. Right now, she longed to take a nice warm bath and put on clean clothes. She remembered how it felt when the warm water streamed over her body when her mama washed her back. She shook her head and quickly occupied her mind with something else. Every memory of her family brought such pain that she tried to put them aside. She had more pressing things to think about.

She was aroused from her reverie when the cats scampered down the ladder into the barn. They were responding to the approach of the boy who milked the cow every day. She could see him through the gaps between the floorboards of the loft where she silently remained. She dared not move for fear of being discovered. It was Dan Wertz come to do the morning milking. The cats all gathered around for their morning milk. He put down his bucket and small pan beside the cow. "Good mornin' Bessie" he said. "and good mornin' to you too" he said, looking at the cats, patiently waiting by the pan. Although she did not understand his words, she smiled as he squirted milk directly from the cow's udder into the small pan for the cats. She had observed this morning ritual many times so she was not surprised when the cats began to leap above the dish trying to catch the milk in midair. Dan laughed. It was a game he played with the barn cats every morning and to a lesser degree at the evening milking. She imagined how good a glass of milk would taste right now. She began to salivate and her stomach growled. It was so loud she hoped he had not heard it. She was relieved when he went on about the business of milking. When he was finished, he returned the milking stool to the peg on the wall and carrying his bucket in one hand, led Bessie out to the fenced-in lot beside the barn. As he left, he turned and said, "See you later, ladies." She wished someone would speak to her in her own language. Her heart ached for conversation—it had been almost three years since she had had verbal communication in her own language. It was like being in a dark hole and clawing to get out by following every ray of light. Dan Wertz was a ray of light. His regular appearance in her world provided her with entertainment and a reason to smile. As she observed him at his work, she reckoned he was not much younger than she was. He looked to be about 14 or 15 years old. She liked him. She liked the sense of humor that he showed as he played games with the cats. She liked his gentleness with Bessie, the cow, as he milked her, fed her and brushed her down and covered her with a blanket at night. She liked the way he talked to the animals and desperately wished she could know what he was saying. He would always say, "Good mornin' Bessie." She could tell by the animals' response to him, he was a kind person. She liked that.

To practice her new language, she said, "Good mornin' Bessie". She repeated, "Good mornin' Bessie." Then standing up very straight she cleared her throat and in her most serious voice said, "Good mornin' Bessie." She fell down in laughter when Bessie responded with a resounding "MOOOOOOO!"

She had too much time to think. She wished for some work to do. She hoped something would appear when the weather got warmer. She could do garden work, house work, laundry and ironing. Her mama had taught her to do all those things. But now her efforts were needed to find food, stay warm and most important of all to stay hidden. She was not ready to be discovered.

She wondered if he—Angel--was trying to find her. She had only walked a few miles from the cabin—maybe three or four. She wondered what the big explosion was—the one she heard when running from the cabin. She had hidden in a cave the first night because it was raining so hard. It was not very far from the cabin. He could have found her if he had tried. The thought terrified her. She must not ever go back to that cage.

The next morning she had begun walking along the railroad track, which ran along beside the river. She walked until she saw this barn. It was just a few yards from the track and she remembered struggling to climb the ladder to this place that had now become her haven. She arrived weak and cold. She covered herself with hay and some horse blankets she found. Her search for water took her to the well.

She remembered almost every day someone would come to the cabin to see Angel. When they knocked on the door, he would go outside for a while and talk with them. Then they would leave. Marika did not know why they came or what they talked about when Angel went outside with them. She only knew that one of those men had become her rescuer. Her day of liberation came when Angel was gone. He had been gone all day. A knock came on the door. She began to scream in her language. "Help me! Help me!" The door rattled as the person tried to get in. Finally the door pushed open and a man stood in the door. He began to yell and kept repeating words she could not understand. It was obvious he was angry and incredulous about what he had discovered in the cabin. She was frantically pointing to the key that hung on the nail by the door. The stranger took the key and unlocked her cage. When the door was opened, Marika grabbed some things hanging on a peg and ran through the open door. She had never run so fast and so long. She stumbled on roots and pushed branches aside as she made her way through the dense woods and kept running. She remembered hearing a big BOOM. What was that? She did not know what it was but she never looked back she just kept running. The man stood in front of the cabin, yelling, "Wait, I will help you! Wait, don't be afraid!" Marika screamed and kept running across the black top road and down the hill and along a ridge till she found a cave below the road. There she stopped to rest. Such was her panic and need to escape, she had not realized that rain had started and was coming down hard by now. She stayed in the cave during the downpour that lasted all night. All night she had tried to remember what the man looked like. She had seen him but she was in *such a panic to get away she didn't really look at him. As she thought about it, she wanted to thank him. She had despaired of ever getting out—he let her out and she didn't even say, "Thank You."*

At the first light of dawn, her solitary figure covered in black made its way down the hill toward the river and then along the tracks. As she walked she wondered if the train could be her escape. She had seen lots of trains where she used to live with her family. They came to take the coal away. But there had been no coal for a long time. How could she know the roads to take her back to her home? She had been so scared that night she did not notice the roads he took to this place. Her thoughts were interrupted when she had seen the barn. Even though she kept thanking God for deliverance, remembering the details of the day she ran through the woods and the night in the cave made Marika shiver from fright. What if he brought in dogs to track her? Would the man who broke down the door try to find her? Would he tell people about it? What was the loud BOOM she had heard as she ran? She did not want to be found—she wanted to find her own way. It had been over a month now and no one had come to find her.

*The battle with fear was her greatest struggle. "I must not let my mind go there" she thought. "I **will** be positive God will show me the way out of this hole."*

From her loft position, she watched the woman come out of the house, take a key from a nail beside the door and walk a short distance to a door which appeared to be lying on the ground. She unlocked a padlock and lifted the door to reveal a large hole in the ground. Then she descended into the hole. When she came up out of the hole in the ground, she was carrying a basket of vegetables. Before she closed the door, she returned inside the hole and immerged with some apples folded in her apron. She added them to the vegetables in her basket. Then she closed the door and locked the padlock, returning the key to the nail by the door. Marika continued to watch as the woman went to the hen house. When she saw the woman return with a basket of eggs, she wished she could have a scrambled egg the way her Mama used to make them. She had eaten nothing all day. She wondered what the woman was making for supper. She hoped that there would be some leftover for her. As she thought about all the nights she had eaten from the box on the porch of the house, she was thankful. She thanked God He provided this meal every day. She also thanked God the woman of the house was a good cook. God provided food and it was wonderful tasting food.

She was sure the woman was aware of her presence but she was not afraid of her. In some strange way, she seemed like a friend. She wished she could talk with her. Talking with her was out of the question since they spoke different languages. How could she communicate with her without language?

For the rest of the day, she continued to observe the activities of the Wertz family from her loft. She heard the bus stop on the road above her position and she knew that soon the man would be coming down the path. There was another man with him today and they were struggling to carry a large box into the house. From the back porch, John waved and yelled, "Thanks, Hubie, thanks for the help" as the man disappeared up the hill to re-board the waiting work bus.

She made a mental note that the word "thanks" was an important word to learn. It was an easy word for her to say. THANKS! She decided that she would practice it with the cats and with Bessie when she had the chance. From now on, that would be her goal for each day—to learn at least one word. The word for today was "Thanks." She liked to hear the sound of her own voice—it made her feel like a human being. She wasn't sure what the word thanks meant exactly but she was going to try it when and if she ever had the chance.

After a while, she noticed a young man come out and walk around the perimeter of the house. He came down to the barn, turned around and walked past the house and well as he followed the board walk away from her position past the other houses. He disappeared around the bend and then reappeared after about a half hour. She did not recognize him. He was tall and thin and very handsome but he seemed weak as he walked. He was older than the boy who did the milking every day—quite a bit older. He was intriguing, she would watch for him.

She wished she could walk with him and tell him all about her life and what had happened to her. As long as she did not speak the language, she knew she could never fully explain or make anyone understand what she had experienced with the kidnapping and all the things she had endured in that cabin. She shuddered when she thought of it. She wished for normalcy—to live in a house again like she had with her Mama and Tata. Her heart longed to be in a family where you never wondered if you really belonged—you just did. She wanted to be where she belonged to someone and someone belonged to her. She knew she was not meant to be alone and trying to make it on her own. She needed people—at least one other somebody to whom she was special and who was special to her. She shook her head as if trying to shake the thoughts out of her consciousness. "There's no use wishing" she said to herself, "I've got to figure this out on my own."

It seemed like just another day in Marika's life. Bessie had been brought into the barn, the milking was done and supper was over, the woman brought the food box to the porch and returned inside. It was twilight when she dared to leave her loft and go to the well for some water. This had become her routine. Get a drink at the well. Since the air in the barn was not always pleasant, she liked to sit by the well for a while to get some fresh air. As she sat by the well, she listened to the sounds of the evening—crickets were chirping and frogs croaking. *A sure sign of spring coming, she thought.* She could tell something special was happening in the house. They were laughing and were louder than usual. Then there was a noisy blast. She nearly jumped off her seat by the well. Then the noise became music. *Ahh, music. I remember music. My mama loved music. We used to dance around and around the room and laugh and clap our hands.* Tears fell down her cheeks as she remembered dancing with Mama and little brother.

When the music in the house stopped, she moved from her post, to retrieve the food box and make her way back to the loft. Tonight there was another surprise lying next to the box—it was a coat. She grabbed it without hesitation along with the food box and ran back to the barn. As she slipped the coat on, she discovered something sticking out of one of the pockets. IT WAS THE SHOE! In the other pocket were some woolen socks. What a special day—a new coat and her shoe AND socks! As she pulled the socks on her sore feet, she whispered, "Thank you God for these blessings." The cats were especially friendly tonight.

They had smelled her dinner before the box was opened. They joined Marika as they all dined on ham loaf, potatoes and carrots. Then she found her favorite—a baked apple with honey. "Sorry, friends, but I will not be sharing this with you," she said with a laugh. Deciding to use her word for the day, she just said "Thanks". She did not know if it was appropriate or not but it certainly seemed right at the moment.

She determined she would try to find a way to pay this nice woman back for all her kindness. Before it got totally dark, Marika slipped down into the main room in the barn. She went to the section where the tools were stored. There was a workshop table. She straightened it and found nails and pegs to hang many of the tools. She put all the other tools in the tool box—organizing them by compartment. Then she raked the barn out and spread fresh straw in Bessie's pen. She threw the manure on the garden plot and spaded it into the soil. When she was satisfied that everything was in order, she retired for the night—she and her friends. Every day from that day until Marika left her home in the barn, she did something to either clean, till, weed, water or help the Wertz family in some small way.

She had been very careful not to leave her things lying around when she left the loft. She had learned Dan's routines for milking and feeding. She just had to be alert for unexpected visitors to her loft. To ensure her belongings would not be discovered in her absence, she needed to find someplace to hide the things she was accumulating. She discovered a shelf where the rafters met the roof. There was a narrow gap where she could hide her things. She folded her quilt flat and pushed it to the rear of the shelf toward the roofline. It was barely visible. Meager though they were, she hid the things she brought with her in the same way on that shelf. As the weather got warmer, her coat found a home on that shelf as well. It proved to be an excellent place to hide things.

Unfortunately, as the winter weather began to moderate, it meant the bales of hay stored in the loft were decreasing in number. With each bale that was removed, the likelihood of being discovered increased. As the bales were being used up, she was losing her shield and her protection. Also, as the weather warmed, she wanted to move around more and be more active. She had to figure out what she could do next. She considered trying to find a new location. That would be her next adventure.

In the evening as the sky was losing light, she made her way around the bend toward the church and schoolhouse. She had never ventured this far from the barn before. She looked for hiding places—either in empty houses or barns. After her unsuccessful first excursion to look for a new place, Marika thought perhaps her best option was to stay where she was in the loft. She was pretty sure the family in the house knew someone was in the loft. They would be looking for explanations for the cleaned barn, hoed garden, etc. All the little chores she did would eventually be noticed and explanation sought. She realized her time in the loft haven she had made for herself was coming to an end and she wondered what lay ahead.

And so it was in Marika's world. She continued to hide in the loft and the Wertz's continued to provide food for her and pretend they did not know she was there. That is until the day Marika slipped up and blew her cover.

When you are bewildered and afraid, take heart, you are still being held by the Everlasting Arms.

The Everlasting Arms

CHAPTER THREE

Two Worlds Collide

It happened on a day when Dan went to the barn earlier than usual and found her brushing down Bessie. He walked in quietly and asked, "What are you doing?"

Startled, she turned to see him standing smiling at her. She had the look of a deer in the headlights.

He held up his hand and said, "Wait!" She knew that word, she had heard it before. Visions of the cabin came flashing back. It was the man who rescued her. He had said "wait" but she had run. This time she did not run. She stopped and waited. She feared no danger from Dan. She knew him. She had gotten acquainted with him over the past two months. She did not know his name but she knew him and she liked him.

He approached her and held out his hand and said "come!" Without hesitation, Marika took his hand and they walked slowly back to the house. When he entered the back door, Jim was sitting at the table doing homework while Aggie was finishing supper preparation. She took one look and said "Well, looky what we have here! I reckon we're gonna need some hot water. Jim, would you fetch a couple of buckets of water from the well? Put it on the stove to start a-heatin'. I'll stoke this fire up so's we can get this here water heated quick. Ya' Dad will be home soon. Dan, get the bathtub off the porch, I've got work to do before your dad gets home."

That's what Aggie said but she thought, *"I've got to get this girl cleaned up. She smells terrible. I wonder when she had a bath the last time. Whew, let's get the water heated and fast."*

In fifteen minutes time, Aggie had found some of Louanna's cast offs, towels, and her best soap and was waiting for the water to heat. When the water was warm enough, Aggie shooed the men out of the house and told them to intercept their father and keep him outside until the coast was clear. To give privacy, she drew the shades at the kitchen windows. Aggie fought the urge to gag as she helped Marika out of her dirty, stiff and smelly clothes and into a tub of warm bath water. Aggie observed she was very thin and had sores on her body. *Aggie was a strong woman who could work hard and there weren't many things that could really shake her up. But when she looked at the condition of this young girl's body, she was boiling inside. She had suffered much for one so young. How could this have happened to her? She knew she needed to maintain her composure to get through this. She would vent her anger and frustration later in her prayers. Now the task at hand was to get this poor girl cleaned up. From her appearance and scent Aggie reckoned that it had been a very long time since she had bathed. Then Aggie paid attention to marks on her abdomen--they were stretch marks! That was curious.* She was younger than Aggie had originally thought when she had seen her at the well. Now Aggie reckoned that she was no more than 16 years old. As she let her body relax into the water, Marika began to weep. She laughed and cried at the same time. Aggie laughed with her. She had never before seen someone so elated to have the opportunity to bathe. As she washed Marika's matted hair, the girl put her face in her hands and began to moan. "Mama, Mama!" she cried over and over again. This was the saddest happy time Aggie had ever witnessed. It was clear to Aggie this young woman had been separated from her family and that it was a grievous thing. It was also obvious she had been abused. Had some horrible thing happened to her mama? Could she have been forcibly taken from her family? Heaven forbid, could she have been sold? Every new possibility Aggie's mind entertained seemed more horrid than the last. She was deeply grieved in her spirit. She determined to find out what had happened to this girl.

When the bath was finished, Marika quickly dried and dressed in Louanna's old clothes. She laughed because they were too big on her but with belts and ties she was able to make them work. She combed her dark hair with the comb that Aggie gave her. She tied it back with a ribbon. Aggie thought she looked lovely. Marika came to Aggie, put her arms around her and said, "kocham cie" (I love you). Aggie did not know exactly what "kocham cie" meant but she was sure it meant something wonderful and special. She said to Marika, "kocham cie". Marika laughed and spun around until her skirt flared out around her. Aggie fought to keep the tears back. Marika became her daughter in heart that day.

After the bath, Marika helped Aggie put supper on the table. Aggie put a new plate on the table. When someone got a plate at the Wertz's table it meant they were included in the family. But of course, Marika did not know that. So as the family sat down for supper, she remained standing much like a servant waits for the master's instructions. When everyone was seated, she introduced herself. "Moy Marika Szlatchta", she said with a smile and slight curtsy. She pointed to Dan, who responded, "I'm Dan." And so all around the table they introduced themselves, "I'm Jim." "I'm Alvin." "I'm John." "I'm Aggie." Marika smiled at each and then went around the table placing her hands on each person's shoulders. She first placed her hands on Dan's shoulders and said, "Dan?" He responded "Yes." Next came Jim, "Jim?" He responded, "Yes." Next was Alvin. "Alvin?" He responded, "Yes." Next was John and then Aggie who each responded "Yes."

Then Marika surprised them as she repeated her trip around the table placing her hands on each of their shoulders in turn: "Dan Yes", "Jim Yes", "Alvin Yes", "John Yes", "Aggie Yes." The boys could hardly contain themselves. Finally Jim burst out, "She thinks our last name is Yes." They all laughed. Marika looked like she was ready to cry. What had she done? Dan took her by the hand and led her to the place set for her at the table and pulled out her chair and indicated that she should sit. She understood his kind gesture. Then he looked directly at her and pointing to himself, said, "Dan Wertz". With a question in her voice, she repeated, "Dan Wertz?" While nodding his head, he said very firmly, "YES." She smiled and said "Dan Wertz." They all applauded.

When Marika saw the whole family bow their heads, she quickly bowed her head. John prayed, "Dear Lord, Thank you for our blessings which overflow. Thank you for the abundance of food on our table. Thank you for a new friend to share it with. We thank you for your provision of eternal salvation and the promises we have in Your Word. Amen.

As John prayed Marika recognized the word, 'thank'. It was her word for the day. She felt as if she were beginning to understand what it meant. Right then she decided to give it a try.

When John passed the food to her, Marika took it and said, "Thank". John kindly corrected her, "Thank you" he said. She smiled. *The next time she would say "Thank you". What fun to have conversation she thought. What fun to hear your own voice.*

When the food was in front of Marika, she wanted to scoop it all onto her plate. But she realized it was to be shared. She took a small portion and passed it to Aggie. "Thank you!" she said with a smile.

When Aggie took the platter of food from Marika, she quickly spooned another serving onto Marika's plate and said, "We need to feed this girl. She's way too skinny."

With a little giggle, Marika said, "Thank you". *She wondered if "thank you" was some kind of magic word. She decided she would say it at every opportunity. Good things happened when she said "Thank you."*

This was Marika's first day inside the Wertz's home. Although she knew that she came from another family and another place and would never truly be at home here, today it felt like home.

At bedtime, it was decided she could sleep in Joseph's room. It had been Louanna's room before she was married. When she left home, Joe had taken over that sleeping space. But now since he was gone for extended periods of time, the room was vacant. Marika's delight at having a bed to sleep in was tempered by her memories. The last time she slept in a bed was the night she had been stolen away while she slept. That was the last time until now, she felt secure going to sleep.

So much had happened to her since then—that other bed was a world away. It was in the world of her memory. She knew she was going to have to walk back through a dark place to open up that memory. She didn't want to make that journey but she wanted to find out who she was and she wanted to find her family. As she snuggled under the layers of quilts into Joe's bed, she thought, *I like you Joe, your bed smells fresh and clean. Is that how you smell, Joe?*

The Everlasting Arms are often experienced through the kindness of loving people who are sharing God's love.

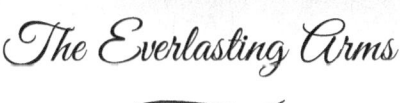

The Everlasting Arms

CHAPTER FOUR

Beginning the Path toward Discovery

Alvin's response to Doc Bondy's "miracle drug" had indeed been remarkable. In a matter of a week, he was feeling like his old self again. On Thursday, he walked over the swinging bridge to see the Doctor and waited his turn. He was a little nervous about what the doctor would say about his heart. When he walked in, it was apparent to Dr. Bondy the sulfa drugs had done what they were intended to do. "Well, Alvin, I think I will send your picture as a testimonial for a Prontosil advertisement in the medical journal. I wish I had a picture when you were layin' in the bed, too sick to raise your head. Boy, what a difference. Stand over there by that wall." He said pointing to the wall opposite the window. "I want to try out my new camera. Now, smile, my friend, this may be your only chance to become a model."

After the photo was taken, the doctor got serious. He sat down on a wheeled stool and rolled up to face Alvin. "Now open wide and say Aah." When Alvin obliged, he shined a light down his throat and said, "Well, I don't see any sign of infection in there. Your tonsils look clean and all the pus pockets are gone. This is remarkable. I can't tell you how pleased I am. The other two patients I told you about are making progress but nothing as remarkable as this."

The doctor continued with his examination by looking in Alvin's ears and examining the nodes in the neck and under his arms. "Nodes all look good" he commented. Now let's have a listen to your lungs."

He wheeled his stool behind Alvin and placing his stethoscope on his back, said, "take a deep breath and hold it. Now exhale. Again. Good. Lungs sound good."

Moving to the front of his patient, Dr. Bondy listened carefully to Alvin's heart. He moved the head of the stethoscope to 3 separate spots and listened. Then he pushed back and looked at Alvin. "Alvin" he said, "I still hear the same thing I heard last week. It sounds about the same. It is a murmur in the aortic valve. It's very slight and I don't hear any swoosh. A swoosh would indicate a backflow of blood into the heart itself. I think this murmur is a result from rheumatic fever which slightly damaged the aortic valve. It's not something to get overwrought about--It's just something we need to keep an eye on. I'd like to see you again next week. I want you to finish the Prontosil. The last thing we need is a relapse so take it all."

Alvin said, "Thanks Doc. I can't believe how good I feel. I'm ready to get out and go but I promised Mom I would wait until after I saw you today."

Doc laughed and said, "Your mom is like a momma lion when it comes to her children. You know, she has been really worried about you. If you want to get out, I've got to go to Welch after I finish office hours, would you like to ride with me? I've got to pick up something at the Flat Iron Drug Store before they close at 5. While I am in town, I was going to grab a bite of supper at the Carter Hotel. You could ride in my new car and I'd enjoy the company."

"Thanks, Doc. I would enjoy that," Alvin said. "What time you reckon you'll be finished?"

"Oh, probably about 4:00 if nobody else shows up at the last minute."

Alvin replied, "Okay, I'll be ready. You might have to tell the Momma Lion I have your permission to go. She's got a powerful strong Scotch-Irish streak—if you know what I mean."

Doc laughed, "We always called that just plain stubbornness." Alvin nodded and laughed.

As Alvin left the office, he turned around and said, "Oh, Doc, could we stop by Hemphill and say hello to my sister Louanna. I ain't seen her for a long time and I know she's been worried about me."

The Doctor answered, "Sure thing. See you a little after 4."

As Alvin walked back home that day, he had one big problem. How was he going to pay for his supper? All the money he had in the world was a few dollar bills tucked in the corner of a dresser drawer and some change he got from selling scrap iron. He hoped it was enough to buy his supper.

When Doc arrived to pick up Alvin, Jim and Dan were just coming home from school. They were really impressed with Doc's new automobile.

"That there is a mighty fancy car, Doc." Jim said as he ran his hand along the front fender. "Where's the rumble seat?"

Doctor Bondy grinned. *There was nothing like a new car to attract a boy's attention, he thought.* "You don't need a rumble seat. This is the new Buick Roadmaster. It has a back seat. This car is all closed in because it has a heater. Heat from the engine warms the inside of the car. That's good in the winter time." He opened the back door to reveal the black leather interior.

"Ooh!" said Jim, "can I sit in it for a minute?" Then without waiting for the doctor's response, both the boys had climbed in the back seat to inspect this new marvel.

Doctor Bondy was thoroughly amused when he heard Jim say, "If that don't beat all. It's even got a radio. Now ain't that somethun'?"

Dan, who was walking around the car and examining the headlights and grille, asked, "Can you listen to music from New York City while you're ridin' along?"

When Alvin came out from the house, he said, "Okay boys, it's time to git started on your chores. We'll be back after while. If you mind your manners, maybe Doc here will give you a ride sometime. See ya'll later."

"Reckon how fast it will go." Dan said to Jim as they walked toward the house.

When they were on their way toward Welch, Alvin and Doc talked about a lot of things. It was about 5 miles along a curvy mountain road—a drive that took about 20 minutes. Alvin knew Doc was intelligent, well-traveled and experienced in things Alvin knew nothing about. He knew about the world while Alvin had no experience beyond these valleys. So Alvin listened. He wanted to learn as much as he could. He needed to figure out how he could earn a living.

Doc's father had been in mining in the early days. He was a "big shot" in one of the companies which pioneered the mining industry in McDowell County. The Bondy family had lived in the most prestigious home in Davy and were considered by the majority of folks in town to be wealthy. Doc's mother had died when his little brother was born back in '15 leaving his father to raise six sons on his own. A couple of years later, his father married a widow woman who had 3 sons of her own. In all, they had a blended family of nine children, all boys. It was a brief marriage because his father died in the epidemic of '18, leaving six sons, the youngest being 3 years old. Although the Bondy brothers had been born into relative affluence, they each had to work hard to make their own way. Three of the six went away for college and chose to earn their living in places far from Davy. Doc and his brother Tim went away to school and came back to work and live in Davy. The youngest of the family lived in dependence on the older brothers.

"Doc", Alvin said, "I've been told I will never be able to work in the mines because of my health. Let me ask you, am I too weak physically to be a miner?"

The doctor thought for a minute before he answered. "Well, Alvin, you might be able to work in the mines, but why do you want to? Just because your father is a miner, you don't have to follow in his footsteps. You don't have to do what everybody else does. You don't have to be a banana—you know 'one of the bunch.' Find something you like to do and give it a go. Test yourself. Examine your leadership ability. Become an entrepreneur. Now is the time to do it before you have the responsibilities of a family. Buy and sell something—anything people need or want. There was an article in the AMA Journal last month about a study of coal miner's health in general. According to that study the average life expectancy of a deep coal miner is about 55 years. That doesn't take into account the mining accidents which are so common. In my short medical practice, I have seen so many miners who are affected with some sort of illness that can be traced right directly back to the mines. I grew up around coal mining but I didn't realize what miners had to endure day after day. A lot of miners are dying from lung disease. They are calling it "black lung." Maybe you could invent some sort of breathing apparatus the miners could wear in the mines to protect them from breathing in the coal dust."

He continued, "This is an important decision time for you. Even if you were considering working in the mines, the future of coal mining is uncertain. Did you know almost every mine in McDowell County has been shut down now for at least two years? There is no guarantee mining will ever come back. And this union thing—if the United Mine Workers take over, mining will be changed forever. They want to break the control of the companies."

Alvin, who had been taking in all that the doctor was saying, asked, "Do you think unions is the way to go?"

"I do think the coal companies wield too much power over their employees' lives. So it turns out to be a question of control, doesn't it? Do I control my own life or does my employer control my life? As it stands now, it's almost like the coal company owns the miner. It is very nearly a slave economy. That's what the unions will try to tell the miners—that they are slaves. But my fear is the mining community will shake off one control only to be controlled by the unions. I don't know what the answer is. I just know that I am uneasy about the whole thing. I came back here to practice medicine because I thought there was a need. I'm not sure what will happen when the unions take over as I think they will. The United Mine Workers is pretty solid in Mingo County but they fought a war to do it. I don't want there to be bloodshed here in McDowell County."

Then he added, "One thing I know for certain, if the mines are unionized, the cost of mining coal will go up, I think dramatically.

That means two things: the first is the mines will bring in machines and diggers to replace men to cut costs; the second is the cost of coal will increase causing the steel companies and other users of coal to look for new sources of energy. So, it's a mixed bag. I can see problems on each side of the issue. The best idea I think is stay out of coal mining."

"Looky here, Doc, we've been a-talkin' on and on so much, we are already comin' in to Welch."

Doctor Bondy found a convenient parking spot near the Flat Iron Drug Store. Alvin stood outside, smoking a cigarette while Doc went in to take care of his business. When Doc came out and noticed that Alvin was smoking he said, "That's another thing, Buddy, those things will not make your heart better. They will kill you in time."

"Yeah, that's what my Mom says, too."

"Listen to your Momma. She's a smart lady, that one."

They walked the block to the Carter Hotel and entered the dining room. The man at the door said, "Good evening, Doctor Bondy, where would you like to sit."

Alvin was impressed. *He even knows people in Welch he thought.*

As Alvin surveyed the menu, he decided on the cheapest dinner, which was just under the amount in his pocket. After he knew he had enough to buy his dinner he could relax and enjoy himself.

On the drive back toward Davy, Doc turned onto the road that led to Hemphill bottom. When they drove into the alley next to the Lovins' house, Louanna came out to greet them. When she recognized Alvin, she ran to him, "O honey, it's so good to see you up and about. You sure look better than the last time I seen you."

Alvin responded, "You're looking good yourself, Sis. As a matter of fact, marriage agrees with you."

"Whose your friend? Where's my manners? Come on in."

Alvin said, "Sis, this here is Doc Bondy. He is the reason I am looking well today. He gave me a new met-cin and I declare it must be a wonder drug. In one week, I feel like my old self." He continued, "Doc, This is my sister, Louanna Lovins."

Louanna turned and held her hand out to the doctor. As they shook hands, *Doctor Bondy thought, She is pregnant. She has that look.*

After they were seated in the living room, Louanna offered them tea and cake. While they ate their cake, Alvin told her about Marika. All she could say was, "Oh honey, that's awful. You mean to tell me she lived in the barn for months before she was found out?"

"It would take an hour to tell you all about it. Mom first saw her at the well—it was a figure all dressed in black. It was when I was so sick and Mom thought she was the death angel come to take me. That may seem funny but it wu'den funny to Mom. She was seriously worried about me. But Doc brought that miracle drug and here I am. Anyways, Dan was the one who found her and brought her into the house. Mom had water heated and that girl in a bath lickety split. Mom said she was real skinny and had sores on her body. She reckoned it was from fleas or bedbugs maybe. She's sleepin' in your old room. Another thing, too. She don't speak no English and we don't know what language she's a- speaking. So she can't tell us what's happened to her. We can't figure out where she came from. I ain't ever seen Mom so mad. She says somebody has abused that girl and she is determined to find out what has happened to her. She has nothing. The clothes she was wearin' had to be burned they was so dirty. Mom said she hadn't had a bath for a long time."

He continued, "Mom was wondering if you could ask your friend Lucy if she has any clothes she is getting rid of or if you know of somebody. The girl is not very big. Mom had some of your old stuff for her but it's all way too big. Lucy is about Marika's size. She needs shoes too. Find what you can. She has nothing and I mean nothing."

Taking a deep breath, he continued, "That's mostly what's been going on at the house. What's happening with you and Reg?"

Louanna looked a little embarrassed when he asked the question. Dr. Bondy interrupted, "Can I take a stab at the news?" Louanna nodded. Then he looked at Alvin and said, "Alvin, let me the first to congratulate you--- you are going to be an uncle in about 6 ½ months. Am I right, Louanna?"

Louanna laughed and asked, "How did you know, I ain't really showin' yet?"

Doc smiled and said, "I am a doctor. I've seen that motherly glow many times. When I was sure I was going to go into family practice back home in Davy, I took some extra work in obstetrics and gynecology. Figured it might come in handy. By the way, Congratulations! Pregnancy becomes you, you're glowing. I'm sure you will have a beautiful healthy baby. Let me ask you this, have you seen a doctor since you found out you were pregnant?"

Louanna said, "I saw Dr. Calhoun here at the Hemphill Clinic. He delivers babies at Number One Hospital in Welch. I reckon I'll have the baby at the hospital since we're so close—can't be mor'n 2 miles away. He gave me vitamins to take—says they'll be good for me and the baby."

Dr. Bondy looked pleased and said, "that's good, Louanna, remember it's important to take care of you. You are carrying the next generation."

As they got ready to leave, Alvin hugged his sister and said, "Congratulations, Sis, I am so happy for you and Reg. I know you will be great parents. Mom will be so excited when she hears the news. She's goin' be a grandma—can you believe it? She'll want to tell you everything to do or everything not to do. You know how she is. But, I reckon she does know about havin' babies, she's been through it 6 times. I hope this depression is over soon so Reggie can come home. You two need to be together now. Tell Reg hello for me when you see him."

When Doc pulled the car back onto the Davy road, he asked Alvin to tell him about the girl that was found in the barn.

"Well, Doc, they's not much to tell that I didn't tell Louanna. Mom thinks she ain't no older than 16 years old. She also thinks something horrible happened to her that separated her from her family. We dunno what it is 'cause she can't tell us. We need to take some kind of action to try to find out who she is. What do you suggest?"

Doc thought for a little while before answering. "Well, Alvin, this is a ticklish situation. She could be a runaway who doesn't want to go home. If that's the case, she'll probably run away again. And then, on the other hand, she could have been taken away from her home—kidnapped. It could have been a relative or it could have been a total stranger. Boy, that's a tough one."

Alvin said, "She seems real smart and friendly. But I think she has been really scared and afraid of people. Why else would she have hid in the barn so long? I think she was trying to see if she could trust us. What do you think should be our first step?"

The Doctor said, "Bring her over to the office next Thursday and let me examine her. You might expect someone who has been on the run to be skinny. But I just don't like the sound of sores all over her body. We could treat those and make her more comfortable. We need to make sure she doesn't have some kind of parasite. If we find out where she came from and she goes back, I'd like for her to go back healthy. Another thing, if I try to talk to her, I might figure out what language she's speaking. When I was in St. Louis, we dealt with a lot of different languages. Maybe I can recognize the language. You might not be able to understand what she's saying but you could tell if it's French or Spanish. Each language has its own sound. If we know what language she's speaking we can try to find someone who knows that language. You've got to start somewhere."

They rode along for about five minutes in silence. As he was turning off the Davy road to go down into Mohegan, Doc asked, "Did you say she calls herself Marika?" Alvin replied, "Marika and some strange sounding last name. Let me see if I can remember it. Marika—Marika Szlatchta. That's it! Szlatchta."

Doc rendered his opinion. "That sounds like Polish to me. Where around these parts would there be a lot of Polish people who speak only Polish? Gary. That's it--Gary! U. S. Steel at Gary brought a lot of miners from Eastern Europe to work in the mines up there. I think Gary might a good place to start making inquiries. Maybe the Catholic Church would have some information—most Pollocks are Catholic."

"Oh! Another idea is to go the County Sheriff's office and inquire about missing person's reports. If she is from Gary, there may be some record in the county office. They might be able to track her family down."

As Alvin exited the car, he leaned in and said, "Thanks, Doc, for the ride in your new automobile. You're right, she is a beaut. Thanks, too, for the advice about mining and about Marika. It gives us a place to start to unravel this Marika mystery. I think Mom will go crazy if she don't get some answers soon. Take it easy, Doc. See ya soon!"

When Alvin walked upon the back porch, he could see that the family had already started their after supper Bible Study. He would have rather skipped it tonight, but instead, he walked in the back door and took his place at the table.

John looked up from his Bible which was opened on the table before him and said, "Oh Alvin, you are jest in time, Son." Then he said, "for the past few days we've been talkin' about being saved. We discussed how we are saved by grace through faith. We are saved by faith in who Jesus Christ is and what He's done in His death on the cross, His burial and His resurrection. We talked about how we don't have to do nothin' to get ourselves saved cause Jesus Christ already did it all."

Continuing, he said, "Well tonight I thought it would be a good thing to talk about the blessings of bein' saved. Ephesians chapter 1 is special to me and Aggie. Aggie pert near knows it by heart. Honey, can you remember verses 3 and 4?"

"I reckon I can, let me see. Foller along with me out of your Bible and see if I get it right, okay?"

"Okay." John responded. He turned to Ephesians 1 and found verse 3. Ready?"

Aggie stood at her place, cleared her throat and began to recite, *"Blessed be the God and Father of our Lord Jesus Christ, who hath blessed us with all spiritual blessings in heavenly places in Christ. According as he hath chosen us in him before the foundation of the world, that we should be holy and without blame before him in love."* She looked pleased as she took her seat. "I never made no mistakes, did I John?"

He said, "No, my dear, that was perfect."

Marika stood up and said, "Thank you!" She looked at the puzzled expressions around the table and said "Thank you!".

Marika thought, I know these are not the right words but I hope they will get the idea. I wish they understood me—I wish I understood them.

Everyone around the table had the look of bewilderment. *What was this about?* Not willing to give up, she pounded her forefinger on the open Bible and said, "Thank you!"

Jim said, "She is trying to tell us something. What is it?" Then he said, "Maybe she wants to hear it again. Why don't you read it again?"

John read slowly, "Blessed be the God and Father of our Lord Jesus Christ." When John got to the words Jesus Christ, Marika jumped up and began to clap her hands. "Yeasus Creeztos" she repeated it over and over. It was obvious that she recognized the name Jesus Christ. *That's a good sign, John thought.*

Before anyone could respond, Marika took Daniel by the hand, leading him away from the table, she beckoned him to stand in front of her. Daniel did not seem to know what she was doing but, because of her serious demeanor, he became a willing participant.

She positioned his arms so they were extended straight out on either side of his body from his shoulders, turning his palms outward in the process. It was clear by now that she was trying to demonstrate something.

The whole Wertz family sat in silence, watching Marika as she went through motions which mimicked hammering nails into Daniel's open hands and then his feet.

In a tone just above a whisper, Aggie said, "She's a-showin' the crucifixion, I reckon. This is amazin'."

Marika, not seeming to notice anyone else in the room continued her pantomime as if she were removing something from off herself and placing it on the body stretched out before her. She went through that motion three more times.

Aggie said, "Look! She's puttin' her sins on him."

John said, "I reckon you're right, Aggie."

Then as they watched, Marika took Daniel's head in her hands and pulled it forward and downward until it took the appearance of Christ as he appears on a crucifix.

Aggie said, "And he died."

Then she pantomimed very carefully taking the body from the cross and laying it on the floor. She crossed his arms on his chest and then covered his face with a dish towel. She sat down on the floor beside Daniel and cried.

As if she were giving a running commentary of the event, Aggie whispered, "And then the burial."

After a few minutes of absolute stillness, Marika jumped up. She held up three fingers with her left hand while pulling Daniel into a standing position.

"And of course, the Resurrection!"

She began singing a song. The others did not recognize the words, but because the melody was familiar, they all joined in.

He arose! He arose! Hallelujah! Christ arose!

Marika jumped up and down and clapped her hands with joy. Then she stood to one side and extended her right arm toward the bewildered Daniel and said, "Yeasus Creeztos!"

She fell on her knees and made no move to stand again until the whole family joined her.

John, moved by this spontaneous worship, began to pray. "Thank you, Lord for what you did for us through your death on the cross and your resurrection. Thank you, too, for bringing this young woman into our home. She has showed us You in a remarkable way. Even if she don't speak our language, she showed us You. We are blessed tonight and we praise You for eternal blessings we have because we are "in Christ." Amen.

Everyone stood silent for a few moments. Daniel finally broke the ice by saying to Marika, "Thank you. That was a blessing." He knew she could understand some of those words.

She smiled. Then pointing toward Daniel, she said, "Thank you, Daniel. Blessing."

John finally said very quietly aside to Aggie, "I reckon she knows who Jesus is. She just acted out the gospel for us. I don't know about you but I feel like I been to church."

Aggie responded, "'Cept it was a lot better'n some church services I've been at. It was beautiful. I reckon that's what you call worship."

"Yeah" John said. "I was gonna talk about our spiritual blessings but we already seen it acted out right in front of us—*for he hath made him to be sin for us who knew no sin that we might become the righteousness of God in him.* I reckon we'll git to Ephesians chapter 1 next time."

Alvin said to Jim, "That was amazing. That girl has an imagination that won't quit. She is really smart and always seems to find a way to communicate. I can't wait till we teach her more English. I think there will be some interesting conversations 'round here."

Jim said, "I don't reckon she'll be round here too long, do you? I think they're gonna find her family and then she'll be gone. I gotta say I will miss her."

The next morning, Alvin joined his mother at the kitchen table for coffee. Marika was busy in the barn helping Dan with chores before he went to school.

Since Marika was out of the house, Alvin decided that this would be a good time to discuss her situation with Aggie. "Mom," he said "I was thinking about Marika last night. You know how quiet she is most of the time but when she wants to communicate, she seems to find a way. I think she's real smart."

Aggie replied, "Yeah, Alvin, she's generally quiet but she ain't one bit shy—especially when it came to lettin' us know she loves Jesus. What she did last night was a blessing and that's a fact."

"I ain't ever seen anything like it. What I really wanted to tell you is what Doc and me talked about on the way home from Welch last night. He had some ideas for places to start to find out about Marika—like where she come from and how and why she showed up here out of the clear blue sky."

Aggie was all ears. "Tell me. I'm dyin' to find out. We need somebody who can understand her and tell us what she's a-sayin', don't ya think?"

"Doc reckons we should go to the Sheriff's office in Welch and ask about missin' persons. And Doc wants to hear her talk. He thinks he might be able to tell what language she's speakin'. He said when he was training in St. Louis he had a right smart of experience with different languages. He said all languages have their own distinct sound—them's his words. I sure never know'd that."

Aggie thought about that for a minute and said, "I reckon he's right. They might be a missin' report—what did you call it?"

"A missin' persons' report. If she run away from home or if she was kidnapped, her family's prob'ly been lookin' for her, I reckon."

Alvin added, "Another thing, Mom, Doc wants to examine her. I told him what you said about the sores all over her body. He reckons she may have a parasite or something. I told him I would try to get her over to see him. Do you think she would go?"

"That's a good idee, Alvin. They's somethun' else I took notice of that is real personal. I don't want to embarrass her but I want Doc to check it out. It's somethun' I never told nobody about. I'll take her over Thursday to see Doc. She won't even know where she's goin' till we get there."

Later as Aggie was preparing supper, she let out a shriek, dropped her spoon and ran out the door straight into the arms of Joseph, her son. "Oh Joseph, I had no idee you was comin' home! You should'a wrote and told us."

"Calm down, Mom" he said. "Ever'thins' all right." The project over in Panther just ended up and the next one don't start up for another month. So I jest decided to come on home and help out 'round here. We need to get the garden ready to plant and I reckon you'll always find somethun' for me to do round here", he said with a grin. "So throw another tater in the pot 'cause you got another mouth to feed."

Joseph put down his suitcase and gave his mom a proper hug. As Marika stood in the door watching Aggie welcome her son, *she wondered who he was. She thought he must surely be a member of the family to receive such a warm welcome. She couldn't take her eyes off him.* She watched as they approached and then stepped back and held the door as Aggie and Joseph entered the kitchen. When Marika caught Joseph's eye, she smiled, he returned her smile. "Who is this young lady?" he asked. Aggie, who was at the stove checking on her supper, turned and said, "Oh, I'm sorry. Lots has happened since you been gone, Joe. This here is Marika. We'll fill you in on her later." Then she said, "Marika, this is Joseph, my son. He's been away at work."

Before Aggie could finish her introductions, Marika stood in front of the newly arrived Joseph. Looking him directly in the eye, as if to signal she was going to say something of utmost importance that he must hear, she said, "Moy Tata Yosef". She kept repeating, "Moy Tata Yosef! Moy Tata Yosef!!" With her arms extended, she nearly danced around the room repeating over and over again, "Moy Tata Yosef!!" After about five minutes, Joseph took her arm and stopped her. Looking like she might burst into tears at any moment, she pressed her forefinger into Joseph's chest and said, "Yosef! Yosef! Moy Tata Yosef!"

Aggie explained, "She don't understand no English. She just come here and we don't know nothun' 'bout her. She's a-tryin' to tell you somethun'. Maybe somebody in her family's the name of Joseph but they call it Yosef. Who is Tata?" Then she added, "I reckon it's a father or brother—whadda ya think?"

Joseph said, "She got pretty excited about the name. So I reckon it must be somebody special to her."

Aggie explained to Joseph all she knew about Marika and how they planned to find out who she was and where she came from. "She helps out around here without being asked. It just seems like she knows what to do. She cleans the barn, spades the garden plot, carries water, cleans, irons—so she ain't one little bit lazy. She seems like a nice girl, but she's been abused and treated bad, Joe. I can't figure how she found her way to our barn. I reckon she lived in the loft of the barn for about 2 months and it bein' winter and all. I reckon the bales of hay protected her some. I put out food at night and she took it. I left a quilt and shoes one night and she took them. Another night I left Louanna's coat she wore in school. Dan was the one who found her and brought her in the house. In all my born days, I ain't ever seen no body as filthy as that girl, I declare, it was awful. I don't reckon she'd had a bath since who knows when. I feel sorry for her. I think we need to help her, if we can. I try to treat her good 'cause I know she ain't been treated good, at least not of late. I don't wanna scare her 'cause if she gets scared, she might run away."

"I'd like to help too. This sounds like a real mystery. If she got that excited about my name, I want to see what she does if she is reunited with her family."

Then Aggie said, "I reckon a body would say she is dramatic. You got a taste o' that fer yourself."

"And one more thing, Joe, she took your bed. We didn't know you'd be home so soon. We'll have to find you another place to sleep."

With a laugh he said, "Well! That there goes to show's how I rate 'round here, don't it? A body leaves for a few days and some girl comes and you go and give my bed away." With a wink, he said, "Aah, don't you worry about it, Mom. I reckon I can bunk with Dan and Jim or Alvin. I can sleep on a pallet on the floor or on that ol' dy-van if I have to. I've been sleepin' in a tent at Panther. So I reckon I ain't too pa-tic'lar."

When all were gathered around the table for supper, Marika surprised them all. She went around the table and while speaking the person's name, placed her hands on the shoulders of each member of the family. When she came to John, she put her hands on his shoulders and said, "John. Tata!" Then patting his shoulders, she repeated, "John. Tata!"

Dan jumped up from his seat and shouted, "She's a-tellin' us that 'Tata' means father. I know it! That's what she's a-tryin' to do—tell us that her father's name was Yosef. I reckon it must be the same as Joseph in her language."

Joseph said, "You know, she really is trying to communicate with us. She wants us to know why the name Joseph was so special to her. It is her father's name. You know, I think besides being industrious, she is right smart, too. We have to try to teach her how to talk in English. That's the best thing we can do for her."

Aggie agreed she was smart. As a test, she took Marika's hands and put them on her shoulders. Looking at Marika, she said, "Aggie, Mama." She repeated it until Marika said, "Mama, Zuzanna!" "Mama, Zuzanna!" Aggie smiled as she watched Marika dance around the kitchen as she done earlier –this time repeating, "Mama, Zuzanna!"

Dan laughed and said "Her mother's name is Zuzanna! I wonder if that is like Susanna in English."

Jim joined in the conversation. "Maybe, the different letters are pronounced different in whatever language it is. This could get mighty interesting before it's done. We need to start teaching her the names of things—ever'thin' she touches.

This firmly convinced Aggie that Marika had a family somewhere. She wondered if that family was missing her as much as she was missing them. She was more determined than ever to try to help her find her family.

When all the excitement had settled down, Alvin said, "I've been waitin' all day to make an announcement. Mom and Dad, you are gonna be grandparents. Louanna is gonna have a baby in about five months. She is absolutely fine—in fact she looks beautiful. Doc says she has the motherly glow. She's missin' Reggie and wantin' him home. The CCC project he's workin' on is in Hillsville, Virginia. But besides that she's a-doin' fine."

Aggie was full of questions, "Has she seen a doctor?" Alvin assured his mother that she was doing well medically and was taking vitamins. "She's going to be fine, Mom."

When Dan and Marika walked into the barn on Monday morning, the cats ran to greet them—especially Marika. They wound their bodies around her legs. She laughed and reached down to pet them. "Good morning, ladies" she said. She walked into Bessie's stall and greeted her "Good morning, Bessie" she said.

She catches on real fast, Dan thought. We'll have her a-talkin' English real quick like.

While Dan occupied himself with milking, Marika climbed up to the hay loft. From her perch in the loft, she noticed Joseph approaching the barn. Marika watched him until he had disappeared from view into the barn beneath her vantage point. *As she backed down the ladder, she thought, his legs are too long for the rest of his body.. and he slings that left foot when he walks so as you think he might trip over his own feet.. and his ears are funny.. they look too big for his head.. and he is the most beautiful man I've ever seen.*

"Good morning, Yosef" she said as she entered the barn behind him

Dan said, "I reckon she learnt that on her own from listenin' to me."

Joseph nodded. Then he said, "I come to tell you Mom has breakfast ready."

Dan said, "I'm almost done here. Why don't you and Marika go on and eat?"

Joseph turned to Marika and motioned for her to follow, "Come, Marika, let's eat breakfast."

"Breakfast?" she queried. With a grin, he mimicked the act of eating by pretending to lift a utensil to his mouth. "Eat" he said. "Eat breakfast." She skipped along in front of him repeating, "Come eat breakfast! Come eat breakfast!"

Joseph couldn't keep from smiling as he watched her skip toward the house. *She can sure make life interesting, he thought.*

The incredible peace of answered prayer is an indication you are being held in the Everlasting Arms

The Everlasting Arms

CHAPTER FIVE

Marika's Secret

After Dan and Jim left for school and the dishes were washed and stacked ready for lunch, Marika turned to Joseph and said, "Come!"

Not sure exactly what she meant, Joseph hesitated. She repeated "Come!" Then holding out her hand to beckon him to follow, she said, "Come, Marika."

She led him behind the barn, along the railroad tracks and river. After they had walked for about a mile, she left the railroad and followed along a ridge up the hill and entered a cave just below the black top road. As they climbed, Joseph's mind was racing. *Where in the world is she going? How does she know about this place? She knew exactly where she was headed—strange! Is she trying to show me how she got to our barn?*

After a short rest to catch their breath, Marika once again beckoned for Joseph to follow her. "Come, Yosef!" she said.

Joseph followed her through the woods on a path that ran parallel to the road above. Pushing branches aside, they walked for about a mile before they came to the black top road at a point where the road made a horseshoe bend. She quickly looked both ways and then ran across the road onto a lane which ran uphill and disappeared into the woods. *This is Peter's Branch Holler, he thought. I ain't never heard nothing good about this place.* They walked up the side road for at least a mile and there she stopped. She grabbed Joseph's hand as if she feared to go farther alone. They moved into the densest part of the woods and walked until they came upon a clearing and a cabin. She stopped. Joseph could sense this place held terror for her. He didn't know how to explain her actions otherwise.

This cabin has something to do with her and the story about how she ended up with us, he thought. How in the world could she have gotten to this cabin? Somebody brought her here and it was dreadful for her. I can see she is afraid to go closer. It seems like she's trying to overcome her fear and face whatever it was that happened here in her past. Mom started seeing her about Christmas time and it's early March now. She hasn't been away from this place for more than about 2 months—three months maximum. She wants to let somebody know what happened. This is her way of communicating with our family. She must trust us—she must trust me--she wouldn't have brought me here if she didn't trust me.

Marika stood behind Joseph and pushed him toward the cabin. As if she feared to be seen, she hid behind him. When they got within a few feet from the porch, she jumped upon the porch and looked in the window. Joseph noticed the door was ajar so he pushed it open. The inside of the cabin was a shambles. There was a broken down bed, a table with food scraps on it, a single chair with a broken leg, a pot belly stove and a cage. When Marika entered the single room of the cabin, a blood curdling scream came from the depths of her being. She could not control it. There was the cage. She trembled so violently she grabbed the edge of the table to keep from falling. When her legs would carry her, she went into the cage and closed the door.

Grabbing the bars of the cage with both hands, she shook it with all her might, calling out, "Help me! Help me!" in her own tongue. Joseph did not know what to think or do. He watched as her body slumped to the floor of the cage. Acting on impulse, he flung open the cage and carried Marika out of the cabin. He didn't know for sure what had just happened but he did know she was overcome by the memory of what had happened in this place.

Whatever happened in this cabin represents the darkest thing a girl can experience, he thought as he gently carried her out of the woods and away from that cabin forever. She showed him where she came from but he did not know how she got there.

He carried her home following the black top road, a route which proved to be a much shorter way than the journey they had taken earlier to get there. When he carried Marika in the door, Aggie jumped to her feet. "What in the world happened?" she asked.

Joseph responded, "Bring a glass of water and a cool damp cloth. I'll tell you later."

When he laid her limp body on the bed, she was barely conscious. Joseph began to wipe her forehead and face with the cloth. She revived and looked at him. She sat up and laid her head on his shoulder and whispered, "Thank you, Yosef. Thank you."

He had the urge to hold and protect her and tell her no one would ever hurt her again. But instead, he offered her a drink of water, which she took willingly. She smiled and said, "Thank you, Yosef. Thank you."

He realized those were the only English words she knew to express appreciation. He thought to himself, don't worry Marika, someday we will be able to talk about what happened today. He longed for the time when she would be able to express her feelings and thoughts in English. He didn't have any idea when that would be but he had faith that it would happen someday. He would make sure it did. He wished that he could tell her but he must be content to let his actions speak for now.

Joe sat by her bed until she fell asleep. He watched her sleep for a little while. "We will unwind all this and find out what happened to you and why," he whispered. "But for now take heart and know you are being held by the Everlasting Arms."

Aggie was full of questions when Joe returned to the kitchen. He said, "Mom, that was the strangest, scariest thing that happened—I don't know how to even say it."

He described in detail how Marika had led him through the woods to the hidden cabin. His voice trembled as he told his mother about the cage. He described the cage and sobbed as he told her about Marika getting into it. He could hardly speak when he tried to tell about Marika's shaking the bars of the cage and yelling something in her language and how she had shaken the bars so hard she fainted. He reckoned she was trying to show him she had been locked in that cage and it was horrifying for her.

His mother was shaken and wondered, "Do you really think somebody locked her in a cage?"

"Like an animal" he managed to say.

"What does this all mean?" she asked.

"I was thinkin' 'bout that all the time as I carried her back." Joe said.

"You mean you carried that girl all the way back here?" Aggie asked.

"It wudun all that far, Mom. The cabin's in the woods up Peter's Branch Holler. I walked back on the road. It was a lot shorter way than by the railroad and up the mountain. Besides, she was in no shape to walk. She was like a rag doll."

After a few minutes, he said, "I know one thing. Something evil happened to her in that cabin. Somebody evil took her there and I need to find out who that was."

"Don't you think we need to go see the sheriff?" Aggie asked.

Aggie had never seen rage fill her son's face as when he said, "Yes, I do. And right now."

"Mom" he said, I've got to find a car so's I can get to Welch to talk to the Sheriff. Do you know anybody who could carry me up to Welch today?"

Aggie thought for a minute and said, "Sam McGrady would probably carry you to Welch if you asked him. You should offer to pay for gas—you got any money?"

"Yeah, Mom, I got five dollars extra I was saving to get me over to Beckley for the work project next month. But this here is more important. I'll figure out how to get to Beckley later."

"Mom, would you go over and check with Sam while I find Alvin. I want him to go with me. I reckon he knows a little bit more about how to handle this kind of thing. And would you mind waiting here with Marika. She may be upset when she wakes up. She trusts you."

Within thirty minutes, Sam McGrady was driving his Model T Ford toward Welch accompanied by the Wertz brothers who were nervously rehearsing what they would say to the sheriff. They tried to bring Sam up to date about what was happening without revealing all the very personal information about Marika.

When they walked into the courthouse, a deputy directed them toward the jail wing on the second floor where they found a very serious looking woman dressed in a police uniform. When they asked to see the sheriff to inquire about a missing person, she led them to a private room where she asked them to be seated. When they were all seated, she said, "Let me introduce myself. I am Sgt. Mary Weaver and I am the person who usually deals with lost children and missing persons. Could I have your names and your relationship to the person you are inquiring about?"

Alvin looked at Joe and then said,"I am Alvin Wertz and this here's my brother, Joseph. We live in Mohegan. This is a strange situation. About two months ago—I reckon it was around Christmas time—my mom started seeing a strange woman dressed all in black hanging around our well in the evening and early morning. Nobody else ever saw her. My mom—she's a little superstitious—thought she was a ghost the first few times she seen her. This figure in black would mysteriously disappear when she tried to get near her. Well, it turned out she was a-sleepin' in the hay loft in our barn. I reckon the hay bales blocked the air and she could keep from freezin'. And she found an old horse blanket in the barn. It turns out she is right smart."

Joe interrupted Alvin. "Let me tell the rest, Alvin. Well finally my younger brother brought her into the house. She was filthy and my mom gave her a bath and some clothes to wear. Another thing is she can't speak no English. But she did tell us her name is Marika Szlatchta. It sounds like Sh-lat-ka or something like that. We ain't got no idee what language she's a-talking but our Doctor thought maybe it was Polish. On account of the language and all, we ain't been able to find out too much."

Joe continued, "So you can see why we want to find out who she is and where she come from. We figured we ought to come to the Sheriff."

Then Joe stopped for a minute and looking at the sergeant, he said, "The strangest thing happened today—that's what I really want to tell you about. She led me along the railroad tracks and through the woods up to Peter's Branch holler and showed me an ole cabin. They weren't nobody around but she was so scared of that place, you could jest feel the fear. But the scariest thing of all to me was the cage. There was this cage-- jest tall enough for her to stand—and she's little, not even up to my shoulder, I reckon. She could sit in it with her knees up to her chin—so the thing weren't too big. Well, anyways, she went in that there cage and shut the door. I watched as she began to take hold of the bars of the cage and she shook 'em with all her might and screamed somethin' over and over. I reckon she was a-yellin' 'help me' in her language. I reckon she was a-showing me what it was like for her in that cage. Then she flat fainted away and slumped down in the cage. I carried her out of the place and back to our house. I don't know where she come from or how she got there or even how she got out but I reckon some God-awful things happened to her in that cabin. I don't know how she managed to stay alive. The good Lord was sure lookin' out for that one."

By the time Joe finished telling the story, he was out of breath. He sat for a moment to catch his breath before he asked, "Sergeant, do you have record of anybody lookin' for a young girl who might have disappeared?"

The sergeant, who had set quietly listening to the story, said, "Well, gentlemen, this is a pretty fantastic story. How do I know what you are telling me is not some kind of hoax?" As she was speaking, she watched the expression on the faces of the two brothers. Joe's lower lip quivered and he looked like he was going to burst into tears. From their demeanor she surmised these young men were serious about this.

After making notes on some cards she had taken from her pocket, she said, "Gentlemen, this is what I'm going to do. We have a ledger where we enter every inquiry and make notes on unsolved cases. Let's have a look."

She led them into another room that looked like a room for storage of records. The previous room had appeared to be an interrogation room but this room was lined with file cabinets. She went to a desk and seated herself before extracting a thick ledger book out of a drawer. She turned to Alvin and said, "This is the ledger for misplaced, abandoned, missing persons, etc. Every case is written up in this book with the date. If and when the case is solved, it is marked out. You don't have any idea how long ago this would have been, do you? How old did you say she is?"

"Well, ma'am, we only know how long we've been seein' her round our place. We ain't got no idee how long she was in that cabin. My mother thinks she's about 15 or 16—no older than that."

She leafed back through the book, slowly scanning each page. She knew this was going to be a tedious process. Her job was to reunite this girl with her family if it was possible.

"Ma'am," said Joe, "I don't want to interrupt your lookin' but I jest thought of somethin'. I think her father's name is Joseph. She called him Yosef but she calls me Yosef, too. So I'm figurin' that Yosef must be the same in her language—whatever it is-- as Joseph is in English. And I think her mother's name is Zuzanna—must be like Susanna in English but she pronounced the 'Z' real plain when she said it. Zoo-zanna. That might help. Now, I'll be quiet while you're a-lookin;"

"I'm back into 1935 and I haven't found anything yet. Wait, here's somethin' of interest. It's dated November 21, 1934. A man from Gary claims his little girl was taken in the middle of the night from her bed. There was nothing else taken—just the child. She was 12 years old. Her name is Marika. The family name is Stanislas—Joseph Stanislas. Gentlemen, I think we've hit pay dirt. Somethin' else noted in the book—there is a photograph in the file on this case. Here's the file number. Let me pull it out."

She went to a file cabinet far back in the corner of the room. "Kinda' dusty back here" she said. Don't look like these files have been bothered for a long time. She opened a file drawer and pushed the files forward with her fingers until she said, "Aha, here it is. Let's see what else we can find out."

She brought the file to the desk and opened it. There on top of the paperwork lay a black and white family photograph of a man and a woman who was seated and holding a baby. Standing to the left of the father was a young girl with dark hair. Beside the mother stood a boy, who appeared to be a few years younger than the girl. He had his arm draped around his mother's neck. From the photo, one would think this was a normal loving family.

Alvin and Joe studied the picture for a few moments. Alvin said, "That girl is Marika alright but she is a lot younger. It's her alright! Look at her widow's peak. That's the first thing I noticed about her. No doubt in my mind."

Joe said, "Widow's peak? What's that?"

"It's when the hair grows into a 'V' in the middle of the forehead." Alvin explained.

"Well brother, you pay much more attention to girls' hair styles than me, I reckon." Joe quipped. "Did you notice how much she looks like her mother?"

Alvin was quick to respond, "Not really, I reckon I don't notice older women too much."

Joe grinned and said, "Yeah! Yeah! Yeah! I hear you!"

Though she was amused by the brotherly banter, the sergeant got back to business and began to read from the papers in the file. "They lived in Gary, as I said before. He worked at US Steel mine #9 in Gary. They lived in a company house on the main road that goes into Gary. I vaguely remember this case, I had just started working here and I felt so sorry for the man. He was absolutely distraught over losing his little girl. At first the sheriff was suspicious he might be the culprit and he was making a show of grief to take suspicion off of hisself. But I was sure he was genuinely grieving. I felt so bad that there was never no trace found of her. I remember thinkin' to myself, 'that little girl is dead'. Some monster has kidnapped her and thrown her off the side of the road. To top it all off, here on this paper it said that the father had just lost his job in the mines. Mine #9 had just shut down in 1934. There was no sign of her—she had disappeared without no trace. I remember when the sheriff told the deputies to keep a look out for circling buzzards. If they seen any, they was to check out the area. He thought she had been killed and thrown in the woods, too. I know the sheriff will remember this case and he will be happy to report the news."

Joe's mind was in a spin. What to do next? Then the thought hit him. What if this isn't the solution Marika wants. What if that happy family picture is deceiving and it wasn't a happy family at all. What if she had sneaked out of the house and got picked up by someone who turned out to be a monster. With those thoughts came more uncertainty.

He said, "Ma'am, could I ask a special favor? Would you please not release this news to the paper until we tell Marika. I would like to try to locate the Stanislas family before this is released. She is very fragile and I would like to continue to protect her from all of this, if possible. What we found out here is just half of the story. We need to find out who took her and how she got to the cabin. Also, what happened to her in that cabin? I think the man was, as you said, a monster who abused her and used her. Something dreadful happened to her. We need to find out what it was. Is there anything in your file about language? We need to find someone who speaks the same language and speaks English, too. That's the only way we can find out what happened in that cabin. Right now it's just guess work. The investigation is just beginning. I want to keep it quiet until we can know the whole story."

"You are so right, sir." The deputy said as she looked in the file again. "Right here it says that he spoke broken English. But, it's funny, because I remember this case. I don't recall him being hard to understand. He certainly could communicate his loss, at any rate." Then she added, "I'm gonna see if the sheriff is in. He will want to get in on this for sure."

Within a few moments, Deputy Weaver reappeared with the sheriff and another deputy. The sheriff shook hands with Alvin and Joseph. "I am Jerry Chatham" he said, "I'm the sheriff of McDowell County and this here is Chief Deputy Jim Dalton. We both were involved in this case back in '34. We had figured that this was what you call a cold case that would never be solved. Usually things like this are family issues and are resolved within a few weeks. But this one was a real heartbreaker and a mind boggler. We could find no trace of the girl. We did find some tire tracks but lost them as soon as they got to the black top road. Nobody ever reported seeing her or noticin' anything suspicious. She just dropped off the face of the earth. We questioned all the neighbors but none of them saw anything or heard anything that night. We interviewed members of the family and friends and never came up with a motive. We found nobody who had a grudge against the family or the girl. Every avenue we investigated turned out to be a dead end."

The sheriff pulled out a chair and sat down at the table across from Alvin and Joe. He quickly looked over the items in the file and then said, "So, there is a girl who showed up at your house and you're trying to figure out where he come from?"

Joe replied, "Yes, Sir, and after lookin' at the photograph in your file, I'm sure it's Marika. But there's more to the story than that. This girl has been abused. She was stayin' in our barn loft for about two months before we discovered her. We told all this to the deputy. I think, Sir, if you could go with us for an hour or so, we could show you what we found in this case better than we can tell you."

The Sheriff looked at Sergeant Weaver and asked, "What do I have scheduled for the rest of the day?"

As she opened the door, she said, "I'll check your calendar, Sir." She reappeared a moment later and said, "Sir, you are supposed to give an interview to the newspaper about that robbery up in North Welch. Otherwise, you are free."

Picking up the file from the table, the sheriff motioned for the brothers to come with him. "Deputy Dalton can handle the newspaper thing. I'm goin' with these boys. This case has been hangin' too long."

As they were leaving the courthouse with the sheriff, they found Sam McGrady waiting for them. Joe went over to where Sam was waiting and shook hands with him, placing the five dollar bill in his palm. "Thank you, Sam. You have been a good neighbor and friend. We're going with the sheriff to look at some things. I would appreciate it if you would tell Mom where we went. The sheriff will bring us home when we're done."

Within a few moments, Joe and Alvin were riding in the police car heading toward Peter's Branch.

Joe, who was doing most of the talking, said, "I want to show you where she took me this morning. We walked from our house in Mohegan along the railroad tracks and then climbed the ridge to the black top road. She don't speak no English and I reckon she wanted to show me how she got to our house. Well, that wodden no easy walk. And it turns out she didn't have no shoes or coat and it was winter and all. She must be pretty doggone strong, I reckon."

After a few moments of silence, Joe said, "When you get to Peter's Branch, take the side road that goes up a hill—it's off to the right. You know, right in the middle of the horseshoe bend. Okay?"

The Sheriff said, "I know the road. There was a moonshiner who blowed hisself up and almost set the woods on fire in that holler about two or three months ago. It was a lucky thing that a rainstorm moved in or we'd have had a big forest fire on our hands."

Alvin asked, "Do you happen to remember the name of the moonshiner?"

Joe quipped, "Know a lot of moonshiners, do you, Alvin?"

Alvin replied, "I dunno, jest wonderin'. Thought I might happen to know him or heard of him."

The Sheriff said, "If you knew him, you knew one rough customer." He continued, "And I might be going against police protocol talking about this case. But, what the devil, he can't hurt anybody now. I don't think I'll ever forget that name—it was Angelo Purilli. He didn't speak much English—had a real heavy Italian accent. Don't reckon I know how he come into these parts in the first place. He was a great big man— stood about 6 feet 5 or 6 inches, I reckon. And he was known to us in law enforcement as mean, brutal and dangerous. He was somebody you did not want to tangle with unless you had a firearm. He was illusive. He came and went off the scene in the Welch area. He would hang around the beer joints and pool halls for a while and cause some kind disturbances and then disappear. As hard as we tried, we never could get anything to charge him with. But eventually, he done hisself in."

There are so many things I need to ask Marika, Joe thought. We have got to find somebody who speaks Polish. It seems like there could be a connection here. I just have that feeling.

"Sheriff Chatham, do you know anyone who speaks Polish who could translate for us?" Joe asked.

After a few minutes of thought, the Sheriff said, "No, Joe, I don't but I know somebody who probably does. I bet the priest in the Catholic Church in Gary would know. And he would probably know about the Stanislas family, too. I will go visit him and find out what I can."

When they got to the curve in Peter's Branch, the sheriff turned the police car onto the dirt lane and drove slowly up the hill. "This is sure familiar" he said as the car moved slowly until Joe said, "Stop right here. This looks like the place where we walked into the woods."

Pushing brush and branches out of their path, the three men made their way into the woods until they came to a clearing. There sat the cabin which Joe had left a few hours earlier. The sheriff was reluctant to go inside the cabin. "This is the strangest thing," he said, "how could we have missed this cabin? This is almost certainly where Angelo lived. I reckon the still that blew up wasn't more than ½ mile from here." He walked around the small space and thinking aloud, he said, "This is a vile place. It smells like an outhouse in here." Then he said, "Wonder what he kept in the cage?"

Trying to control his rage, Joe said, "I can tell you what he kept in the cage! Marika! That's who. He kept Marika caged up!"

"Oh, my gracious goodness" escaped the sheriff's lips. "I think I'm going to be sick." He ran out the cabin door. Alvin and Joe could hear his wretching in the woods just outside the cabin.

Alvin said, "Joe, do you mean to tell me that you think he kept Marika in that pen like an animal? That is sickening. I wonder how long she was in that thing."

Joe could hardly contain himself. "What difference does it make how long? The fact she was in it at all is unhuman and cruel beyond words. No wonder she fainted today when she put herself back in the cage to show me. She just wanted me to know what had happened to her."

Alvin said, "I ain't ever seen anything so filthy and revoltin' in my life. Look at this bed. It's broke down but it looks like somebody bled in it. I mean a lot of blood. I can't even allow myself to imagine what happened to Marika in this cabin."

Joe staggered out of the cabin and sat down on the edge of the porch. He put his head in his hands and sobbed like a baby. *How did she endure this? What is the blood all about? What kind of monster could be so cruel?*

Oh, Lord, help me! Oh Lord, heal Marika! She has so much darkness to put behind her. Help me be an instrument of forgiveness for her. Give us both the heart to follow your example of forgiveness. He remembered the verse: Be ye kind one to another, tenderhearted, forgiving one another even as God for Christ's sake hath forgiven you. That's Dad's verse, he thought. This is going to be a hard one to forgive. We are supposed to be kind to the cruelest person we ever knew about? We are supposed to be tenderhearted to someone who has a black heart. Oh, Lord!

When they returned to the police car, none of the three said anything for a while. The Sheriff finally spoke. "I want to thank you for bringing me here. I commend your family for taking her in and helping her. I will continue to investigate this and attempt to reunite Marika with her family. I am 99.99% sure Angelo Purilli is the culprit who did all this to Marika. He is dead and buried and can never hurt her again. The best thing you can do for Marika is to be kind and try to make some good memories to replace the recent horror in her life. Try to help her return to health. I think a good medical examination is in order. She may have worms, TB or who knows what after being in that filthy place."

Alvin said, "We had planned to take her to see Doc Bondy on Thursday. My mom will take her. She noticed some women's stuff she wants to talk to the Doctor about."

The Sheriff said, "That's good, Doctor Bondy is a good man. He really cares about his patients."

Alvin replied, "I know that all too well. I am one of his patients. He got a new drug from Germany to help me. He goes the long mile to help somebody."

He continued, "After you go to Gary and talk to the priest, I would appreciate if you could come and talk to our family. We are very anxious to find an interpreter. There are things only Marika can tell us. I have this feeling we have taken a couple of giant steps in unwinding Marika's past but we have a ways to go. We want to help her put this behind her. She is so young and she has had so much hurt. So, anything you can find out will be helpful."

When the Sheriff pulled off the black top road into Mohegan

bottom, Joe offered directions. "Turn left at the first road and take it all the way to the end. We're the last house before the railroad."

Alvin asked, "Sheriff Chatham, would you like to meet my mom and Marika? My Dad is working in Davy—WPA."

When the sheriff answered in the affirmative, Joe and Alvin waited for him to exit the vehicle and follow them into the house.

"Mom, where are you?" Alvin yelled when he entered the back door. "Got someone I want you to meet."

There was no answer. "That's strange, I wonder where she went. She's always here this time of day."

As they turned to leave, Aggie and Marika came up the path from the garden. Aggie explained, "Been gettin' the tater patch ready. Won't be long before we plant taters, onions and cabbage. I been watchin' the moon."

Alvin said, "Mom, this here is Sheriff Chatham." Then he said, "Marika, you won't understand what I'm sayin' but this here is the man who's gonna help find your family."

Marika looked at him and smiled. Then very sweetly said, "Gettin' tater patch ready! Watchin' moon!"

Joe thought, she is smart. She's learning to make conversation even if she doesn't know what she's saying. How cute!

Aggie shook hands with the sheriff and Marika curtsied and smiled.

What a charming young lady, the sheriff thought. We do need to find her family. Her absence has left a hole in their hearts, I'm sure. I can't imagine losing one of my daughters like that. This deal is a tragedy every way you look at it. I'm glad she happened upon the Wertz family. It's like someone was directing her path to this place.

Miraculous escapes and happy accidents provide evidence of the Everlasting Arms.

The Everlasting Arms

CHAPTER SIX

An Interpreter

As the Sheriff drove into Gary, the thing that struck him was the lack of activity in this once busy mining center. The U. S. Steel mine in Gary West Virginia was the largest producer of metallurgical grade coal in the United States but on this day it sat idle. The rows of empty coal cars rusting in the rail yard served as a reminder that this facility was shut down. He wondered how long it would be so. Crossing under the empty conveyer bridges that spanned the valley, he arrived at Our Lady of Victory Catholic Church, which sat on a hill overlooking the now-nearly desolate town. Exiting his patrol car, he made his way along a sidewalk which led to a side door marked 'PARISH OFFICE'. When he rang the bell, it was answered by a middle-aged man dressed in black wearing a cleric's collar. Assuming this person to be the Parish Priest, the Sheriff said, "Sir, I am Sheriff Chatham. I would like to speak with you about a situation you may have information about."

The Priest invited him in and led him to an office in the back of the building. The office windows provided a view of the playground at the attached school. Offering the sheriff a chair, the Priest said, "My name is Father Paul. What can I do to help you?"

The sheriff took off his hat and sat in a chair facing the Priest, who had taken a seat behind a large desk. "I need to get some information about a family from Gary. Do you know a family by the name of Stanislas—Joseph Stanislas? I am investigating a case which is almost three years old. Joseph Stanislas filed a missing persons' report for his daughter Marika on November 21, 1934. The girl was 12 years old at the time and was reportedly stolen from her bed during the night. Sir, does any of this sound familiar to you?"

The priest looked puzzled and said, "I have only been at this Parish for about a year and a half so I was not here when this happened. The previous priest told me about a tragic case of a girl from this Parish who was abducted from her home. He said they presumed she was dead. He said the parents gave up hope of ever finding her again and they moved away after the mines shut down."

This was what the sheriff had expected when he began the search for the Stanislas family. So many out-of-work miners left the county that some coal camps had the appearance of a ghost town. After a moment's thought, he remarked, "I am not surprised they have moved away. Do you have any way of finding out where they moved? You see, we have located the missing daughter—at least we are 99% sure it's her. Do you know if they had friends or neighbors who stayed in the area who might be able to give us an address or even a city?"

The priest sat for a moment or two drumming his fingers on the arms of his chair. He said, "I don't personally know who their friends were when they lived in Gary. But what I can do is to put an announcement in our newsletter asking for information about the Stanislas' current address. I will mention it when I make announcements at Mass tomorrow and on Sunday. Right now, that's all that I think I can do."

The sheriff replied, "That could prove to be helpful. We have to start somewhere. Maybe they have stayed in touch with someone in the community. Is there a community bulletin board? Could we post a notice there? Does U. S. Steel have any office staff left in Gary? Could they have left a forwarding address with the coal company? I plan to put a notice in the Welch Daily News but I am looking for ways to get a-hold of Mr. Stanislas as soon as possible."

The Priest queried the Sheriff, "Just to make sure I do not reveal any information just for the police, what should I say in the announcement?"

The Sheriff thought for a minute and then said, "Do you have a pencil and paper? You can write out the information that is for public knowledge."

When he noticed the Priest had a fresh sheet of paper in front of him and pencil poised, the Sheriff asked, "Are you ready?"

When the priest nodded, the sheriff said, "The Sheriff's office in McDowell County West Virginia is seeking to locate Joseph Stanislas and his family who previously resided in Gary, West Virginia. The Sheriff's office has uncovered new information concerning the disappearance of their daughter on November 21, 1934. Anyone having information about the current location of the Stanislas family should immediately contact the Sheriff's office in the McDowell County Courthouse, Welch, West Virginia."

"I think that covers the announcement. I don't want to get their hopes up too high although I really think we have found her alive. I really appreciate your help. Now there's one other thing I need help with for this case."

The Priest couldn't think what it could be, asked, "What else can I do for you?"

The Sheriff continued, "This girl, Marika, does not speak English. She has learned a few words but she has very little understanding of English. Do you have in your church records anything about the nationality of the Stanislas family? We are assuming Marika is speaking Polish but we are not sure. The family she is living with would like an interpreter so Marika can communicate to them what she has experienced in the past over two years."

"Let me see" the priest responded. Rising from his chair and going to the book shelves, he retrieved a large tome which looked well worn. He leafed through the pages to the 'S' section. He scrolled with his finger down the page and stopped at the name Yosef Stanislas. "Interesting," he said, "here is the notice of their membership in the Parish—Josef and Zuzanna Stanislas. The christening dates for two children are recorded. Here's what you were interested in. Mr. Stanislas was born in

Warsaw, Poland. So you were right, they are Polish. But it is interesting Mr. Stanislas came to America in 1922. I wonder why the daughter speaks only Polish. He and his wife must have stayed to themselves and spoke only Polish at home. Marika should catch on to English quickly because she surely must have heard it at church and school. Oh, and one thing, they resigned this congregation on March 31, 1935 and we have no record of another Parish ever confirming transfer of membership. Hmm, March 31, 1935 is about 4 months after Marika's disappearance. I think that means they had given up on ever finding her."

The sheriff thanked the priest for the information, and commented, "She never gave up on getting back to her family. I think this girl has great faith and a tremendous amount of grit. She has been through a lot."

As he arose to leave, he said, "One of the main things I came for I almost forgot. Do you know of anyone who could act as an interpreter for Marika? I really would prefer if it was a woman. I think there are some things that Marika would not be comfortable discussing with a man. Could you check it out for us? This is just as important as finding the family. There are a lot of holes in this story we need to fill in. Only Marika can tell us."

After thanking the priest again, the Sheriff made his way back to his car. When he arrived back in Welch, instead of going to his office at the courthouse, he continued on to Peter's Branch Holler. He drove past where they had stopped the car yesterday. When he finally brought the car to a stop and walked into the woods, he came upon the site of the still explosion three months prior that had killed Angelo Purilli. He walked around the site which had already begun to grow over with weeds and grass. *As he walked, his mind was going in all directions questioning his own police work. I can't reckon why we didn't find that cabin when we investigated the explosion. Were we too preoccupied with cleaning up and getting the remains of the body out of here? That body was blown to pieces. Why did we identify those remains as Angelo Purilli? Did we make assumptions based on reports of Angelo moonshinin' somewheres around here? Or did we go by the fact it was the body of a really large man? I remember looking at the large size of the feet and hands—did we make assumptions based on that? We didn't have any of his fingerprints in our files. I remember taking prints off of one of the hands. They must be in our files on this case. I guess we should have sent them to the FBI for identification but that takes months and months sometimes. The face was too damaged by the blast to recognize. Could it have been somebody else? I wonder if we had located the cabin on that day if we would have found the girl. How did she escape out of that awful stinking place? Someone had to let her out. Somebody unlocked the cage. I don't think it was Angelo who freed her—he was too mean for that--not after he had caged her up for so long. Somebody else had to let her out. Could the person who let her out be the one who got blown up? God forbid Angelo Purilli is still walking around. Who was it that opened the cage? That will be something we ask the girl. Who let her out? Did she hear the explosion? Unless, she was deaf, she would have heard it in the cabin, so she knows something about it. Maybe she escaped the same day the explosion happened. Whoever let her out knows something about this. He saw the girl and knew she was caged. Why didn't he come forward and report it to the Sheriff's office? The brothers were right—we need an interpreter.*

When he had walked around the site of the still looking for things he had missed before, he noticed the pieces that were not destroyed, jotted down some notes about his observations and wrote some questions he wanted to ask Marika when and if they found an interpreter.

As he drove back to Welch, he decided he would stop by the newspaper office and place a want ad in the paper. He would be happy to pay someone for their time if they could untangle this mystery about Marika, Angelo Purilli and the cabin.

After placing the advertisement for an interpreter, he turned to leave when he remembered his other errand at the newspaper office. She asked the lady at the desk, "Can I place a classified ad to inquire about the whereabouts of someone who used to live in Gary? The Sheriff's Department is looking for Mr. and Mrs. Joseph Stanislas. I would welcome any information that leads to locating them."

The woman in the advertising department said, "As you know, Sheriff Chatham, there is a standard form we use in legal ads. Do you consider this a legal ad or a personal ad?"

After thinking for a moment, he replied, "I guess it is a legal ad since it has to do with a police investigation. We need to locate the Stanislas family in regard to a three year old missing persons' case. When you consider that, I reckon it would be a legal ad."

"That was my thinking, too" the woman behind the desk replied. "Let me get some more information. For a legal ad of this nature, I will need the case number and the date that it originated. If you would call me with that information, we can get this in tomorrow's paper. So, let me understand. You are trying to locate this couple because you have new information about the referenced case. Is that correct? Also, you have the option of sending this out over the Associated Press wire. Do you want to do that? It will appear in newspapers all over the United States."

The sheriff nodded in agreement. "Absolutely, I want to do that. I am sure this family is now not living within the circulation area of this paper. I will have Sergeant Weaver call you with the information you need. I'd like to get this going as soon as possible. ASAP as we say at the courthouse."

When he walked into his office at the courthouse, Sergeant Weaver told him he had a phone call from a Father Paul at the Gary Catholic Parish. Picking up the phone, the sheriff spoke into the receiver, "Sheriff Chatham, here." The voice on the phone asked, "Have you found an interpreter yet, sir?" "No, Father, I haven't. I just placed an ad in the newspaper for an interpreter. You got any news?" The priest said, "I have a member of my Parish who was raised in a Polish household so she understands the language and can tell you in English what the girl is saying. Her name is Lena Babinski. She lives 3 or 4 houses away from where the Stanislas family lived."

The Sheriff said, "That sounds exactly like the person we are looking for, don't you think? When can I meet her?"

Before the sheriff could answer, the priest added, "One more thing, sheriff, since this lady has lived in Gary for many years and lived in the same neighborhood, there is a good possibility she knows the Stanislas family. I did not reveal the nature of the case or give any names, since I did not have permission to reveal the details."

The Sheriff replied, "Well, sir, that was good work. I did not expect such a quick response. I would like to come up to Gary and speak with her. I also need to speak with the Wertz family—that's the family who is sheltering the girl in question. There are a few details we need to work out. Would you be available to go with me to meet Mrs. Babinski? Say, tomorrow afternoon at 2?"

The priest responded, "I think a better idea would be if she came to the Parish office. I will ask her to come around at 2 o'clock. How does that sound? Also, she asked about pay. She probably needs the money. Most people in this camp have the bare necessities."

The sheriff responded, "That sounds perfect. I had decided I would offer to pay the person we found to interpret. I will talk to her about that tomorrow. I will see you tomorrow afternoon. Also, I will be bringing Sergeant Mary Weaver, who has been assigned to this case. Thank you so much."

The next day as Sheriff Chatham accompanied by Sergeant Weaver drove toward Gary, the sheriff said, "I brought you into this case for a couple of reasons. First, you were the person in the department that the young Wertz brothers spoke with when they came to report this situation. I think you have an idea about the character of that family. It appears to me they are genuinely interested in the well-being of this young girl. They have gone to some extreme measures to help her. What do you think?"

Sergeant Weaver agreed. "I, too, think the Wertz's are looking out for the best interest of the girl. They are trying to connect her with her lost family. I was impressed by their sincerity. I would like to be part of seeing this case brought to conclusion. It would be especially gratifying if we could unite the girl with her family and mark this case off the books."

The sheriff continued, "Another reason I wanted you to be involved in this case moving forward is the feminine angle. That young girl will no doubt open up to you and a female interpreter more than any of our male officers. I want you involved in any interviews of a personal nature. Another thing, it seems Marika—that's her name—is attached to Mrs. Wertz. So be sensitive to that connection as you move forward. I think this case has a lot of hidden angles. I need you to try to find out exactly what happened to that girl and who was responsible. One more thing, if it turns out this girl is not the Stanislas' daughter, we still have to find out who she is and what happened to her."

Wishing to sound a note of caution, the sheriff continued, "I know you are new to this kind of investigation and I want to caution you they rarely turn out the way you want them to. We have to deal with them with compassion but not let compassion blur our judgment. This is a case of kidnapping. But at the same time it is a family tragedy—a family divided who may never be reunited even if they come together in the same room. In a sense, the family trust has been broken. This girl may have the deep-seated feeling of being betrayed by her family—especially the father, who was supposed to protect her. And the parents may have doubts about the abduction itself—couldn't she have done something to get away? It would be easy to get emotionally involved in this case. Remember, the Stanislas family is innocent—they are victims. The only thing the Wertz family is guilty of is charity. Marika is innocent—a victim. So, this is a rare case when the perpetrator of the crime is not in the picture. We believe he is dead--killed in an explosion of his moonshine still on the same day Marika escaped. But we still have to follow this case and bring it to a satisfactory conclusion if at all possible. We deal with facts not feelings—okay?"

For Sergeant Mary Weaver this was a new experience. She was glad the sheriff had enough confidence in her to include her in this investigation. Although she had achieved the rank of Sergeant, all her previous duties had been of a clerical nature. She had always felt like "Sergeant Secretary". Today she felt like a real law enforcement officer. It was a good feeling. She turned her face toward the side window and smiled.

The Sheriff continued, "I think I need to take you to the cabin where Marika was held. She took Joseph Wertz there to show him where she had come from. It's an evil place, but I think you need to see it so you will understand what this girl has been through. We'll stop there when we go to Mohegan."

Arriving at the Parish church, the sheriff and deputy were ushered to Father Paul's office where he was waiting for them. In a side chair, sat a woman, who the sheriff thought to be about 50 years old. She was introduced as Lena Babinski. After, a brief discussion about the details of the case and the nature of what Mrs. Babinski would be doing, the sheriff told her she would be paid for each session with Marika. They made arrangements for a meeting on Monday of the following week. As they closed the meeting, the sheriff asked the priest, "Could you get a message to Mrs. Babinski if we made a telephone call to the Parish?" The priest assured him he would do that. When all arrangements were complete, the sheriff and deputy made their way back to the car.

On Thursday, Dr. Bondy arrived at his Mohegan office a few minutes earlier than usual. He was surprised to see Ronnie and Audrey Ball waiting for him to arrive. Audrey was carrying a young baby who appeared to be less than six months old. Doc wondered about the baby. He had delivered a baby for the Ball's about eight months ago—but it wasn't this baby. They followed him into the office when he unlocked the door. He took them into the examination room immediately.

After closing the door to the waiting room, the doctor turned to the couple and asked, "Whose baby is this? I know this is not the baby I delivered around 8 months ago. What's the story?"

When the couple looked at each other, it was clear each wanted the other to tell the doctor what they had come to tell him.

The doctor could tell they were reluctant to begin so he took the child from Audrey Ball's arms and laid her on the examination table. "This is a handsome child. But I don't think it's what you came about today. Is this child ill?"

Ronnie Ball said, "This is how it is, Doc. This ain't our baby and we don't rightly know who it belongs to and we don't rightly know how to find out. We reckon we don't have no legal right to this child but we reckon this here is a miracle---it's a miracle-- God just dropped her into our arms. My wife and me are about to go crazy tryin' to figure this thing out. We's a-hopin' you can hep us."

The doctor handed the baby back to Mrs. Ball and then pulled out chairs for them all to sit down. "Okay, Ronnie, let's hear the whole story."

Ronnie took a deep breath and began "It happened back in the fall. My brother and me was a-comin' out of the woods—we'd been hunting up on the ridge above Peter's Branch. Well, anyways, we was walkin' out and we heared a baby cryin' and it was close. We was puzzled so we started lookin' for where the cryin' come from and we found this little thing wrapped in an old nasty looking piece of blanket layin' on the ground by the path. We looked around for somebody and we couldn't see no sign of anybody anywhere and we couldn't in our Christian hearts leave that little thing just lay there and die. So I wrapped my jacket around it and carried it home and give it to Audrey here."

Ronnie stopped and Audrey began, "This little girl had jest been borned I reckon. I mean the afterbirth cord and all was still hangin' on the poor little thing. They was somebody wanted to get rid of this little one but I reckon the Good Lord done stepped in and protected her. I've pondered this whole thing a lot and I reckon it was the daddy who done it cause the mother wudden able to get up and walk in the woods so soon after birthing her baby. I mean this here little girl was about as newborn as you can be. She weren't cleaned off or nothin'. She had a lot of black hair and it was matted with dry blood by the time Ronnie got her to our house."

The doctor was stunned, "Well, I want to tell you that nothing I learned in Medical School applies to this situation. I don't honestly know what legal ramifications there are. I believe the police would have to give her over to the State and she would probably end up in an orphanage somewhere in West Virginia. I'll talk to a lawyer about this. Meantime, let me ask you, does having another mouth to feed pose a big problem for you folks?"

The couple looked at each other. Audrey Ball said, "Well I was lucky I guess. Since I was already nursin' our baby, I had plenty of milk for two babies. So she's been real healthy and growing—I reckon it's a miracle. She's a happy baby and we've jest been treatin' 'em like they was twins. We could raise her up like our daughter cause we're mighty fond of 'er already."

The doctor smiled and reached for the baby. He laid her on the examination table and talked to her softly as he examined her. As he looked at her stomach, he asked, "Who tied the cord off?" Mrs. Ball indicated she had done it. "You did a good job. Couldn't have done better myself." The baby smiled and cooed at the doctor. "This one could win your heart real quick—and that's a fact. She certainly doesn't seem to have suffered any ill effects from the rough beginning. She has all the appearance of a healthy baby girl. I will have to agree with you—it is a miracle."

Placing her back into the arms of Audrey Ball, he said, "One legal issue I can think of right now is she needs a birth certificate. There is no record of her birth. I will talk to the lawyer about how to handle that. Have you named her? Would you be in agreement to have your names on the birth certificate as the parents of record?"

Audrey spoke up, "I'd like to call her Zoe. I looked it up and Zoe means life. She fought to live and I think that would be a good name for her. I reckon Zoe Grace. She has life by the grace of God, who protected her and led my husband to find her. Her name tells the story of ever one of us: Life by the Grace of God.

He continued, "That's beautiful, Audrey, I think you have the soul of a poet. Now listen, folks, I want you to think about if you want to legally adopt her. I will get legal advice on that for you, too. I don't want to jump in where you don't want me to. It is all right if I do that, isn't it? Or do you want to talk to a lawyer on your own?"

Ronnie Ball spoke up, "No siree, Doc, that's why we come to you today. We didn't know what to do or where to turn. We're glad to know she's healthy but we already thought she was by the way she eats and how she's growing." Then standing and extending his hand to Doctor Bondy, he said, "I feel so much better after talkin' to you, Doc. My wife and me will be waitin' to hear from you. We appreciate the way you always want to help people. We are blessed to have you for a doctor but even more as a friend."

Doctor Bondy was visibly touched by the kind words, he said, "Well, Ronnie, you made my day. I think this is the reason I became a doctor—to help people. You folks have a great day. And take care of your little ones. You are doing a fine job as parents."

Since there were no other patients waiting, Dr. Bondy sat down to read the medical journals he had brought to the office with him. But he had trouble concentrating on the words because his mind kept going back to the story Ronnie Ball had told about finding the baby in the woods.

He went to the phone and rang the number of Ben Sizemore, an attorney in Welch. When he answered, Doc said, "Ben, this is R. C. Bondy and I have a very unusual situation here tI need some legal advice about. As you know I have offices in Davy, Asco, Twin Branch and Mohegan. I am at Mohegan today. This morning there was a couple waiting for me when I got here. They had a six month old baby girl they say the husband found in the woods last fall. It was a new born with cord attached—it had just been born. Evidently, it had been wrapped in a piece of blanket and just laid on the ground. Well, to make a long story short, the husband took the baby home and they have been taking care of it ever since. What are the legal ramifications of this situation?"

The lawyer, stammered a little when he said, Well, I…..I… I think you do have a situation. Has anyone reported this to the authorities?"

Doc replied, "No, Ben, I'm sure they have not. The only ones who know about it is this couple, his brother, who was with him when he found the baby and the person who put the baby there. The name of the couple is Ball, Ronnie and Audrey Ball. They are good people— they have been taking care of her like she was their own. They have a baby boy themselves who is a couple months older so they are treating them like twins."

Ben Sizemore had been in practice for a number of years and thought he had seen or heard of everything. But this was a new thing. He finally said, "R. C., are you still there?"

"Still here, Ben, waiting for your wisdom."

"Well, my wisdom tells me to think it over. I'll look at some case law and precedents on similar situations. It's a real puzzler—one you don't come across every day. I am going to have to roll this one around in my brain for a bit. What say, I get back to you tomorrow? Where are you tomorrow?"

The doctor responded, "Friday is my day off. I'll be hanging around home in the morning and then I was going to run to Bluefield in the afternoon. I could stop by your office tomorrow about 11 am, if that would fit your schedule."

Ben replied, "I have an appointment at 10 but I should be finished with them by 11. You might have to wait for a few minutes but I think 11 would work. See you then."

Just as Doctor Bondy hung up the phone, someone came in the office. He turned his attention to his next patient.

As the afternoon rolled around, Aggie Wertz came into the doctor's office with Marika. From her body language, it was obvious Marika did not want to be there. Aggie had spent the morning trying to communicate with her the importance of going to be checked out by the doctor. Joe had stepped in and somehow, without the benefit of spoken language, persuaded her to go with Aggie to see Doc Bondy.

When the door to the examination room was closed, Dr. Bondy turned to Aggie and said, "Can you help her disrobe and put this gown on? I'll go in my office and wait. Just knock on that door over there when you are ready."

Marika did not want to undress but Aggie finally got her to cooperate, put on the gown and sit on the examination table. When Aggie knocked on the office door, Doc appeared immediately.

"Marika?" Doc asked. She shook her head to the affirmative. In a very calm manner, he continued, "I want to look at your arms and legs." He took her right arm in his hand and turned it over while pressing on the multiple lesions he found. "It looks like she has ringworm, Mrs. Wertz. I have some good medicine that should clear that up." He listened to her lungs. He took a deep breath and let it out slowly, he did it again. Finally after about the fourth time, she mimicked his breathing. They both laughed. *Good girl, he thought, you are a clever one, you are.* "Well, her lungs sound pretty good. What she needs is what she's getting: good food, good rest in a clean environment and plenty of exercise. With gardening season coming on, she will get exercise, for sure."

"Now let's listen to your heart, young lady. He placed the stethoscope on her chest and listened. Then repositioned it and listened. He put the ear pieces in Marika's ears and let her listen to her own heart beat. She sat transfixed and said "Ooh!"

Doc laughed and then added, "I guess that says it all."

He carefully positioned her for a pelvic examination and although she held back at first, it was obvious she did not feel threatened and she trusted him. After he had finished, he took her hand and brought to a full seated position. "You did great, Marika." Then he turned to Aggie, and said, "Mrs. Wertz, I can tell from the pelvic examination she has delivered within the past 6 months. There is a lot of scar tissue which tells me she was torn during delivery. The fact there is a lot of scarring also indicates that it probably was a full term pregnancy. The birth was probably unassisted without any medical care or supervision. That's my best guess. Did you notice the stretch marks on her abdomen?"

Aggie indicated she had noticed them when she bathed her that first night. "I knew she had been through a lot. I suspected she had a baby because of the stretch marks. That's one of the reasons I wanted her to see you. Will the scar tissue hurt her? I mean if she has another baby. Will she be able to have children? I feel sorry for her because I don't think she brought this on herself. And Doctor, the next question in my mind is: What happened to the baby? Did it die? Did he kill it? My heart is breaking for her. I wonder if she knows what happened to the baby. So many unanswered questions. The sheriff is trying to arrange an interpreter—I hope it's soon."

The doctor said, "Mrs. Wertz, she is in remarkably good health. She is a strong young lady. I don't know about the baby but I will try to find out. There is no way I can tell by examination if the delivered infant was born alive or stillborn. As far as the scar tissue is concerned, it will need to be surgically removed and the area cleaned up. That is a minor procedure that takes just a few minutes to perform. I can do that at #1 Hospital after about another 6 months. It's always better to wait for a few months. After the surgery heals, it should not prevent pregnancy or delivery as long as she has proper medical supervision. Do you have any more questions?"

Aggie thought for a minute and said, "No, I don't think so. Thanks Doctor Bondy. Don't forget the medicine for those sores."

He smiled, "Oh, I won't. This is a salve that should be applied liberally to each of the lesions on her body. You may have to help her for areas where she cannot reach. This salve has a chemical that will kill the fungus that causes the condition. Do this several times a day until the lesions are dried up. Don't let her pick at them. They will eventually peel off and she will have smooth skin. If she picks at them, she could have scars on her arms and the rest of her body. Okay?" Aggie nodded. "All right, I'm going to step out and she can dress again and you'll be ready to go. But don't leave until you get the salve. I'll have it in the outer office."

It was a slow day for Doctor Bondy. *I guess most everybody in Mohegan is healthy this week, he thought.* His mind was preoccupied with the story Ronnie and Audrey Ball had told him. He strongly suspected there was a direct connection between the baby that he had seen earlier and Marika but he couldn't connect all the dots.

It was about 3 pm when Alvin Wertz came by for a follow-up. "Sorry, I'm running a little late today, Doc. I've been lookin' for a job. I think I could get lots of truck drivin' jobs if the mines were workin' but they ain't. I been thinkin' about all the odd haulin' jobs I could get if I had a truck of my own. The problem is I ain't got no money to buy anything—let alone a truck. I'm tryin' to work it all out. Got any idees?"

After the doctor had examined Alvin and pronounced he was well. "I still hear that murmur in the aortic valve—but I honestly think it sounds less pronounced today than last week. I just want to keep checking it. We got that sulfa drug just in time to prevent serious damage to your heart. I can tell you are feeling 100% better. Am I right?"

"I reckon you're right, Doc. I got a lot of energy and I need to earn some money. The railroad ain't hirin' and besides I don't reckon I'm strong enough to swing a sledge hammer all day long—I ain't feelin' that good" he said with a grin. "I probably never will feel that good. A sledge hammer don't fit my hand too good, if you know what I mean."

Doc Bondy, pushed his wheeled stool back and said, "Alvin, I was

B E V E R L Y   S C E L L A T O

planning to go up to Bluefield tomorrow afternoon. A buddy of mine from medical school is practicing up in Princeton and he has two extra tickets for a concert tomorrow night. We would stay the night at his place and drive back to Davy on Saturday. I was wondering if you would like to go. I've got to make a stop in Welch for an appointment at 11 before going on to Bluefield. The appointment shouldn't take more than an hour. I've got some ideas I would like to talk to you about."

Alvin looked at the floor for a moment, then replied, "I have a problem, Doc. I ain't got a red cent to my name. I can't afford to run with your kind. I ain't had a job for about a year. My parents are eking out a living and I've been livin' off them. So I'm gonna say, I can't go nowheres now. I appreciate your asking but I'm goin' have to say no."

Doc had a serious look on his face when he said, "Alvin, I have confidence in you. In a matter of about 10 years I predict you will be one of the wealthiest men in this valley. You have the heart of an entrepreneur---you are going to figure out a way to make money—and a lot of it. I don't know how you will do it but I do know these hard times will not last forever. Better times are coming."

After he finished with his pep talk, Doc pulled his wallet out and extended a twenty dollar bill toward Alvin. It had been a very long time since Alvin had seen such a large bill. He recoiled from it and did not take it. "Consider this a long term loan. I expect you to use it very strategically and to pay me back twenty one dollars within the next two years. This will be plenty for the weekend and money left over. How about it, Buddy? I think it will be good for you."

The challenge of stretching that $20 bill and make it work for him was tantalizing. He thoughtfully took the bill from the doctor's hand and put it in his pocket. "Thanks, Doc. You have challenged me to do something special with this money. I accept the challenge. I'm gonna make me a budget for spending—that's the easy part. The hard part is figuring out what strategically means!"

The doctor laughed and said, "I think you already have a good idea of what it means. I'll pick you up tomorrow morning about 10:15 or so. Don't forget to take an overnight bag. Now get out of here, sounds like I've got some sick people in the waiting room—who need a doctor."

Aggie was not happy when she got the news Alvin was going out of town with Doc to go to a concert. It would be different if he was going to work. She realized he was a grown man who needed to make his own decisions--but doing something just for fun did not fit into her image of what a man should do. Especially as she put it, "somebody who did not have a pot to pee in."

When Alvin told her Doc had loaned him $20 she went on a rampage. "Alvin Wertz, whatever possessed you to borrow that much money from the Doc? How are you ever gonna pay back that much money? I declare that there's enough money to put a down payment on a Model T, I reckon."

Alvin just said, "I have a plan, Mom." *But he thought, did she say down payment on a car? Hmm!*

Aggie stared daggers at him and said, "We'll see."

Things were tense all through supper that evening in the Wertz household. After supper John took out his Bible for the usual Bible Study. Knowing he did not want to add an element of discord to the Bible Study, Alvin was looking for a way to excuse himself when the back door flung open. "Hey folks, look who's here!" It was Louanna and Reggie laden down with boxes.

Good timing, Sis! Alvin thought.

Aggie jumped up to embrace her daughter whose baby bump was beginning to show. She said, "I was beside myself with sheer happiness when Alvin told me about the baby. You do look beautiful. Alvin was right, motherhood is becomin' on you."

After everybody hugged Louanna and Reggie, Aggie said, "Louanna, this here is Marika. She's livin' with us now. She has your old room."

Marika stood from her seat. "Louanna" she said but her eyes were fixed on Louanna's stomach. She whispered "Jitscaw". Then she went over to where Louanna was standing and put her hand on Louanna's stomach all the while saying, "Jitscaw!" "Jitscaw!" Over and over with increasing volume, she said "Jitscaw!" Within a few seconds, she was holding her own stomach and shouting and the shout turned into sobs. "Jitscaw! Jitscaw!" she cried and then she collapsed onto the floor.

Joe picked her up and carried her to the bedroom. He was puzzled, why did Louanna's pregnancy throw Marika into such a frenzy? He wiped her forehead and stayed with her until she fell sleep.

When Joe reappeared in the kitchen, the family was having a discussion about Marika. Aggie began, "Joe, I've been waiting for you to come back to tell ever'body what the doctor said about Marika today. She is in good general health. He gave her medicine for the sores on her body. It should dry them up. But the most interesting thing that happened and might explain what happened here tonight is Marika has delivered a baby within the past six months, the doctor reckons. He said he thinks it was a full term delivery since they's a lot of scar tissue where she was tore on the inside when the baby come."

With a puzzled look on his face, Joe asked, "What happened to the baby?"

"That is what everyone is asking? Where is the baby?"

Then she added, "If the baby was born in the cabin you described, what do you think happened to it?"

Joe thought for a few minutes and then looked at Alvin. "What do you think Alvin?"

Alvin very thoughtfully said, "I don't know much about delivering a baby. Let me say that another way. I don't know nothing about delivering a baby. I've always thought there was a lot of blood. I remember the blood—or at least what looked like dried blood on the bed. Did you notice that, Joe?"

Joe nodded. *I wonder if he took the baby after it was born and threw it in the woods. Maybe it was stillborn. Doc said it was probably full term. I wonder if we should look around the area for the body. If it happened six months ago, there is no way the baby could have survived. Wild animals would have eaten the baby—dead or alive. The thought of it sent shivers down his spine. He put his head in his hands—he could not bear the thought of it. Thinking about what she must have experienced was hard enough to endure but he could not bear to think about a dead baby, too. No wonder she had such a hard time dealing with the memories of the cabin.*

The thoughts were almost too much for him to bear—what she must be going through. He was beginning to understand her emotional response to Louanna's pregnancy. He was deep in thought when he suddenly realized he was crying. Tears were running off his chin.

Alvin's words penetrated Joe's thoughts. "I think I am beginning to understand why Marika was so afraid when she was hiding in our barn. She was afraid he would find her. What he did to her was unthinkable."

Louanna, who looked like she was going to cry, too, said, "Oh, honey, I had no idea. This girl has been through so much. I don't want our happiness to cause her pain."

Aggie said, "No, no, Louanna, you must not think that a way. It's not your happiness that gives her pain—it's her pain that causes her unhappiness. It is not your fault."

Louanna replied, "I know it in my head but my heart is heavy for her. I feel sorry for her but she will have to find a way to deal with this pain every time she sees an expectant mother. She is going to have to find a way to put it behind her. It won't be easy because there are always going to be expecting women around. I wonder what we, as a family, can do to help her."

Aggie said, "The sheriff is arranging for an interpreter to come and talk to her. We are hoping she can tell us exactly what happened there in that cabin. Maybe if she can talk about it she will allow somebody to help her. I wonder how long she was there in that wretched place. The way I see it is she has been through hell and right now she is in a dark place. I reckon it's our Christian duty to help her climb out of that darkness and see daylight."

Alvin spoke up, "I reckon she was there over two years. According to the police report, she disappeared in November 1934. Here it is March 1937. It was right around Christmas time last year when Mom saw her for the first time. So she's been around here over 2 months so it figgers she was in that cabin over two years. Two years of hell, I reckon."

Looking at Reggie, Louanna said, "You know, honey, it's a miracle she escaped from that cabin."

Marika entered the room very quietly. She went over to Louanna and put her arms around her and said "Shay-prasham. Shay-prasham." Then she turned and sat in the empty chair next to Joe.

Louanna said, "I accept your apology, Marika. We will be friends, I know it."

Marika smiled.

Louanna brought out the boxes of clothes which she and Reggie had brought. It was like all the birthdays and Christmases Marika had ever known rolled into one. Marika pulled out dresses, shoes, coats squealing with delight with each new piece. There were everyday clothes and dress clothes. She was so proud. She had never had such beautiful things.

She sorted through the boxes and finally picked the one with the most ruffles. It was light blue—her favorite color. She dismissed herself and reappeared in a few minutes. Joe couldn't take his eyes off her as she modeled her new clothes.

Joe felt a strange pride in her composure especially after her breakdown earlier. Her unprompted apology to Louanna showed humility. She is certainly resilient, he thought. It takes a very strong person to endure what she's been through and maintain her sweet spirit. She has been so hurt—both emotionally and physically—she is grieving--but I don't see any bitterness. She's going to get over this and she will lead a normal life, I know it. Heartbreak and pain that have defined her last few years will one day melt into the past. Weeping may last for the night, but joy comes in the morning. He decided that he would pray that for her from now until the day he could see joy in her eyes.

Aggie commented, "I reckon that them clothes cudden-a fit her any better if they was made special for her. I knowed that your friend, Lucy, was about the same size as Marika but I reckon she is the exact same size. Make sure that you tell Lucy how happy Marika was to have these wonderful clothes. She'll be so proud to wear them, I reckon."

Marika went around the room, showing off her new dress. She made her way to where Louanna and Reggie were seated. "Thank you, Louanna", she said. "Thank you, Reggie".

John explained, "Thank you was the first English words she learned. I reckon them's good words to know, don't you?"

John continued, "since they's so much goin' on tonight, it don't look like we're gonna git to have Bible Study, I'd like for us to pray together before Louanna and Reggie have to leave."

They all bowed their heads and John prayed:

"Dear Lord, we are feeling so blessed tonight as we think about a new addition to the family. We pray You would keep Louanna safe through this time and the child that is growing inside her would be healthy and whole. We all got Marika on our minds, Lord. She has become a part of this family and she's got troubles we don't know nothing about. There are things about her situation that only You know, Lord. If it be Your will, we pray that we would be able to discover the hidden things tormenting her soul so we can help her. Bless our family as we try to honor You in all we do. Amen."

After picking up Alvin on Friday morning, Dr. Bondy pulled onto the black top road to make the trip to Bluefield via a stop at a lawyer's office in Welch.

On the way, when they reached the horseshoe bend at Peter's Branch, Alvin said, "It was up that there holler where Marika was held in that cabin. She took my brother Joe over there last Monday. Then Joe took me and the sheriff to see it on Monday afternoon. I tell you Doc, it was worse than awful. I ain't seen nothing like it before. It was filthy and it smelled like an outhouse. But the worst part is that she was put in a cage just big enough for her to stand or squat but not lay down. I think she was treated like an animal. The bed was broke down—it had an old blanket on it that looked like it had been soaked in blood. You found out she had delivered a baby so I reckon the blood was from that. It's amazin' that she never got infected and died. Doc, do you think the baby survived?"

"I guess everything is possible but I think it is definitely a longshot. The chances are not too good. Do you think we could stop and look at the cabin tomorrow on our way back?"

Alvin said, "I don't know why not."

Doc had not heard about the cabin before today. He was especially interested in the location. He kept remembering what Ronnie Ball had told him about where he found the new born baby. *I don't think I'm going to tell Alvin what I know about the baby yet—not until I'm sure. After I talk with the lawyer I should have a better idea of which direction to go.*

As they drove into McDowell Street in Welch, the doctor said "I've got to talk to a lawyer about a situation with a patient. I figure it will take me about an hour. You can stay in the waiting room or take a stroll around Welch."

Alvin replied, "Think I'll walk around for a little bit. It's a pretty day. I'll mosey back over here at noon and wait by the car."

In the second floor corridor above the Men's Smart Shop, Doctor Bondy found the door marked: Benjamin Sizemore Attorney at Law. When he opened the door, he was greeted by the attorney who invited him into his office. Seated across the desk from his client, Ben Sizemore took out a yellow legal pad and said, "Okay, doctor, what can I help you with?"

Not sure exactly where to begin, Doc Bondy said, "This is a complicated situation and I need to know what I am legally required to do. I told you about it briefly on the phone yesterday. A couple, who are patients of mine, came in my office yesterday with a baby who does not belong to them. The husband said he found it in the woods last October. He heard a baby crying so he went to check it out and found this little baby girl lying on the ground wrapped in an old dirty blanket. It was a new born with the cord still attached. He took her home and they have been taking care of her ever since. The baby is healthy and seems to be thriving. I examined her and she seems like a happy baby who is well cared for. The question I have for you is: Can this couple claim parental rights and get a birth certificate for this baby?"

Ben straightened in his chair and said, "Well, this is a hard one. If that couple just raised that child without saying anything to anybody about it, after a few years—I think it's seven-- they could claim that child by a law similar to one which deals with common law marriage. The child concerned would be considered an abandoned child according to the law."

The doctor said, "But if that happened in this case, the child still would not have a birth certificate. Right?"

"Correct. But if they want to get a legal birth certificate, it would have to go through the courts. It doesn't necessarily mean it will be in open court but rather a judge would have to decide about legal parentage. How that works is that a legal notice is put in the paper and it has to run for 6 weeks, I think it is. The notice would state the petitioning parent's intention of claiming the child as their own. In this case, they would naturally claim parental abandonment at birth. If there are no challenges to their claims, the judges normally finds in favor of the applicant. The court system is looking out for the welfare of the child. It looks to me like this child had divine protection and has been placed in a good home with some good parents. I, personally, don't think the courts could do better for this child. This could make a person believe in miracles!"

Doc Bondy asked, "If a woman came forward and claimed parentage of the child who had been cared for by this family, how could she prove she was the biological mother? I know sometimes they will try to use blood type as proof of parentage. However, current medical wisdom goes against using blood type alone to determine biological parents. In the future I think there will be scientific means to establish paternity but that's a long way off."

"Another question is: if this couple wants to get a birth certificate like we talked about and claim this baby as their own, do they still have to go through adoption proceedings with a judge, etc?"

Doc Bondy continued, "Do I have your word our conversation today is confidential?"

The lawyer looked up from his notes and said, "Absolutely, everything that is said here stays here."

The doctor shifted in his chair and said, "Okay, here goes. Just yesterday I came across information which leads me to believe I know the identity of the biological mother in this situation. This story is so unbelievable I don't know how to start. There is a young woman whose name is Marika—she is probably not more than 16 years old who was sleeping in the barn of one of the families in Mohegan. The family discovered her and took her into their home. She doesn't speak English so we can't ask her a lot. They have reported the situation to the sheriff and they think she was kidnapped during the night out of her home in Gary nearly three years ago. They have discovered she was held in a cabin in the woods in Peter's Branch holler against her will. She was actually kept in a cage. The cabin where she was held is very close to the spot where the baby was found in the woods."

The lawyer looked up and said, "I have a feeling there's more."

"Right, this is where my problem rests. Yesterday, not three hours after the couple with the baby left my office, Aggie Wertz—she's the woman who took this girl in—brought Marika for an examination. Outside of having ringworm, I discovered she is basically a healthy young woman. That's another miracle when you think about it. Anyway, I did a pelvic examination and discovered she had delivered a baby about 6 months ago, according to my estimation. She has some tissue damage which is common in unattended births but otherwise she is fine."

He hesitated and then continued, "so when I put this all together— the baby, the location, the cabin, the young woman who recently delivered, the dates that match up—I can only come to one logical conclusion. The child in question is the one born to Marika in that cabin. So—you can see my dilemma. What is my legal responsibility? If I report this to the sheriff, it's my guess they will take the baby away from a very good home and place it in institutional care. I don't want that for the child or for those parents who have bonded with the child and consider it like their own. I didn't tell you they have a baby of their own who is a couple months older than the infant in question. They are raising them together like twins."

He looked up at Ben Sizemore, who was writing furiously on his yellow pad and then he continued.

"I'm sure Marika believes her baby died. She surely seems to be grieving. She has no idea what happened to it. She must have delivered the baby unattended and her captor took it and left it in the woods. Her captor has to be the father, also. That is the only scenario that makes sense. The men who saw the cabin talked about the covers on the bed being blood-stained. She must have delivered in that filthy bed. It's a miracle she didn't pick up an infection and die herself."

Then he added, "I have this information. As far as I know, I'm the only one who has put all this together. What do I do?"

"Another thing I forgot to mention—the sheriff is arranging an interpreter to talk to Marika in her language. When she is able to tell her story we will know a lot more. Do you think I should tell the sheriff what I suspect happened? I really have only circumstantial evidence. But the circumstances tell a lot."

Taking his glasses off and laying them on top of his yellow legal pad now filled with scribbled notes, Ben Sizemore looked at the doctor and said, "having this kind of information is heavy, isn't it?"

The doctor just nodded and murmured, "yes, it is."

"Well, Doctor, you came to me for advice. So here is my best judgment for now. I think it would be wise to wait until the interpreter talks with Marika. You should write some questions for her to ask. You should ask for information about the birth, baby, etc. As I was listening to your story, I was thinking about what Marika would need to show as evidence this was her baby. There is only one thing that connects that baby with the cabin and it's the old dirty blanket the baby was wrapped in. You should find out if the people who found the baby saved the blanket. It probably got burned up or thrown away—that would be my guess. But, if that lady was like my mom, she may have saved it—you know washed it because she might need it someday. Find out about it and if it still exists, see if you can obtain it. If you do, just wrap it up and put it away. I know this is far-fetched but that piece of blanket could come into play as evidence. It is the only thing that connects Marika and that baby. The next thing is to connect Marika and that blanket from which the piece was cut."

The lawyer continued, "Some of these details don't fit. In my experience with cases of child molestation or abduction, there is always a connection between the family and the perpetrator. Do you know what the connection between Marika's family is with the man who held her in the cabin? Do they even know the identity of the man who took her? Whoever took her to that cabin didn't just drive by the house one night and decide to take her. He had to know about her and something about the family. We were talking about connecting Marika and the baby—how do we connect Marika and her abductor? You say the baby is about 6 months old but the abduction case happened almost 3 years ago?"

Dr. Bondy replied, "I had not thought about that. I've been focused on the infant and Marika. I guess that is a question for Marika. Did she know her captor beforehand? He knew her or at least he knew about her. He knew where she slept."

Doctor Bondy looked at his watch. It was nearly noon. As he stood to leave, he said, "I came to you for answers and I go away with more questions. It looks like this is a twisted knot that will take a while to untangle."

Accompanying him to the door, the lawyer said "Give me a call after the interpreter talks with Marika. Be discreet. Everybody doesn't need to know what you know—as a matter of fact, nobody else needs to know what you know. It will all come out in due time. We want to use this information to help the situation and not hurt anybody involved. That's a fine line."

After shaking hands with the lawyer, Doc Bondy walked out into the dimly lit hallway.

As he slowly made his way down the stairs, he thought. This has me in a knot. If I reveal what I know and the baby—little Zoe-- is taken from the Balls they will be heartbroken. They have taken such good care of her and she is a happy, healthy baby. They are excellent parents. On the other hand, what could Marika give the baby now? She has so many issues of her own to work through. She has no home and no means of support other than the Wertz family. I know biological parents have God-given rights but they also have responsibilities. Marika believes the baby is dead. Maybe it would be better if it stays that way. But on the other hand, who am I to play God? This may drive me crazy. And now, there's this connection angle Ben brought up. Is it possible Marika's own father had some involvement in this? How did the kidnapper know about the child? Pedophiles usually stalk their victims—but where and how did he ever even see this girl? He shook his head as if to clear the thoughts. *I'm glad we're going to the concert tonight—maybe I can think of something else.*

When the doctor got to the street level, Alvin was waiting near the car smoking a cigarette.

Doc said, "Alvin, I tell you, those things are going to kill you. You need to give it up."

Snuffing out the cigarette on the ground, Alvin said, "I know, I know."

"I'm hungry" the doctor said, "all that legal mumbo-jumbo has given me an appetite. Let's go across the street to Franklin's and have a sandwich before we head toward Bluefield."

"Sounds good to me" Alvin replied.

On Saturday afternoon, Alvin led Doc Bondy to the cabin in Peter's Branch. As they approached, Alvin realized he had not adequately prepared Doc for what he would see. But it was too late now.

Doctor Bondy's first response was revulsion. "I thought that I had seen the worst but I was wrong. This is truly more vile than I ever could have imagined." He walked over and looked at the bed. Realizing that a human being had been brought into the world in this bed made him shiver. *Wild animals have cleaner birthing places, he thought.*

When the doctor turned around, he discovered Alvin had stepped out to the porch. "Alvin", he called. Alvin came back in the cabin and said, "I needed a breath of fresh air. Sorry."

"That's understandable." the doctor said and then he asked, "do you think I could take that blanket? I'd rather not say why I want the filthy thing but I do have a good reason for asking."

Alvin thought for a moment and said, "I don't know why not. It seems to me the sheriff would have taken it if he wanted it. I'll let him know you took it--jest in case he needs it for evidence or police property. Here let me help you fold it up."

As they folded the blanket and rolled it up, the doctor commented, "this makes a body wish he carried surgical gloves with him at all times.

I hate to even consider what the germ content of this thing is." As they folded, the doctor also noticed a large section from the corner of the blanket had been cut away. *The newborn must have been wrapped in that section, he thought. Mission accomplished. I think with this blanket, we could make a good case for Marika's parentage, if we need to. That is if Audrey Bell kept the other section. Little Zoe has to be Marika's baby—no doubt in my mind. And she doesn't know the baby survived. I bet she never even saw her or if she birthed a boy or a girl for that matter.*

"Well, Alvin, I think I've seen all I need to see."

Alvin asked, "Did you notice the cage? I wanted to make sure you looked at that cage. That thing, to me, is a torture chamber."

The doctor said, "Yeah, I looked at it. And I noticed that the rags in the bottom were soaked with blood, too. I hope he didn't put her back in that thing after she delivered." Then he added, "but I fear that's exactly what he did." *Remembering the crying infant laying on the ground in the woods*, he said, "What kind of monster does something like this?"

After putting the blanket roll in the trunk of his car, they continued the drive toward Mohegan.

Alvin said, "Doc, I hope this has not upset you because this is really not your problem. But remember you asked to see the cabin."

Doc replied, "Alvin, I try to make it a practice to not get personally involved in the problems of my patients. I think it's too late for this one. I am involved more than you know. I hope very soon I can share with you all the details I already know about Marika's situation. Right now, I think it would be too heavy for you to carry. It will all come out soon. My hope is that Marika's parents will be found soon and they will be able to help sort this out. It is not really the responsibility of your family. Marika just happened to find her way to your barn when she somehow escaped from that dreadful cabin. It seems to me there was a divine hand guiding her to a nurturing family like yours. Finding the interpreter will give her the opportunity to unburden the heaviness which she has endured and allow her to begin the healing. Remember, she has not had the chance to tell anybody about it. We have pieced some things together about a scenario that seems logical—but we do not know for sure what happened. It is my hope she can put this behind her although how one does that is beyond my knowing. I think it will be hard for her to ever trust a man but I also believe since God delivered her, He will also provide a man who will love her selflessly and lead her into a happy marriage and contented life. This is in God's hands."

"Wow, Doc, I couldn't have said it better. I know Mom and Dad are praying for her. They are very concerned. In many ways she has been a blessing to our family. She is really smart and is picking up English words real quick. You know, besides all that happened to her in the cabin, she has the grief of losing her baby, too. That's a big burden."

"Uh-huh" Doc said, as he turned into Mohegan bottom to drop Alvin off at home.

The doctor said, "Alvin, make sure you wash up real good when you get in the house and put on clean clothes. That blanket was nasty. It was not wise to allow you to handle it. We're probably both loaded with germs. Your resistance is not very strong."

"Thanks for everything, Doc. I really enjoyed the concert. Those big bands put on a good show. It was good to get away overnight. I liked your friend. But if I'm gonna hang out with you fellows, I gottta figure out a strategy to make money. See you! Thanks, again."

As the doctor turned his car toward home, *he thought, somehow this is all going to work out and that fellow is going to make it—I just know it.*

Before he pulled on the black top road, he took a left turn and pulled up in front of the Ball's house. He sat in his car for a few moments, thinking about his approach to the Balls. *If they ask why I want the blanket, I have to be truthful with them. Nothing is gained by lying about it. They have to know there is a possibility that the birth mother may try to claim the baby. I can't control this just because I have decided how I want it to turn out. I'll just be truthful and leave it in God's hands.*

As the doctor approached the front door, Ronnie Ball came out to meet him. "Hi, Doc", he said. "We're alright. They ain't none of us sick. Reckon why you came by."

Doctor Bondy responded, "Well, Ronnie, I have an unusual situation on my hands. I come to ask you if you saved that piece of blanket the baby was wrapped in. It would be helpful to me."

Ronnie grinned and said, "Of all the things I figured you come about, I never thought it would be fer that old piece of blanket. You sure you want it Doc—it's filthy?"

Then he continued, "I'll have to ask my wife. I don't know what she did with it. She might'a throwed it away or on the other hand she might'a washed it to save for quilt pieces. Problem is she ain't here right now. She and the babies are visiting with her maw and paw over in Premier. I gotta go fetch 'em after while. I'll ask her and if she still has it, I'll bring it over to your office on Thursday. That's the best I can do for now."

As the doctor turned to leave, Ronnie Ball asked, "If you don't mind me askin', what do you need with that old dirty piece of blanket?"

Doc replied, "I'm going to be honest and straightforward with you, Ronnie. I don't know for sure if I'll ever need it. I know you have thought about the possibility the birth mother could appear at some time and want to take the baby. The way I see it, that blanket is the only link between the mother and the baby. It is my belief, unless we get further evidence to the contrary, the birth mother never saw the baby and in all probability believes the baby is dead. She did not abandon her baby—it was out of her hands. There is the possibility that piece of dirty blanket could provide an avenue to get the mother with the right baby. I know if the situation were reversed and you had lost your baby you would want to be dealt with fairly. That's what the piece of blanket does—helps the birth mother have a fair shake. Does that make sense?"

"Yeah, I guess so. But I don't even want to give no thought about losing Zoe. It seems like she belongs to us. We had her since the day she was borned. If I hadna found her out there in the woods she would have died, I reckon. Me and my wife should have some say in this, don't you think so, Doc?"

"I do think so, Ronnie. I'm obligated to obey the law and if I know something that would legally clear up a situation, then I need to deal with it honestly. That's what I'm trying to do. You think it over and decide how you want to handle it. Come by the office on Thursday and let me know what you decided. Okay?"

"Okay, Doc. See you Thursday."

When Ronnie went to bring his family home, Audrey had the children ready to go. As they put them in the car, Ronnie asked, "What did you do with that dirty piece of blanket the baby was wrapped in when I brung her home?"

She replied, "I should'a got rid of it but I never did. I washed it and put it back. I thought I might find a use for it sometime or tuther. Why you askin'?"

As they drove toward Mohegan, Ronnie related to his wife everything Doc Bondy had told him. As he talked, he could feel the tension growing in his usually relaxed wife. When he finished, he asked, "Well, hon, what do you think?"

When Audrey looked at him, he could see sheer terror in her eyes. *She's terrified she is gonna lose her little girl, he thought.*

Then he said, "The Doc, he don't know if you kept it or not—cause I didn't know. So you can decide what to do with it. I don't want you to throw it away but you don't have to give it to the Doc. That's up to you."

She glanced into the back seat to see both of the babies were sleeping. "Oh, ain't that sweet? They played pretty hard with their Mamaw and Papaw. I guess they's just wore out." She began to silently weep. "Don't she feel just like your little girl? Can you tell me for honest that you don't love her as much as you do her brother? Look at me! I'm calling them brother and sister. I can't bear to think about letting her go. In my heart, she is our little girl—our Zoe."

Wanting to help ease Audrey's anxiety, Ronnie said, "Honey, according to the Doc, without that blanket piece they ain't no way to connect the birth mother to the baby I found in the woods. Doc knows about the blanket piece and he seen where it was cut out of the blanket the baby was birthed on. But he can't prove nothin' if'n he ain't got the piece."

Then he added, "I thought it was good when Doc said he was going to be truthful with me—he didn't try to trick me and get the blanket piece. So he told me exactly how it would be used—that is if the birth mother wanted her baby and that's a big if. I don't think he's going to bring it up to her. I'm not even sure he knows who she is but he knows about her. He assumes the birth mother thinks her baby is dead. This is a big decision 'cause it's so important for little Zoe."

They drove along quietly for a while. Ronnie could hear his wife sniffling. It was getting dark when they pulled off the black top road into Mohegan bottom. Audrey blurted out, "I made my decision. I'm a gonna' tell Doc Bondy I don't have it no more. I'm gonna say I got rid of it the same day. I wish I didn't have to lie about it but I can't bear to do nothin' differt if it means somebody could take our baby. Even if that somebody is the birth mother—I'm the real mother. I'm the only mother she ever knowed."

Ronnie was disappointed with her choice to deal deceptively with the doctor but he wanted to support her. "If that is your decision, I told you I would go along with whatever you decided. Only don't throw it away. Just hide it somewhere. Okay?"

"Okay", she said.

Audrey's thoughts were racing. This decision helps me deal with this for right now but I sense that there is heartbreak ahead. Maybe it would have been better if she had died in the woods. She instantly felt ashamed for her thoughts. O Lord, forgive me. I love her—I really do. I would give my life for her—how could I think that way? Fear has taken over my mind. I am going to start having faith that God has a plan for Zoe and pray me and Ronnie will do what God wants us to do. What we do should help prepare her for what God has planned. This is not about me. THIS IS NOT ABOUT ME! I am ashamed of my selfishness. Me and Ronnie has been chose by God to do a special thing in the life of this child. O Lord, help us to know when our job is finished and that we will find joy in doing what is right for Zoe.

Audrey and Ronnie carried the sleeping babies into the house and tucked them in their beds. They kissed each of their children.

Audrey thought, Thank you Lord for each precious day we have with both our children.

On Monday morning, Sheriff Chatham picked up Lena Babinski at her home in Gary. He considered this a very important day in unraveling the mystery that surrounded Marika's abduction and subsequent captivity in a cabin. He wanted to know details about her treatment while she was held in the cabin. He wanted to find out what happened to her captor. Lena Babinski held the key to unlocking the mind of Marika Stanislas.

To this point, Mrs. Babinski did not know the nature of the job she had been hired to do. As a matter of fact, she was more interested in the money she would earn than the details of the task ahead. As they drove along, the sheriff informed Lena of the situation. He reviewed the case without mentioning proper names, beginning with the date Marika was abducted.

"Did you say November 21, 1934?" she asked.

The sheriff confirmed that this case was about something that happened almost 3 year earlier.

"No, no," she said, "I remember—that is the date our neighbor's little girl was stole in the middle of the night. It was awful. The mother nearly lost her mind. The father was so upset he wanted to kill hisself People were sayin' he blamed hisself for not taking care of his little girl. It was the priest-- the old one who's gone now—who helped them. They finally moved away when the mines completely shut down. It must have been about 6 months after the little girl disappeared."

The Sheriff was surprised at the wealth of information that poured out of Lena Babinski. Then he asked, "Mrs. Babinski, did you know the little girl? How old was she?"

She responded, "Oh, Sheriff, call me Lena. Mrs. Babinski sounds so formal."

He smiled and said, "Okay, Lena, did you know the name of this family? Did you know the girl? How old was she?"

Lena said, "Well, I did know them a little bit—their name was Stanislas. His name was Joseph and her name was Susanna. The girl's name was Marika—that's the one who disappeared. They kinda' kept to themselves. The father spoke English pretty good but I don't think they talked English at home. They just lived three houses away but

I didn't know 'em too good—like I said they stayed to themselves. I reckon I knowed 'em just good enough to nod and say 'hello' at church."

Then she blurted out, "Oh, yeah, you wanted to know how old the girl was. I remember when it happened the papers said she was 12 and a half."

The Sheriff said, "Well, Lena, the young girl I need you to translate for is Marika Stanislas. She has been found alive."

"Oh! Glory Be" she exclaimed, "Praise the good Lord in heaven. I never dreamed in all my born days I would ever see that girl again. I bet she's all growed up now. Where in the world has she been? Does she know what she put her family through? Her parents thought she was dead and they had no reason for staying in these parts since they was no work to be had. What in the world happened?"

The sheriff interrupted her and said, "The answers to all those questions is what we need you to find out. I am taking you to meet the young woman we believe to be Marika Stanislas. She is staying with a family by the name of Wertz in Mohegan. She came there about 2 ½ months ago and hid in their barn. When they discovered her they brought her into their home. She's been living with them for about two weeks now. She showed one of the Wertz sons an old cabin in the woods where she was held. She has been through two years of cruel captivity and torture."

Continuing, the sheriff said, "I know this is heavy to lay on you but what you find out is very important for us to know. I have written out a list of questions that I want you to ask her. You, of course, will be speaking to her in Polish. When she gives you her answer, I want you to repeat her words in English so we can record them while they are still fresh. I also want you to promise that you will keep whatever information you learn confidential. This means you cannot talk to other people about what you learn. This is police business and should not be discussed outside of police circles. I want to make you a temporary deputy so you will be paid through the Sheriff's Dept. I will ask you to swear to uphold that vow of confidentiality. Can you do that?"

"Oh, yes sir. I know how to keep my mouth shut, for sure." *What else was I to say, she thought, I need this money so bad.*

The sheriff continued to inquire, "Lena, have you heard where the Stanislas family moved to? We need to locate them as soon as possible. They need to know their daughter is alive. They have been grieving these almost three years—I would like to lift that burden."

Lena replied, "Let me think a minute. I don't know of any specially close friends in Gary that might know—like I said they kept to themselves. The Father at the Catholic Church might know."

"We've already checked with him. They did not give a forwarding address when they moved. And they have not requested a change in their church membership to a new parish. So that was a dead end. Father Paul is going to make an announcement at Mass and put some notices around the town of Gary. He was also going to check with the mine office to see if they left a forwarding address when they moved. I ain't heard nothing on that yet. We also got an ad in the newspaper."

The sheriff continued, "One of the areas I want to question her about is relatives who live in the United States. A lot of folks who left these parts have gone to live with relatives in other states till this depression is over. If we could locate relatives, I think we have a better shot at finding the parents."

When they came into Welch, the sheriff pulled into his designated parking place at the courthouse. He said, "Lena, if you could come with me, we have some official business to take care of before we get to work. I want to swear you in as a temporary deputy who is designated as interpreter on this case."

The sheriff introduced Lena to Sgt. Mary Weaver. "Sgt. Weaver, would you find Chief Deputy Dalton. I need you both to witness Mrs. Babinski taking the oath as a deputy in this case."

When the oath was administered to Mrs. Babinski, the sheriff said, " Sergeant Weaver is going with us down to Mohegan. She is a certified court reporter so she is going to record Marika's response to the questions."

Then he pulled a sheet of paper out of the breast pocket on his uniform shirt and handed it to Lena and said, "This here is the list of questions we need answered. You can read it over while we drive."

Lena read over the list:

1. What do you remember about the night you were taken from your home?
2. Do you know the name of the person who took you? What happened to him? Do you know where he went?
3. Where did he take you?
4. Describe the way he treated you.
5. How did you escape? Who let you out? Where was your captor when you escaped?
6. Did you hear an explosion while you were in the cabin?
7. How did you end up at the Wertz's house?
8. How are you now?
9. Do you have relatives in the United States? Do you know where your parents might have moved when they left Gary?

When she read over the list, she thought, Oh, good, this is gonna' take a long time. More cash in my purse—I need it.

As the sheriff pulled the car into Mohegan bottom, he remarked, "One more thing, Lena, when I hear the answer to one of the questions it could lead to another question I want you to ask. So don't let that catch you off guard. It won't mean you did anything wrong—it just means I need more information. I just wanted you to be prepared. This is the simplest way I can think to do this."

When the sheriff and the two women arrived at the Wertz home, they were surprised to see a smartly dressed young woman waiting for them. Sheriff Chatham thought she looked like a different girl—she had been dressed in rags before. He watched Marika for signs of recognition when introduced to Mrs. Babinski—but saw none.

Aggie invited the group in and suggested that they sit around the kitchen table. "I ain't got no other table" she said "we had to make the dinin' room into a bedroom for our sick son. But he's better now so I reckon we'll be rearranging a-gin soon."

"This will be just fine" the sheriff said. They each found a chair and began to arrange papers in front of them on the table. The photograph of the Stanislas family laid on top in the sheriff's file. He quickly tucked it under another sheet of paper. *That will come later, he thought.*

Aggie offered them tea or coffee before excusing herself to go work in the garden. Before she left the room, she said, "Marika's a little nervous like today. She ain't ever been talked to by law enforcement before. So I hope this goes okay."

The sheriff said, "Mrs. Wertz, you are welcome to stay if you think it would help Marika. What do you think?"

Aggie thought for a minute then said, "I reckon she'll be able to handle it. But I would like to know exactly what happened before she came to us. So, since it's okay with you, I reckon I'll stay and listen. I won't say nothing. I'll be quiet as a mouse over in the corner." Aggie pulled a chair away from the table and sat in the corner of the room just to listen.

Lena sat across the table from Marika. She told Marika in Polish she was going to interpret in English everything she said. "Everything you tell us is important. I want you to answer each one of the questions as truthfully as you possibly can. If it is something that you don't remember, it's okay—just say 'I don't remember'. I'm going to ask you some general questions before I get to the list of questions the sheriff wants me to ask you. One of the reasons we are asking you these questions is to help you be re-united with your family. Is this something you want?" Lena paused to wait for Marika's response, which was slow in coming. Then she said, "I like it here. Aggie and John and all their family have been so good to me. I feel safe. I love my Tata and Mama but I'm happy here, too."

Lena turned to the sheriff and said, "I did not expect that. I asked her if she wanted to be re-united with her family and she said she liked it here with Aggie and John. She said she feels safe. She loves her Tata (Daddy) and Mama but she's happy here."

Then Sgt. Weaver said "it's interesting that she feels safe here. There's the implication of fear in that statement. Perhaps because of what has happened, there is an unspoken fear her family can't protect her. We'll explore that later."

Lena looked at Sheriff Chatham and asked, "Is it alright if I say that her parents have left Gary?" The sheriff nodded.

Lena looked at Marika and reached across the table and took her hand. Speaking to her in Polish, she said, "Marika, I want to tell you that your parents have moved away from where you lived in Gary. They looked for you for several months before they moved. Your father lost his job at the mines and they moved in hopes of finding work somewhere else."

Marika looked shocked and her lower lip began to quiver, "I thought they would find me. I always thought they would find me. They gave up on me." Her voice began to shake as she repeated "they gave up on me. They thought I was dead. Did they really think I was dead? There were lots of days when I wished I was dead." She put her head on the table and sobbed. Aggie handed her a handkerchief and patted her on the shoulder. "Aggie is my friend, she takes care of me." Marika said.

After Lena relayed to the sheriff and deputy what Marika had said, she continued by asking the first question on the list.

"Marika, what do you remember about the night you were taken from your home?"

Lena could tell from her expression this was very difficult for Marika. She felt sorry for the girl. She wanted to be gentle but she could not think of an easier way to ask for the information the sheriff wanted. She had to ask.

Marika, straightening in her chair, began slowly. "The first thing I remember is a hand over my mouth. I tried to bite the hand because it was so tight it was hard to breathe. Then I remember being carried out of my house. I tried to scream but I couldn't make a sound. The next thing I remember is being pushed into a vehicle of some kind. I started crying out and he stuck a rag in my mouth and said something that sounded mean. I didn't understand what he said but I could tell it was mean. It was dark and he drove really fast. I was crying and screaming. He hit me and I fell against the door. I was so scared I just rolled into a ball and cried. When he stopped, he grabbed me out of the truck and carried me into a dirty cabin in the woods. I thought about running but it was dark and I didn't know where I was. I thought my

Tata would come for me. He lit a lantern and when I looked at him I was even more scared. He looked mean. And he was big—I mean real big. There was a cage that looked like it was made for an animal—he threw me in it and locked it. I tried to get out but he just laughed. He was so mean. Then he laid down on the bed and in a few minutes, he was snoring. I was so cold. I had a nightgown and that's all." When she finished, she let out a big sigh as if to say, "I'm glad that's over."

Lena told the sheriff and the deputy what Marika had said. "None of that surprises me" the sheriff said. "We had figured out most of that for ourselves by seeing the setup in the cabin. See if she knows who he is."

Lena turned again to Marika and asked, "do you know the name of the man who took you away from your home?"

Marika began, "he spoke another language—not my language and not English. I could make out that his name was Angelo—or Angel." The sheriff suppressed a laugh. "What happened to him, Marika?" She shrugged her shoulders as if to say, "I don't know." Then Lena asked her, "do you know where he went?" Marika said, "No. He would leave every day—sometimes he would leave for days. He always locked me in the cage when he left. Everyday, I cried. Everytime I heard a noise outside, I screamed and yelled but nobody came. I wanted to get away so bad—but he always locked me in the cage—all night long. I couldn't get out. The key was hanging by the door just out of reach. I would look at the key and think 'if only I had that key, I would run so far so fast.' But I couldn't get it—I couldn't get it." She broke down in sobs, "I couldn't get it!"

Speaking to the sheriff and deputy, Lena said, "it is interesting Marika specified that her captor did not speak English or Polish but another language she did not understand. The poor girl has had language problems all around. She said his name was Angelo or Angel. I noticed you had trouble not laughing at that one." The sheriff smiled and said, "Yeah, I caught that. It was hard to miss even in another language." Lena continued, "She doesn't know what happened to him. He would often leave and he always locked her in the cage when he left—sometimes for days. She doesn't know where he went or what he did when he was gone. Every time she heard anything outside the cabin, she would yell and scream but no one came."

When Lena had finished her explanation, the sheriff said, "Lena, I think she already answered the next question. We know he took her to that cabin. So go on to question number four."

The sheriff looked at Lena and said, "Lena, do you have any knowledge of Angelo Purilli? We believe he is the abductor and we have good evidence he died in an explosion at a moonshine still real close to the location of this cabin. Have you ever heard of him?"

Lena looked puzzled and then said, "No, I don't think so. I'll ask my husband if he knows of him?" She then picked up her pen to write the name, "Angelo? Is it P-U-R-I-L-L-I?" The sheriff nodded, "That's right. Sorry for the interruption, wanted to ask you while it was on my mind—since you were living in the area."

"Marika", Lena continued "How did he treat you? I know he locked you up. When he let you out, was he mean to you?"

Marika looked like she had been slapped in the face. She looked at Lena and said, "I don't even want to think about it." She put her head in her hands and continued in that posture. Lena looked at the sheriff and shrugged. She mouthed, "she doesn't want to think about it."

The sheriff said, "I can understand why she doesn't want to go over it all again. Okay, let's go on to the next question. I think we're getting the picture as she talks."

Lena nodded and said, "Okay, Marika, let's talk about something else. How did you escape? Who let you out?"

Marika perked up at that question. "Angel was gone and I was in the cage, of course. Someone knocked on the door. I started screaming 'Let me out! Help! Help!' and then a man broke the door down. I didn't know who it was or what he came for—I never saw him before. I just wanted out. He seemed really mad about me being pinned up in that cage. He acted like he was mad. I pointed to the key and he unlocked the cage. I grabbed some clothes off a hook and ran and ran and ran. The man who unlocked the cage kept yelling, "Stop! Stop! I will help you! I wasn't sure what he was yelling but it didn't matter. I never stopped running. After I got across the black top road I heard a big Kaboom. I never looked back. I just kept running and running. Then it started to rain and I found a cave where I could stay dry. It rained all night so I stayed in the cave. I don't know where Angel was and I didn't care. I just had to get out of that place as fast as I could. I had to get away from him! I didn't know where I was going but I was leaving that horrible place. I prayed Angel wouldn't try to find me or send some dogs after me."

After Lena very carefully explained what Marika had said to her, the sheriff said, "that was a miraculous escape. I wonder who the man was who unlocked her cage. That may be the biggest mystery we have here. Whoever it was may turn out to be the real 'angel' in this situation. There is something missing about this whole thing. The missing element is a report about this cabin by the man who let Marika out of the cage. Why would he keep it a secret? Does anyone have an explanation for that? He didn't run after her but he did yell for her to stop. "Lena" the sheriff said, "you can skip to question 7. I think she's answered the other ones."

Then he said, "before you go on to question 7, ask Marika how old the man was who let her out? Was he like a brother, father, grandfather in age?"

Lena asked Marika, "how old do you think the man was who let you out? Was he old like a grandfather, sort of old like your father or about the age of a friend?

Marika thought for a minute. Then she said, "I did not notice and that's the truth. I was crazy to get out and I guess I didn't even look at him—I mean really look. But now that I think about it, I don't think he was real old or real young. He was sort of in between young and old—but not like my father—younger, I think. But he didn't hurt me—he let me out. He was kind to me."

Lena turned to the sheriff and said, "She thinks he was medium—not old and not young. She said she really didn't look at him that much. I don't think there's more to learn from her about that."

The sheriff gave Lena a thumbs-up which was her signal to continue. She then asked, "Marika, can you tell us how you found your way to the Wertz house?"

Marika smiled. "I told you I stayed overnight in that cave because it was raining. I was afraid Angel would find me there and I knew I needed to find something to eat. It had been two days since I had eaten. So, early the next morning, I wrapped up in all the clothes I had brought and went down the hill to the river and the railroad. I walked along the railroad till I came to a house that was close to the tracks. There was a barn between the house and the tracks. I saw a ladder on the back of the barn and I climbed up the ladder. When I saw the bales of hay, I decided I could stay there. I looked around and found a horse blanket hanging with the saddles so I took it to try to stay warm. I moved the bales so I could hide behind them and they would block the wind. There was a cow downstairs in the barn. You would be surprised how much heat one animal can give off. And there were about 5 barn cats that came and shared my room with me. They helped keep me warm. I waited till it was almost dark and then I went to the well next to the house and got a drink of water and then I found a box of food on the back porch. I didn't know who the food was for but I took it because I was getting weak from hunger. Aggie is a really good cook so I had a good supper every night. The Wertz family—they love God and they love me. They found me and took me in—they gave me a bath, clothes and a bed." Then she turned around in her chair and looked at Aggie, who had kept her promise to be quiet. "Aggie is like my Mama—she takes care of me. I love her."

Sgt. Weaver wrote the details in her book as Lena related what Marika had said.

Lena thought, the sheriff was right she is bonded to Aggie Wertz. I think she would have a hard time leaving this family. They are her rescuers and her safe place.

The sheriff looked at his watch and gave Lena the signal to continue. Lena turned back to Marika and asked, "How are you now, Marika? I know you have a place to live with the Wertz family but how are you on the inside—in your heart?"

For an instant, Marika looked puzzled at the question and then she said, "Oh, I see what you mean." She twisted the handkerchief Aggie had given to her in her hands, tying it in knots and then untying it and stretching it out on the table.

Lena was not sure if she was going to answer but when she began, it came pouring out. "He was so mean to me—I can't think of another word to use. He would take me out of the cage and throw me on the bed and hurt me. He did it almost every day. I would cry because it hurt so bad—he would laugh like he was happy. But he always put me back in the cage."

After taking a momentary break, she continued, "One day he put a baby in me. My stomach began to get bigger. At first I didn't know what was happening because I didn't have much to eat and I knew I wasn't getting fat. Then one day I felt a movement inside me and then I knew I had a baby growing inside me. When he saw what was happening to me, it didn't make him any nicer—he still treated me the same. I think he was even meaner—it seemed like he was mad because I had the baby inside."

Aggie brought her a glass of water and set it on the table in front of her. Marika smiled and said, "Thank you, Aggie."

The sheriff said, "I thought she didn't speak English."

As she was returning to her seat in the corner, Aggie replied, "We've taught her a few words. 'Thank you' was the first words she learned."

Lena prompted her, "What happened next, Marika?"

Marika continued, "One day I started hurting real bad. I thought I knew what it was because my Mama told me about the ways of women and having babies. The pains kept getting stronger and there was more and more pressure. I yelled for him to let me out because I couldn't get my legs apart in the cage. He took me out and threw me on the bed. I almost passed out from the pain and pressure. I pushed and pushed and I remember a little dark head between my legs. I must have passed out then because I don't remember anything else until I heard a baby crying. Then I could hear it crying in the distance. I tried to get up to go find the baby but he pushed me back in the bed. It cried and cried and then it didn't cry anymore. It was my baby—it cried till it couldn't cry anymore. He took my baby and threw it in the woods. It cried and cried til it couldn't cry anymore." The tears that had been running down her face turned into sobs. "It cried till it couldn't cry." After she wiped her face and regained her composure, she said, "He must have cut a piece out of the blanket on the bed to wrap the baby in cause I noticed a big section of the blanket was missing. I think it died—my baby must have died in the woods. I am about to go crazy when I think about my baby being eaten by wild animals."

Lena told those in the room what she said about the baby.

The sheriff said, "Does she know how long ago that was?"

Lena asked her in Polish and Marika thought about it for a while. Then she said, "it was after summer and before winter. It was not real cold yet."

The sheriff said, "Must have been in the fall, I'm guessin' October—deer hunting season. Could a hunter have found it?"

Marika was not finished, she continued, "Some nights God gives me hope somebody found my baby. And I like to think that he or she is happy with another Mama to hold her or him. Sometimes I just hold my pillow at night and pretend it's my baby—I rock and rock and sing lullabies like my Mama used to sing to me. You ask me how I am. I make it through the days but the nights are filled with memories and questions and a lot of prayers to God. I pray if my baby is still alive that God will protect it. And I pray that if it is in Heaven that God and all the angels will love it till I get there to hold my baby." By the time she had finished, tears were once again flowing down her face and her voice had become near a whisper.

As Lena told those around the table all she had said, Marika watched everyone else in the room wiping tears from their eyes.

When Lena finished, she was emotionally spent and sat in silence.

The sheriff thought, I didn't know about the baby. This presents a new situation. I wonder if Aggie knew. If she knew, how did she find out? The doctor! He has to keep patient information confidential. This thing is getting deeper. All this adds to the depth of the mystery. What did happen to the baby? We know it was born alive because she heard it crying. When the crying stopped, what happened? Did someone find the baby? But I'm still wondering who let her out. How does this all fit together? Why would somebody break into the cabin, be upset over what they find—she said he was mad—and not report it? What reason would that person have for not reporting it? Why would anonymity be important enough not to report this girl being held captive in a cabin deep in the woods? I wonder if it was somebody coming to buy moonshine from Angelo. I'm going to have to give this some more thought. I think we have to try to find the baby—but how? There's no scientific way I know to trace parentage. I need to talk to the doctor. Didn't they say that he kept office hours in Davy on Monday?

Marika was moved by their empathy and said, "Thank you, friends, for sharing my grief. Aggie and John and all the Wertz family have been with me but because I can't talk to them in English, they had no way of knowing the depth of my hurt. I love them all and thank them. They did everything they could do."

Lena regained her composure and told those at the table what Marika had just said. Then Lena said, "I have one more question to ask you, Marika."

Marika looked at her as if she were ready. "One more thing, Marika, do you have any relatives in the United States? We are trying to locate your parents. Do you have any idea where they might have moved?"

Marika sighed and slumped down in her chair. She was glad she could talk about something different. "Lena, I don't know of any relatives in the United States. My Mama has a sister in the old country. My Tata and Mama talked about wanting to go back to the old country but said they could not go back. I think that's the reason I never learned English—they thought they were going to take us back to the old country. There were some other people Tata knew in Gary who moved to Ohio, but Ohio is probably a big place. I'm sorry."

The sheriff thought, I think she is becoming more and more attached to the Wertz family. She needs to be reminded about her family.

The sheriff opened the file he had carried with him. He took the photograph of the Stanislas family and laid it on the table in front of Marika. Then he said to Lena, "Ask her if she knows who that is?"

Marika picked the picture up and looked at it. She held it to her heart and smiled.

She took it to where Aggie was still seated and began to point out the individuals in the photo. "Tata and Mama." Then pointing to the other individuals in the photo, she said, "Marika, Jakub and Anatol. This is my family."

Marika asked Lena, "Could I keep this picture?" The sheriff, figuring out what she had asked, said, "Tell her to keep the picture—it is hers."

All the while the sheriff was asking himself the question: Where does Angelo Purilli fit in this picture? He seems like the unseen presence in this picture, to me. How did he have access to a 12 year old girl without help from somebody—at the very least he had to have information about her.

The sheriff could see Marika was proud of her family. He took that as a positive sign that although Marika was not threatened at this time and she was content, he should continue to search diligently for her family. He knew it would not be easy to find them."

Puzzling times and perplexing life questions cause one to seek refuge in the Everlasting Arms.

The Everlasting Arms

CHAPTER SEVEN

Pulling it together

Life in the Wertz household was changing again. Joseph was away working on the CCC project at Babcock State Park up in Fayette County. He was not due to be home for several months. It was evident that Marika was missing him. She had begun to depend on him for moral support. They had developed a close friendship.

Daniel was teaching Marika English. Every night they would review vocabulary and learn how to put each new word in a sentence. Daniel made this observation, "She sure picks up things fast. I reckon by Easter she'll have about 150 new words."

Aggie said, "I reckon I should have you teach me to read words. I don't have no trouble talkin' words but I jist don't know how to read words."

Daniel said, "Mom, that is a good idee. Why don't you study along with Marika? We could have us a regular English class ever' night. We could call it 'Night School'."

Aggie stopped what she was doing and looked at Daniel, "I reckon you're serious about that. Do you think your old mom is smart enough to learn after all these years?" she asked.

Daniel said, "Aw, Mom, you're the smartest woman in this valley.

You just ain't had nobody to teach you. You're so smart you got along just fine without reading."

Aggie said, "I reckon you're right about me gettin' along alright without readin'. The only thing I really miss is readin' the Bible. I always wanted to read it for myself. How I would love to be able to know that God is speakin' to me just because I could read it for myself. Now wouldn't that be a blessin'?"

"Well," said Daniel, "I reckon that's where we'll start--reading Bible verses. How's that sound?"

Aggie looked at her son and said, "Daniel Wertz, you are becoming a fine man. You have a great heart. I couldn't ever be no prouder of you than I am right this minute. I love you."

"I love you, too, Mom", he said with a grin. Aggie turned away because she didn't want him to see the tears welling up in her eyes.

When John came home that day, he had news about the next job assignment. This job was going to last a long time, he said. He hoped it would last until the mines opened up again. There were rumors that Capels and Gary #9 and #4 were going to open up soon. But so far, it was just rumors.

"Well, John, are you gonna' tell us about the new job?" Aggie asked when they all sat down for supper.

"I reckon we better pray first" he said, as he bowed his head. "Lord, it's been a good day. We thank you for all the blessings we have. We thank you for work we can do and we thank you for letting us see the benefits from our work. Thank you for the food you set before us this fine day and I thank you for the hands of my dear wife who prepared it. Amen."

Marika echoed "Amen."

"That was a fine prayer, John", Aggie said, "I 'ppreciate the mention." They both laughed.

As they passed the plates of food around, Alvin asked his father, "Dad, what is the new WPA job?"

John sort of stammered, "Well, uh, uh, I ain't sure it's proper supper talk."

Alvin said, "How bad can it be? We ain't high falutin' 'round here."

John replied, "Okay, you asked for it. I reckon we're gonna build new outhouses for ever' body in this valley. They have delivered truck loads of what they's callin' sanitary bases. They's all formed concrete with the seat built in and they have a ventilation pipe out the back so the air moves through and keeps the thing from gettin' to smell too bad. It's all one piece. Ever' one of them has got a number on it—so they's registered. I reckon that's how the gov'ment works—everything is registered somewheres. How we're doin' it is to dig a hole in the ground the size of the new foundations. Then we take the old outhouse off and set it over and hook it to the new foundation. We use the dirt that we dug out of the first hole and fill in the old hole. It sounds pretty easy. We got machinery to dig the holes and move the dirt. So they tells us we can do about 20 of these things a day--but they's just so many of them all up and down these hollers. They's a lot of people who don't want their privies moved—even fer a few feet. They don't reckon they's anythin' wrong with old ones. And then they's gonna have to put in new paths and all. I'm gonna' be supervisor of what they're callin' the Davy sector. I think one of my big jobs is to sell the people on the whole idee. Even if it's free and won't cost 'em nothin', our first job is to make 'em think they need this new thing."

"That would be a good job for Mom, I reckon" said Jim. "If you give her fifteen minutes, she can make you think black is white." Everybody laughed—including Marika.

Aggie said, "Yeah, I hear you. I'll get ya fer that, Jim Wertz. Don't come around sweet talking me the next time you's gets hungry for sticky buns. It will do you no good." She laughed and winked at her son.

John continued to describe his new job. "We will start in Asco, move down the holler toward Davy, then up Little Davy holler, and on like that till be get all of Davy. After we get Davy, we move down toward Marytown and Hensley and on down to Rodiefield."

Aggie asked, "Is this what they's callin' Miz Rosievelt's folly?"

John grinned, "I reckon it is. I heared that it was her idee. She said they's lots of people gettin' sick on account of their outhouses. This is s'posed to make outhouses healthier. But I reckon if we's gonna' go to this much trouble, we ort'a be puttin' them new flush toilets in the houses. It ain't gonna' be many years till all folks are gonna have flush toilets anyhow."

Alvin opined, "And then all the outhouses sittin' on the sides of these hills with their special numbers are gonna' be useless. 'Cause who in the world would go out to the privy when they can just go in the next room?"

Marika said, "Winter time. Brr!"

Everyone at the table laughed because they knew exactly what she was talking about.

Aggie said, "I reckon we need runnin' water in the house before we can have inside toilets. What do you think about puttin' in runnin' water? Why don't one of you boys learn how to do that?"

John said, "Back to the job--the good news is that I will still get to come home at night. Since I'm gonna' be a supervisor, I'm gonna' have me a truck to drive to work every day. I can use it on the weekends as long as I buy the gas. I have to pick up a fellow in Big Jenny and take him to Davy ever' morning but that ain't no worry. I think we'll be able to use the truck to go over and see Louanna since it won't be long before the baby comes. I'm kind'a gettin' excited about being a grandpa." He reached over and took Aggie's hand, and said, " How about you grandma? You getting' excited?"

"Indeed, I am. Marika and me's been making some things for the baby. I sure wish I knowed if it was a boy or girl. We made a blue outfit for a boy and a pink outfit for a girl. We made a white blanket that has blue and pink stripes. That should take care of it either way. Marika is pretty handy with a needle and thread."

After supper, Alvin said, "Do you mind if we turn on the radio? It's time for Gabriel Heatter. I'd like to hear the news while Mom and Marika get the dishes done."

After the news was finished, Alvin asked, "Dad, what do you think about this A-dolph Hitler in Germany?

John said, "According to the news I hear on the radio, he's turned hisself into a dictator. I heared he's making laws against the Jews. They have been declared by law to be second class human beings. And they're leaving Germany in droves. They's probly gonna be a lot of them end up in New York City. Jews is smart people. Hitler is cuttin' off his nose to spite his face. Don't he know Jesus Christ was a Jew?"

Alvin replied, "I think it's getting' dangerous in Europe. Reckon Germany's gonna start another war over there?"

John answered, "I hope not, son. But I know they's building up their army and weapons. I reckon they's tryin' to look fierce to the countries all around them. What do you call that? Intimerdation?"

Alvin continued, "Yeah and ever' time I go to the picture show, I've been seeing pictures on the NewsReel about their army. They do that funny straight leg step when they march—they call it the goose step. They're building up their army for something. I don't want to think about another war—I don't think the United States could stay out of it, do you? Me and my brothers are all just the right age to get drafted."

John continued, "One thing about war in Europe is that the coal mines will start up workin' agin. Because they's gonna need our coal to make steel. I betcha England will start makin' steel in a big way. They's gonna need airoplanes. The last war was jest a taste of what the enemy could do with airoplanes. You know they's just across the channel from Europe—I reckon it ain't more'n 20 mile."

"That gives me an idee," said Alvin, "if the mines are gonna start back up, they prob'ly need to clean up around the tipples and get all the trash and scrap that's layin' 'round cleaned out. If I had me a truck, I'd go try to get some work getting' ready for them to open back up agin. Ever' one of the coal camps in this county has lots of junk just layin' round. If I had a truck."

John thought for a few minutes, then he asked, "Got money to put gas in a truck?"

Alvin laughed and said, "Maybe one tankful. How long you reckon that would last?"

Then John said, "I have a work truck assigned to me. Tomorrow, I'm gonna ask my crew chief if we can use the truck for other things if I keep it in repair and buy the gas. If he agrees, we could have a crew to work evenings till dark—since summer's comin' on, the days are gettin' longer now. And we could work all day on Saturdays."

Alvin look puzzled, "Who is we?"

John grinned, "Of course Jim and me and you. You was plannin' to work, wuddna you? Or were you just plannin' to supervise? We need to get Joe back home, too. Now that's a good work crew. Daniel and Marika will help your Mom with the garden."

Alvin laughed out loud, "I wonder if that's what Doc was talking about when he talked about strategizin'."

John said, "I'm glad to know what city folks calls it. 'Cause I call it work. I call it gettin' somthun' done."

Aggie was excited about the pot-luck supper at church on Easter. There would be a sunrise service to celebrate the resurrection. Everybody would meet at the graveyard next to the church. Years ago, some forward thinking folks had dug a hole in the hillside just above the cemetery and had built a "stone" out of scrap lumber, painted it gray and fitted it to the opening. Every Easter when the folks arrived for the early morning service, the stone was rolled away disclosing an empty grave. This was a Mohegan tradition. After some singing and scripture reading, the folks went into the church for a regular Sunday School and after service with preaching.

The pot-luck supper was planned for 5 o'clock. So after the preaching, all the women in the valley would spend the rest of the day cooking and baking getting ready for the feast. Easter pot-luck had become popular since hard times hit and was fast becoming a tradition among the church-goin' folk in Mohegan. They hoped even those folks who didn't go to church might come for supper. Everybody in the community was invited.

Easter, 1937 arrived with a bright blue sky and the promise of a beautiful spring day. Marika happily found one of the most attractive dresses from her now plentiful collection of dresses. She loved to dress up. She also found a hat and shoes to wear. She wished Joe were there to see her Easter outfit. She felt pretty. This was a coming out party of sorts for Marika. She would be getting to know the people of Mohegan—this was her first social venture. She would be testing her newly developed communication skills.

She felt proud of her accomplishments. Her English lessons were going well. Daniel was a good teacher. She could ask questions and understand answers. She was beginning to conceptualize in English— she didn't always think about the Polish equivalents for words and ideas. She was proud of Aggie, too. She was now reading the Bible to her every day—after breakfast and then after supper with the family.

When the Wertz family made its way to the pot-luck supper Easter day, they were laden down with food. Aggie and Marika had been busy all afternoon. It was a happy parade that made its way to the little church in Mohegan that Easter Sunday—each member of the family carrying a culinary treasure. Everybody contributed what they had—if they had a lot, they brought a lot. If their supply was meager, their contribution to the long food table was meager. Everyone brought their own table service.

Aggie was in charge of the supper. Not long after Marika became part of the Wertz household, she had observed that Aggie was often in charge. That was her personality. She knew how to get things done and that's what she did. This day, she greeted every person as they arrived and gave clear-cut instructions for the arrangement of the various dishes of food. When it was all arranged, she stepped back and smiled. *Everyone would eat well this blessed day, she thought. She noticed the congregation was smaller than at the dinner last year. It had decreased in size each succeeding year since the mine closed. How she longed for the days when this valley was a bustle of activity. How she hoped this resurrection day would signal the beginning of new life in her valley. She missed those who had moved away and hoped for their soon return.*

Meanwhile Marika was watching the people arrive. She knew only a few of them—there was Uncle Jessie and Aunt Hattie. She hoped Aunt Hattie had brought her biscuits and honey. She also knew Sam and Maggie McGrady from next door. They had a daughter close to Marika's age—her name was Mary. She was a student at the nursing school at Welch Emergency Hospital. She lived in the Nurse's Quarters attached to the hospital. She was home for Easter. Marika greeted her.

As she watched others arrive, she noticed a couple with twin babies come in the door. The father was carrying a little boy, dressed in blue and the mother carried a little girl dressed in a frilly pink dress.

The father brought in two homemade miniature chairs that sat on top of the big chairs. He secured each of them with a rope and put the children in the chairs. She watched as the mother tied bibs on each of the babies. Then she handed them each a rattle and half a biscuit which seemed to satisfy them. She sat down in a chair between them.

Marika stood aside and marveled at the efficiency of these parents as they carried in family and food. She was fascinated by the chairs especially when she noticed each had a tray for the children to eat on. How clever she thought. What a handsome family! She allowed a little pang of envy to creep into her thinking momentarily—I wish, she thought. Then she noticed the little girl had dark hair and eyes while the rest of the family was light-haired with blue eyes. She didn't remember ever seeing that in a family before. Usually families all have similar coloring. The little girl reminded her of her baby brother—they had the same shaped face—or something. Anyway, she just seems familiar. My baby would be about that age, she thought.

In the absence of a pastor or preacher, John stepped up to pronounce the blessing over the get-together of the remnant of believers in the Mohegan coal camp.

"Let's bow in prayer and ask God's blessing on our time together" John began.

"Dear Lord, we are ever so grateful for that miraculous day when you came out of the grave alive. Thank you for the hope your resurrection gives us who believe in your Son, Jesus Christ. One of these days we are gonna' rise out of the grave and come to be with you. We rejoice in that promise and that hope and it's all because you came out of that grave alive first. Hallelujah! We have come together this evening to fellowship in love and to enjoy all this wonderful food that has been spread out before us. We thank you for it. We know all good and perfect gifts come from above. We receive those gifts and return to you our thanksgiving. In the name of the one who died but ain't dead no more we ask it. Amen."

Aggie came over and whispered in John's ear, "My dear, that there was some ele-quent prayin'. I loved it and I think God loved it too."

"We'll just keep that our secret, Okay?" John said with a smile. Aggie gave him thumbs up and then went on about the business of seeing that everybody got fed. When the line began to dwindle, the little girl baby began to cry. Marika noticed the parents were in line getting food, so she went to the mother and asked, "Okay, hold baby?" The mother nodded. "I'm Marika, be careful." The mother smiled. Marika carefully removed the baby from her chair. As soon as the child was in Marika's arms, she stopped crying. As she walked back and forth with her, the baby seemed to be studying Marika's face. And then the child snuggled against Marika's chest and went to sleep. She continued to walk, not wanting to wake the child until the mother had finished her meal.

As she walked, she thought, she feels like she fits my arms. What a strange thing to think about! She's just like any baby. She likes to be held. She may be a little spoiled and is used to being held when she's fussy. How could a mother with twins have time to spoil one of them? All in all, I like the feel of a baby in my arms—I didn't know how it would feel.

When the mother was finished eating, she came to take the baby again. "Sleeping" Marika said. What her name? The mother said, "Oh, dear, I'm so sorry. Did you say your name was Marika?"

Marika nodded and said, "Marika Stanislas. With Wertz family."

The mother smiled and said, "Oh, you're the young girl I heard was staying with the Wertz family. My name is Audrey—Audrey Ball. Over there is my husband, Ronnie. Thank you for taking care of Zoe while I ate. With twins, it's hard to eat a meal without interruptions."

As Audrey took Zoe from Marika's arms, she roused and started to whimper. Marika patted her hand and said, "Now, now, none of that." The baby giggled. "What boy's name?" Marika asked Audrey. "His name is David." With that Audrey walked away and went back to her place with Ronnie and Zoe's twin brother. Little Zoe began to jump in her mother's arms as they came near to David. Marika smiled.

As the Wertz family walked home that night, Marika's thoughts were full of the events of the evening. The food had been really good—especially the dishes Aggie brought. Holding that baby had been an unexpected pleasure—what a sweet baby. Zoe! And although she was sure she had never seen him before, the father seemed familiar. Where have I seen him before? His name is Ronnie. I don't remember his face but there was something familiar about his voice. "I've got to figure this out" she said to herself "and I will".

When the Sheriff pulled into the Wertz home on Monday morning, Lena Babinski was with him. He wanted to make sure he communicated clearly with Marika. He had a few unanswered questions.

When he was greeted by Aggie and Marika, he was pleased Marika looked so well. He thought, h*er health is improving with good food, rest and family security. The Wertz family is providing a very nurturing and healthy environment for her.*

When they were all seated around the table in the Wertz' kitchen, the sheriff looked at Marika and said, "Marika, I have not had any leads on finding your family. I am right now working on the assumption they are somewhere in Ohio. Today, I have Sgt. Weaver working on getting information broadcasted on every local radio station in Ohio. She has contacted the Federal Communications Commission, a new government agency for their assistance. So unless your parents are living in a vacuum, they should hear about your situation this week. I will let you know what I find out."

Lena repeated what the sheriff had said. Marika nodded she understood. "Thank you", she said.

She's not too eager to leave this home, he thought. She seems pretty contented at the moment.

Then he continued, "Lena is going to ask you a couple of questions we need the answers for. I want to make sure you understand them. First of all, I need to know if you knew Angelo Purilli before he abducted you. Do you remember ever seeing him before? There has to be some connection between him and your family. He didn't just drive down the road and pick your house. He had to know of your family, the layout of your house, where your bedroom was located, etc. Do you understand the question?"

When Lena asked her, Marika nodded to indicate she understood the question. She had a puzzled look on her face as if she had never thought about this aspect of the situation. "Could he have known my Tata?" she asked. Then she said "I don't know."

The sheriff asked, "Was your father a drinker? Angelo made moonshine and sold it."

Marika answered the question after it was relayed to her by Lena. "Yes, my father was a drinker. I know he did drink moonshine. My Mama got mad at him because he got drunk. One time she poured all his moonshine out in the backyard on the ground. I never saw my Tata so mad. They had a big fight over that. He slapped my Mama so hard she fell down. My brother and me got scared and hid in our bedroom. But I don't know where he got moonshine. He might have got it from Angelo but I don't remember ever seeing him."

That gets close but not a bullseye. If her father drank moonshine and if he bought it from Angelo, it still doesn't connect him to Marika and the house. But it does possibly connect the father to the cabin. Did he come to the cabin to buy his moonshine? If he had been to the cabin, why didn't he connect Angelo with Marika's disappearance? When she disappeared and he was so distraught, why didn't he look in the cabin? I think I would have—at least I think I would. Was he passed out drunk the night she was snatched out of her bed? Or did Angelo deliver his moonshine to Gary? Marika said he left the cabin and was gone sometimes for a few days. Was it to sell the moonshine elsewhere? That makes sense—who could find that cabin? If he delivered to Gary, that could be how he connected to Stanislas. Where would be a logical place to set up business? Out of his truck? Down where the Union Hall is now—that was a company office building when Stanislas was here. The parking lot was empty at night. That made it a perfect place to do that kind of business.

He asked her, "Marika, did your father ever go out at night?"

Marika responded, "Yes, but I don't know where he went. My Mama used to fuss at him over that too. She used to say to Tata, "You always come back home drunk." She would be real mad. She did not want him to go to out at night. My Tata did not act like my Tata when he got drunk. Mama and Tata would get into a fight and then he would go to sleep."

"There's got to be some connection between this Italian speaking Purilli and Polish speaking Stanislas or someone else close to the Stanislas family. If I don't find it, I will never answer all the questions about this case." *Then he thought, I should have done this three years ago. I was negligent and a young girl suffered.*

If Purilli and her father drank together, that still doesn't connect her with Purilli. There has got to be a direct connection between Purilli and Marika. Maybe we should investigate the 'friend of a friend' aspect.

Then he asked, "Marika, do you have an uncle or aunt or other relatives who lived in Gary? What about friends who were close to you or your parents?"

Marika replied, "No, Sir, I don't know of any."

Then the sheriff said to Marika (through the interpreter), "Angelo Purilli was what is called a Pedophile. That is a person who preys on children or young people. He waited for the opportunity to grab you for himself. The mystery I'm trying to unravel is how he knew you and knew where you were. Somebody had to reveal that to him. I will investigate the moonshine aspect but that doesn't seem to me to be a strong possibility. I still feel there is something else we're missing."

Then he said, "Lena, did you know of this man? Have you ever seen him around Gary? Do you think your husband might have some information? Is your husband a drinker of moonshine?"

Lena responded, "Well, sir, I didn't know the man. If I ever saw him, I was not aware of it. He might have been at church sometime when I was there, but I didn't notice him or any other man so as to inquire of their identity. As far as my husband goes, he don't go out at night except on Fridays when he plays poker at his brother's house. I'll ask him when I get home if he knows anything."

Then she added, "Do you think the church could be the connection? There are always a lot of children around the school and pedophiles hang around where children are. The only thing is the Stanislas children did not attend English speaking school."

Marika understood enough of what they were saying to respond, "No, no, Jakub and me church school. Polish school. Tata say no English."

The sheriff said, "Could he have done odd jobs around the church? If he saw Marika there, he still had find out where she lived—which I guess would not be difficult—but to gain access to the home he had to have been on the inside at some time.

The sheriff continued, "In a case like that, you would expect the child to be grabbed at the school not out of bed. Any way you look at it, there is a huge leap in every possible situation we talk about.

As if thinking out loud, the sheriff said, "I think I'll go back and talk to the priest again. He was helpful the last time. He may know something about this Angelo Purilli."

He looked at Lena and said, "We didn't come up with any great ideas on this trip. Let's ask her if she has remembered who let her out of the cage."

Marika understood the words, "let her out of the cage." She replied, "I don't know who. (Then she finished the rest in Polish.) I had an unusual experience yesterday. I met a man named Ronnie Ball. I don't remember meeting him before but there was somethin' so familiar about him. It was mostly his voice, I think, that I have heard somewhere before. I'm not sure. There was just something."

Then she added, "Angelo was an evil man. He did evil things to me. He was so ugly and mean I think I would have run from him even if I had seen him on the street."

On the drive to Gary, the sheriff asked Lena about her observations of activities around the Stanislas home. In rapid fire, he asked, "Did you notice people coming and going on a regular basis? Were there a lot of cars in and out? Did it seem people came at unusual hours? Did the Stanislas' go to church on a regular basis?"

Then he said, "I'm racking my brain trying to figure out how Angelo found this young girl. He had to have some contact with the Stanislas family—not just Joseph. I think we can assume he knew Joseph. And he had to know the layout of the house and where the girl's bedroom was. How did he get that information? What went on while Marika was at school?" Then he paused and took a deep breath. "I guess I'd better take a breath and let you answer." he said with a laugh.

When she finally got the chance to speak, Lena said, "You know my house is about 4 houses from where the Stanislas family lived. I could see their house if I went out on my porch. Otherwise, I couldn't see what was going on over there. Unless they made a lot of noise, I would have no reason for even looking out my front windows or go on my front porch, especially in winter. So, I ain't no help about that. I can tell you the Stanislas family were sort of regular attenders of Sunday Mass. They had a car but they always walked to the church—I would notice that. As I think about it; I don't remember ever seeing the father—Joseph—with them. It was the mother, Marika, a boy and a baby. Don't remember ever seeing the father—even on Easter. That seems unusual—especially since he was the only one who spoke English."

The sheriff thought about what Lena had said, "I wonder what that means? Does it mean anything beyond the father not wanting to go to church? I think I'll go see the priest after I take you home."

Then Lena said, "It sounds like Joseph Stanislas was a mean drinker. Marika said he got drunk and it was a source of conflict in the family. Some people get mellow when they are drunk but some become violent. Some get real quiet and others get real talkative. I've seen very shy people turn into extroverts when they are drinking. I learned a long time ago not to tell the family secrets to a drinker. Could the fact he never went to Mass with the family have something to do with his drinking?"

As the sheriff pulled off the black top road onto the rut-filled side road that led to Lena's house, he said, "Lena, you have given me a lot to think about. I'm going over to go talk to the priest right now. I hope he is in. And I will probably need for you to speak with Marika again in a few days. I'll be touch."

As she exited the car, Lena said, "Thanks, sheriff." *Thank you indeed for the chance to earn a little money—we ain't got nothing coming in, she thought.*

When the sheriff arrived at the church, the priest was saying goodbye to a group of students who had been meeting with him. He invited the sheriff into his office. "What can I help you with today? He asked.

After taking a seat, the sheriff said, "Father, we are still working on the case of the Stanislas girl who was abducted almost 3 years ago now. In that regard, I have some additional questions I would like to ask you."

"Fire away" said the priest. "I don't know if I will have the answers but I'll try."

The sheriff began, "I wonder if the Stanislas family were faithful to come to Mass. I'm especially interested in Mr. Stanislas. Did he come to church often?"

The priest answered, "To tell you the truth, Sheriff, I would have no way of recognizing Mr. Stanislas if I saw him. The abduction of the daughter happened before I came to Gary Parish. It's my understanding they left Gary about 6 months after the sad event. So, I just did not know the family. After you were here last, my curiosity got the better of me and I asked a couple of the lay leaders of the church about the family. They said they never saw him at Mass with the mother and the children. They indicated the local police had been called to the Stanislas' house on two separate occasions because of a domestic dispute. From what I hear, Mr. Stanislas had a drinking problem. When he drank, there was trouble at home."

The sheriff said, "I didn't find any mention of that in the county records. The local police must not have reported it to the county. Hmm! Those things are usually reported."

The sheriff continued, "Another item I would like to investigate is, do you have record of Angelo Purilli on your church membership?"

The priest hesitated a minute and then said, "That name sounds so familiar. Oh, I know, I think he is working on the school grounds today. He volunteers as a handyman and does small repairs and cleanup around the building. He is very helpful."

The sheriff could hardly contain his surprise, he gulped and said, "Did I hear you right? He is working on the school grounds right now?"

"Yes, I believe that he is" the priest replied.

"Let me ask you, sir, what does this man look like?"

"Oh, he's just a normal looking guy about 5 feet 10 or 11. There's nothing outstanding about his appearance. The outstanding thing about him is his character. He has the reputation of being a fine man."

The sheriff breathed a sigh of relief. "What did you say his name was?"

The priest said, "Let me look it up just to be sure. The Italian names are confusing to me. Here it is: Angelo Parello. Isn't that what you said?"

"No" the sheriff said, "I asked about Angelo Purilli. P-U-R-I-L-L-I. It is my firm belief that Angelo Purilli is dead. I think he is the man who abducted the Stanislas girl but I'm having a hard time figuring out how he made contact with the family. The girl said she had never seen him before. But he had to have knowledge of her and how to get her in the middle of the night. Could you look in your old membership logs and see if anyone by the name of Purilli was a member here?"

After looking in an old book, he said, "here is something interesting. Angelo Purilli was a member of this Parish. There is a notation next to his name. It's a hand written note in the margin. It says:

A woman named Susan Donnelly from Welch stated her 7 year old daughter was grabbed in Murphy's by an Angelo Purilli in 1932. He released the girl when the mother screamed. The charges were eventually dropped when the accused could not be located.

The priest continued, "There is no record of his participation in church activities or giving to the church. It says here that he was asked to withdraw his membership because of his lack of participation in the Mass. I didn't know we still practiced forced withdrawals but I guess we do."

As the sheriff stood to leave, he said, "I have a lot of loose ends I want to tie up. It's very likely I will be back again. This seems to be a good place to find out what goes on in Gary. Thank you, Father, for your help."

As the sheriff got back into his car, he was mulling over all he had learned and all he had speculated about. How did it all fit? Facts, facts, facts—all loose ends dangling. I need to find the string that ties it all together. I can't escape the idea that Marika's father knew Angelo—but how did he know him? Was it as a drinking mate? Did he ever invite him into his home—maybe while Susanna and the children were at church? Facts and questions—but so far no connector—no string to tie it all together.

The sheriff drove to the Union Hall which was about a block from the Catholic Church. When he pulled in, he observed there were just a few cars in the lot. He was admitted without membership because he was a law enforcement officer and went into what appeared to be the main room and found the bar. It was not difficult to do since the bar dominated the room. As he approached the bar with bottles of whiskey displayed against a mirrored wall, he thought.

This is a pretty fancy bar setup especially since prohibition was in effect until 4 years ago. I wonder if it is left over from World War I days before prohibition.

There were two men working behind the bar. They were cleaning and obviously getting ready for the night's business. When they noticed the uniformed officer, they stopped what they were doing and came over to speak with him. The first man, who seemed to be in charge, asked, "What can I do for you?"

The sheriff explained in sketchy fashion the case he was working on. Then he asked, "Were either of you men working here in 1934? Then the sheriff realized what he had asked and laughed. This place couldn't have been here yet—the unions were just coming in—slipped my mind. Okay, let me start over."

"I am looking for information about a man named Angelo Purilli. He is a known moonshiner. I wondered if he had any contacts here. Do either of you have any information about this man or know of any connections he may have had here in Gary?"

The first man answered, "There is something. Let me think a minute. You know the men talk a lot when they're drinkin' and when you're tending bar, you hear bits and pieces of conversations. I recently heard about an explosion of a moonshine still someplace over on the other side of Welch somewhere. There was somebody who got blowed up. I think that was the name that was mentioned or one that sounds a lot like it."

The sheriff nodded, "Yeah, that's part of the story. We're trying now to see if there was a Gary connection between Purilli and anybody here. We think he was involved in an abduction of a young girl from Gary almost three years ago but we don't have the connector. Do you know if he ever sold any of his likker here—say from his truck in the parking lot?"

The other man spoke up, "This building was used for company offices back in '34. So, I reckon technically there was no such building as the Union Hall. But as I remember, a lot of men used to hang around this parking lot especially on weekend nights. There was drinking and it got rowdy sometimes. The local police just sort of looked the other way 'cause they knew boys will be boys. They just tried to keep the fighting down. They didn't want nobody to get killed or hurt bad. I vaguely remember when that little girl was taken. I was working with CCC over at Watoga but my parents told me about it. It really scared people around here. I remember my dad said he was going to keep a closer eye on my little sister. It seems like I remember a little girl who was grabbed in Welch, too. But she got away. And just this week, I heard a story and you can prob'ly tell me if it's true or not. Some men talking in the bar said the Stanislas girl had been found alive. Is that true, sir?"

The sheriff said, "I guess we have a leak in the Sheriff's Department. Yes, it is true. She is doing well. That's all I'm going say about it. That is the case I'm trying to wrap up. We did lousy police work back in 1934 when it happened. So we are now finally trying to answer some unanswered questions."

The man behind the bar continued. "When they were talkin' about the girl being found, one of the men said something like, "Old Stanislas got out of here as fast as he could after it happened." It weren't 6 months after that girl was taken that he left town. I know there wudden no work around here but if it was me and my little girl had been taken, I wudda searched every holler in this county to try to find her. I would want to be the one who found her or the one who buried her. I would have to know. I don't think I could live with myself until I found her or found her little body."

He paused, looked around and then continued, "you know he had a drinking problem, don't you? My dad worked with him over at #9. He said Stanislas kept to himself and never said much most of the time.

But once in a while, he was like a magpie and wouldn't shut up. Dad reckons he had been drinking on the job. Said he smelled of alcohol. Back then it was prohibition—so I reckon it had to be moonshine."

The sheriff sat for a few minutes, then said, "you fellas wouldn't happen to have a cup of coffee around here, would you?"

"Yes, sir. How do you like it?"

"Just black, please. I appreciate it. You fella's go about your business. I'm sorry for the interruption. I need to mull this over for a few minutes."

As he drank his coffee, he thought, I remember when the father came and reported the abduction at the sheriff's department. He was distraught. He appeared to be desperate to find her. But he didn't have much information about it. He didn't offer any details about how it could have happened. He didn't have 'if onlys'—like if only I had done this or not done that. Most of the time, people will try to figure out what happened and what they did to either cause or enable it or what they could have done to prevent it. There was none of that. I remember I was suspicious at the time. There was something that did not ring true. Now that I am remembering these details, I think Joseph Stanislas knows more than he let on. I wonder if he was drinking when this happened. I reckon the bartender was right—I would search every nook and cranny if it was my little girl. What did he do? He left town. I wonder what he was doing during the six months before he left. What was he running from? And their's was a troubled household—caused by his drinking. Marika said 'my Tata was not my Tata when he got drunk'.

When the sheriff finished his coffee, he thanked the two men for their help and the coffee. He had a mental list of things that needed to be done at headquarters.

As he was getting into his car, he was approached by Lena Babinski. She introduced the man who was with her as her husband Rudy. "Rudy has something to tell you what he noticed a few days before little Marika disappeared. He never mentioned it before because he did not think it was important."

The sheriff shook hands with Rudy Babinski and asked him what he had noticed. "Well, sheriff", he said, "I reckon the reason I noticed it at all was the Stanislas family stayed to themselves. But I just happened to be lookin' out my front window and I saw Joseph Stanislas going in the house with another man. I don't have no idee what it was they was carrying but it seemed heavy. I watched until he came out—I reckon it was about 20-30 minutes."

The sheriff asked, "Rudy, how would you describe the man?"

"Well, sir, As I recall, he was a big man. He was a lot bigger than Joseph. Other than his size, I didn't notice anything else about him. He was driving a kind of beat up truck—I believe it was a Ford and it was a bluish green but it was rusty and muddy like it had been off the road. I reckon that's all I remember. I was trying to remember exactly when that was I saw him but I don't rightly remember. It don't seem like it was too long before the little girl disappeared. And then I saw him agin, a little while after it happened. Do you think this is important?"

The sheriff inquired, "Are you sure the second time you saw him at the Stanislas home was after the abduction?"

Rudy responded, "Like I said, I don't know the exact date. The first time, it was warmish and they had on just shirts. In fact the big man didn't have no shirt on—just his t-shirt. Then the second time I seen him, he went up to the door my hisself. He was carrying a box that seemed pretty heavy—it was about the size of the other boxes-- but he had on a coat. So it was cold weather. The girl disappeared in November and it generally ain't too cold in November. That's what makes me think it was afterward."

As the sheriff started to step into his car, he said, "One thing more, Rudy, do you happen to remember what day of the week it was when you saw them?

Rudy thought for a minute, and then said, "Yes, I do. I know the first time was on Sunday morning. 'Cause I wanted Lena to see him but she was gone to church. Lena, she don't miss church on Sunday. I ain't so sure about the other time, though."

The sheriff thanked Rudy for the information. "I reckon this will help me as I sort through all the other things going forward. Thanks Lena. You're turning into a regular detective. I'll see you in a few days."

When the sheriff arrived at headquarters in the courthouse, he asked Sgt. Weaver to join him in his office.

When she followed him into his office, he said, "Close the door, please. There are a lot of things I need to sort out and I need your help. Oh, have you heard anything from the FCC about the Stanislas family?"

"No sir, I haven't. I really expected to hear something today, didn't you? We'll just wait and see. Maybe they aren't in Ohio. If we don't hear after tomorrow, I'll expand it to Virginia, Michigan, Indiana and Pennsylvania and prob'ly Kentucky, too."

Then she said, "Sir, do you think there is a possibility they don't want to be found? Do you think this thing is too painful to come back to?"

The sheriff replied, "I just don't know. One of the bartenders at the Union Hall said, "if it was my daughter, I would search every holler in this county. I would not have given up and moved away. I agree with that—how could you leave if your child was out there somewhere? Wouldn't you want to find her dead or alive?"

The sheriff said, "let's make a list of the information we have." He took a piece of paper from his desk drawer. "I'm going to write down the facts I know about the situation."

1. Marika had no knowledge of Purilli before she was abducted.
2. Her father was seen with a man matching Purilli's description prior to the abduction. He was seen going into the Stanislas home on a Sunday morning in warm weather with Joseph Stanislas. They were carrying boxes that seemed heavy.
3. He was seen entering the Stanislas home after the abduction. He delivered a box of something in cold weather. He was wearing a coat. Marika disappeared in November.
4. Mr. Stanislas was a heavy drinker. His drinking was a source of domestic problems. There were 2 police runs by the Gary police to the Stanislas home on domestic disturbance complaints.
5. Angelo Purilli was accused of attempting to abduct a 7 year old girl at Murphy's in Welch in 1932. She managed to escape. No charges were filed because he could not be found.
6. We also have not definitely identified the body that was blown up in that moonshine still explosion. I personally

took fingerprints from the hands of the corpse—or what was left of it. We made the assumption it was Purilli because of the size of the extremities.

7. The Catholic church does not seem to be the connection. Angelo Purilli was asked to withdraw his membership for not attending Mass for a year. Joseph Stanislas was never seen at church although his wife and children attended regularly.

8. There are no known relatives of the Stanislas family in the United States.

Things to Do:

1. I would like for you to go to the file on the explosion and send the prints to the FBI and see if they have a match for them. I could not match them from our records. If he has ever been arrested, somebody has his fingerprints. If he has been in prison, the FBI should have a record of it along with fingerprints. When you send them, make sure you keep a copy on microfilm in our files. Identify them as belonging to Angelo Purilli and ask them for verification.

2. Stay on top of the radio broadcasts in Ohio. After tomorrow, if there is no word, expand the broadcasts, as discussed earlier.

3. Contact the newspaper and find out if this can be put out on Associated Press. I want to get it in papers all over the country—or at least in the surrounding states.

"Can you take care of those three items?" he asked. She said, "certainly, I'll get right on it."

Then he said, "I've got a couple of things I need to do"

1. The baby angle is another thing that is still dangling, as far as I'm concerned. I am not 100% convinced the baby is dead. I think I need to talk to the doctor. That will be my next thing I do.

2. And then I'm going to interview Ronnie Ball. Marika mentioned him. I want to see how he fits into this case."

He folded the paper and put it in his pocket. "Can you think of anything else that needs to be checked out right now?"

She was slow to reply, "I am thinking maybe Ronnie Ball is the man who let her out of the cage. She said there was something about his voice, didn't she? What if she was so blinded by her desire to escape and get out of that cabin she didn't really see the person. It may have been dark in the cabin and when the door opened all she saw was the shape of a man in the doorway. But when she was running away and he yelled. Maybe at some level of her consciousness, she remembers the voice. What was it he said? Was it "Wait! Wait! I will help you!"?

Then she continued, "What if we set up a reenactment of that day. Do you think that would help?"

The sheriff said, "I will never ask her to go back to that cabin. She collapsed when she took Joseph Wertz there to show him where she came from. I just won't ask her to do that again."

Then the sheriff added, "Let me work on that and we will discuss it again." Looking at his watch, he said, "it's three o'clock now. I'm headin' to Davy. The Doc finishes his office hours at four. I'll catch up with you again tomorrow."

When the sheriff arrived in Davy, the doctor was just leaving his offices. When he noticed the sheriff pull up, he waited at the door. "What's up?" he asked.

The sheriff responded, "Wonder if I could have a few minutes of your time? I have some things on my mind I hope you can clear up."

The doctor unlocked the door and invited the sheriff into his office and offered him a seat. When the door was closed, the sheriff said, "Well, Doc, I don't know how to ask the question that's on my mind except to just ask it outright. So what can you tell me about the baby Marika delivered in that cabin?"

The doctor looked uncomfortable. After a few minutes, he looked up and said, "What I know is confidential. If I tell you it would be a breach of the confidence my patients entrust to me. If I thought it was a matter of life and death, I would be tempted to break the confidence. But as it stands, I cannot in good faith share what I know without permission from my patients."

"I respect that, doctor. I guess in my heart of hearts I would have been disappointed in you if you had told me confidential things. I'm trying to sort out Marika's situation. There are a lot of factors here. The baby she had in the cabin is still a mystery—did it survive? If it did survive, where is it? I think you have the answer but I will try another avenue to get to the full truth."

"I am trying every way I know to find her family. I'm using radio broadcasts all over Ohio, since Marika mentioned Ohio. Tomorrow we are going to broaden the scope of the broadcasts to other neighboring states. We have ads in the papers throughout West Virginia. We are in the process of getting Associated Press to put it out all over the nation. The FCC is cooperating with us. We want her parents to know Marika is alive and well."

The doctor surprised the sheriff when he said, "The news Marika is alive and well may not be good news for her family, especially her father. Some family secrets are better buried, if you get what I'm saying. That's all I'll say about that."

The sheriff said, "Some things are gradually coming to light which seem to back up that assumption." And with a grin, he added, "and that's all I'm going to say about that."

As they parted, the doctor said, "Good luck to you in your search for the truth. I think it's buried deep, but you can get at it with persistence."

As the sheriff turned around and headed back to Welch, he decided to make a stop in Mohegan. When he pulled into the Ball's house, Ronnie was just coming out of the door. When he saw the sheriff, he stopped and they talked standing by the car.

Ronnie began, "Sheriff Chatham, there are some things I need to tell you about. First of all, last fall during hunting season, I was comin' out of the woods. Me and my brother had been huntin' upon the ridge above Peter's branch. Anyway, when we was walking down the hill, we heared a baby cryin'. We stopped to see where it was comin' from and we found a baby layin' on the ground right there by the path. It was wrapped in a dirty piece of blanket. I looked around and I never saw nobody and I never saw no houses or nothing. So I just wrapped the baby in my jacket and took the poor little thing home. At that time, me and my wife had a two month old baby boy. When I got home and unwrapped the little thing, I saw that the cord was still attached. It was just borned—I mean just borned. What was we to do? So we's been takin' care of that little girl just like she was our very own. Been treating the babies like twins. My wife was even able to nurse them both. We named her Zoe. She is a sweet baby and we love her just as much as we love our little boy."

The sheriff was moved by the sincerity and honesty of this young man. It was miraculous this baby survived.

Ronnie continued, "That ain't all" he said, "there's more."

The sheriff said, "Go on, Ronnie."

"Well after we had the baby here with us for a while, I got to thinkin' about it so I went back up to Peter's branch and walked back into the woods close to where we found the baby. You see, I knowed if there was a new born baby—there had to be a mother. So I went back to look for her. I found a cabin but it was locked up. When I tried to get in, I could hear somebody screamin 'but I couldn't make out what it said. I broke down the door and saw this young girl locked in a cage. She looked like a wild animal. Her hair was matted and she was nearly naked and dirty. She pointed to the key and I opened the door. She was so crazy to get out of there and away from that place she jest grabbed some stuff that was hangin' on a peg and run. I don't reckon I ever seen nobody run as fast. I yelled at her, 'Wait! Wait!' I said, 'I will help you.' But she kept runnin' and then there was a big explosion and I thought I better get out of there. I didn't want to be blamed for no explosion. So I run and got in my car and took off."

Ronnie added, "I never knowed what happened to the girl. I never knowed until she showed up at the Easter pot-luck supper. She looked so different—cleaned up and all—I almost didn't recognize her. But when she held our little Zoe, I knew."

The sheriff said, "Thank you, Ronnie. That was not easy."

"Yeah", he said, "My wife is gonna kill me for tellin' you before

I told her—about that last part. She don't know I went back up that holler a-lookin' for the cabin."

Then he continued, "We want to keep little Zoe. We love her so much. She has been with us since the day she was borned. She don't know no other momma or daddy. It feels like she belongs to us. It was my wife who tied the cord after I brung her home. Outside of birthing her, you can't get no closer, I reckon. We can't bear the thought of her being with somebody else. I reckon she will have to prove she's the mother, if she wants our Zoe. How can she do that? Just lookin' like somebody ain't proof, is it?"

The sheriff asked Ronnie, "Do you know the identity of the birth mother?

Ronnie looked down at the ground, and said, "Yes'sir, I do."

The sheriff looked at Ronnie and said, "Who do you think it is?"

Ronnie said, "I think it's the young girl who's living with the Wertz family. I hear she just came there and them being good Christian people took her in. I can tell you she was livin' in hell in that old cabin. You can't believe how dirty that place was."

The sheriff replied, "Yes, I can. I was there. You don't know the whole story. Right now I don't think you need to know."

The sheriff shook Ronnie's hand and started to get back in the car. "Ronnie, you just relax and try to stay positive and calm. I have this feeling you are doin' the Lord's work with this baby. He will reward you for your loving care of her. Keep praying God would continue to take care of Zoe like He's done so far. You've got to know in your heart it was God who sent you back to let her out of that cage. She would have died there. God works in mysterious ways. So keep trusting Him and keep doing what you're doing--taking care of your family and your wife. I'll be back in touch."

As the sheriff drove home that evening, his thoughts were crowded— all the facts and emotions of this case came tumbling in at once. *How dare I give Ronnie Ball advice about his relationship with God? That man is head and shoulders above me in understanding about how God works. Who do I think I am that I would become his spiritual adviser? Me! Lord, forgive me! It just came out—I didn't think too much about what I was* saying—it just seemed right. In a lot of ways, I think this case has changed me. I know I am seeing things differently. When this case was brought to me originally, I felt sorry for the parents. But, to my shame, I didn't follow through with it like I might another case. Why? I can't say why. It was just one of those things. I actually forgot about it. It breaks my heart to know Marika suffered so much at the hands of an evil man. It is even more heartbreaking to consider her father—her very own father-- may have been involved in some way. What could I have done to make for a different outcome?

When all this came down, why didn't I think of Purilli? He had been in and out of the rough scene in McDowell County. Everywhere he went and everything he touched turned to chaos and confusion. Why didn't I remember that case in Murphy's in 1932? I was a deputy then, but I knew about it. Why didn't I connect the dots and go looking for Purilli?

But, look—Ronnie Ball delivered her. He just happened to be hunting that morning up on the ridge above Peter's Branch. That was a miracle of God's timing. The baby cried and God sent Ronnie Ball. When Marika was in the deepest despair, God sent Ronnie Ball. He is just a humble man—yeah, a humble man doing God's work. When I think about it all, how could I not see the hand of God moving through these valleys to preserve the life of this young girl and her baby?

I am glad to know for sure who let her out of the cage and it's a miracle the baby survived in spite of Angelo Purilli's evil hand—the Balls are responsible for the beautiful baby girl you see today. If the baby had been left with Marika, both would probably have died.

My next task is to inform Marika that her baby is alive. She may have figured it out already but I still need to tell her the full story. She has a tough decision to make. She will be elated beyond words. She has turned out to be such a beautiful young lady. Ronnie Ball said she looked like a wild animal when he found her. That's another miracle of grace and love. The grace of God led her to the Wertz family and their love restored her spirit and gave her hope.

The joy of discovery for Marika could spell heartbreak for Ronnie and Audrey Ball. As I see it, this child will be loved and nurtured in the future—regardless of how the case is resolved. If she is raised by the Balls *she will be the twin sister of David. I can see her as a happy well-adjusted child with a future. But when I think of her with Marika, I know she will be loved—no question about that—but I can't see beyond that. I am going to have to maintain neutrality. That's going to be hard, he thought.*

When storm clouds are gathering, take
refuge in the Everlasting Arms

The Everlasting Arms

CHAPTER EIGHT

Startling Revelations

W hen the sheriff entered headquarters the next morning, she called Sgt. Weaver to his office. "How's it going this morning?" he asked.

"Oh, fine, Sir" she said. "But I can tell you have a bee in your bonnet. You've got a lot going on in your head. I could tell by the way you walked in the office."

"I think you're right, Sgt. I hope you have something to tell me, too."

She replied "I do, sir. But I think you should go first. It looks like you're going to bust if you don't get it out."

"Okay, kiddo, you asked for it," he said. "Remember the list we made yesterday? I have it right here in front of me. The doctor was no help to me when I saw him yesterday. He said everything that he knew was confidential. So that was a dead end. On my way back from Davy, I stopped at the Ball residence and talked with Ronnie Ball. You said you thought Ronnie Ball might be the key and you were right. He started talking and before he finished I found out the baby Marika birthed is alive. Ronnie found her in the woods the day she was born—she still had the cord attached. She was wrapped in a piece of dirty blanket. He heard the baby crying and found her. He and his wife are raising her like their own. Audrey Ball was able to nurse the baby because she had a two month old little boy already. So now they have twins. They named her Zoe. And that's the short version of a long story."

"Wow!" she said "what a shocker. Does Marika know?"

The sheriff replied "Not yet. I want you and Lena to go with me to tell her. I don't know what to expect when we tell her."

The sheriff continued, "That's not all. Ronnie said later after they had Zoe for a while, he was thinking about Zoe. How did she get out there in the woods—who put her in the woods? —a newborn and all? And those kind of thoughts would not leave him alone. So to satisfy his curiosity, he went back up Peter's branch holler to the spot where he found the baby. He looked around for a sign of anybody and went back into the woods. He found a cabin. When he tried to get in, he heard screaming from inside. He broke the door down and found a young girl in a cage. He said she looked like a wild animal—her hair was matted and she was half naked. She pointed to a key hanging on a peg so he unlocked the cage. He said she came out like a wild person, grabbed some clothes hanging by the door and started running. He yelled for her to stop but she kept running. In just a few minutes, he heard an explosion. He was afraid he would be accused of causing the explosion, so he got in his car and took off. He did not know where she went or what became of her until she showed up at church on Easter Sunday."

The deputy said, "Oh, boy, that brings up a new issue, doesn't it?"

The sheriff replied, "Indeed, it does. The Balls are determined to keep Zoe if at all possible. They say she is their little girl—and she has never known another mommy or daddy. She has a brother. They love her—they named her. He said they have as much right to her as Marika does. She has been with them since she was born—his wife tied the cord off. Marika didn't even know if it was a boy or girl."

"But that wasn't her fault. She was held captive."

"What you say is true but the baby is a separate issue. How can Marika prove she is the mother? I think I need to go back and talk to the doctor. I wonder if there is a biological way to prove parentage. I ain't heard of any—except maybe blood type and from what I read, that ain't foolproof."

Then the sheriff added, "Then there are the legal issues involved.

She doesn't have a birth certificate. There is no legal record of her birth. That's where we need an attorney to help sort through those issues."

The deputy said, "The more we know it seems like the more we don't know."

The sheriff laughed, "When you put it that way, you're right. Everything we discover will lead to new discoveries, I reckon."

Then he looked up and said, "Okay, what have **you** got?"

She began, "We got our first bite from the radio broadcasts in Ohio. A man by the name of Paul Hicks contacted us through the FCC with the following information. He said a little over 2 years ago two couples came to his farm. They said they were out of work coal miners. He has a dairy farm in Sarahsville, Ohio, which is in eastern Ohio. Anyway, one of the couples was named Stanislas. Mr Hicks said that he hired both couples—both husband and wife-- to work at his farm. Joseph worked with the cattle and feed management. His wife Susanna worked in the plant where they produced cottage cheese and buttermilk. They are also living on the farm. He had cottages for his workers to live. The thing is, Joseph Stanislas left about 3 months ago. The mother and two children are still there. The older boy is working on the farm now—he is fourteen. Since there are two people from the family working on the farm, they are still eligible to stay in the cottage. How's that for results?"

The sheriff said, "I declare, it has been a good day already. Would you call the priest at Gary and ask him to get a message to Lena? We'll pick her up about 1 o'clock, no let's make that 12. Then we can get to Mohegan by 1 o'clock. Could you run over to Gary and pick her up and then come back here and pick me up? I'd appreciate it. I'm going to try to get ahold of this Paul Hicks and see if I can make some kind of arrangements to get Marika together with her mother and brothers. I reckon a dairy business would have a phone. You did get a phone number, didn't you?"

"I'm on it, sheriff. The phone number is on the report I just handed you. Do you see it?"

While the sergeant was gathering up her papers, the sheriff asked,

"Did you hear anything from the FBI about the fingerprints? I think that it's too soon to expect it, but I thought I'd ask."

"Not yet," the sergeant replied, "I'll let you know as soon as I hear something."

When his office door was closed, the sheriff picked up the phone and asked for the long distance operator. After giving the operator the necessary information, he could hear the phone ringing on the other end.

After the third ring, a voice answered, "Hicks Dairy, home of premium dairy products. May I help you?"

The sheriff thought, that was a nice way to answer the phone. He said, "Yes, maam, I'd like to speak to Mr. Hicks. Paul Hicks."

"With whom am I speaking?" was the response.

"Oh, I'm sorry Maam, this is Jerry Chatham, I'm the sheriff of McDowell County West Virginia. I am looking for information about a Stanislas family. It is my understanding they are employed at your farm."

"This is Holly Hicks. Paul Hicks is my husband but he is at the auction today. I can give you information. What is it you need to know?"

The sheriff continued, "Your husband contacted us through the FCC in response to a radio alert we had broadcast throughout Ohio. I think I should tell you what the situation is on this end and maybe we can pull it all together. Almost three years ago, a 12 year old child—a girl—was abducted from her home in Gary, West Virginia in the middle of the night. The name of the family was Stanislas. The girl's name is Marika and about 3 months ago we found her alive. She is staying with a family in Mohegan West Virginia. She is doing well at the moment. I would like for the mother to know of the daughter's rescue and find out if she wants to see her. I would like to arrange to bring Marika over to Ohio to see her."

Mrs. Hicks replied, "Wow! That will be tremendous news for Susanna. The problem is we are going to have to find someone to relay this information to Susanna, since she speaks no English. There is a woman in our little town who was born in Poland. I've been wanting to get the two of them together but I haven't done it yet. Trouble is Susanna goes to the Catholic Church when she can go and the other lady goes to the Reformed Church, where we attend. I'll try to locate

Marianne—that's the Polish lady's name—and bring her over to give Susanna the news. If you will give me your phone number, I will let you know what Susanna says. I just know she will want to see her."

Then she added, "You go ahead and make arrangements to get Marika up here and let me know and we will arrange things on this end. What mother wouldn't want to see her daughter after three years?"

She went on, "You say, the girl was found about 3 months ago? That's curious--it was about that time---3 months ago—when Joseph Stanislas disappeared. He was a troubled man—especially when he drank. He got really mean when he got drunk. There was abuse of the wife and the boys—all the incidences happened when he drank. So, when he left, no one was really sorry. The older boy stepped in and does twice as much work as the father—and he has a much better attitude."

The sheriff finished the call by saying, "That agrees with information we had in our files about the Stanislas family situation. Thank you so much, Mrs. Hicks. I will let you know when we can come. I hope it will be sometime within a couple of weeks—if not sooner. Thanks again." After the exchange of telephone numbers, he hung up.

That was a very nice lady, he thought—very accommodating. I would say they were lucky to find that situation. A farm job and housing right there. I wonder what happened to Stanislas. She said he disappeared about 3 months ago. It seems sort of strange about 3 months ago, Marika was found and rescued from the cabin and the moonshine still blew up and her father left the farm in Ohio. I wonder if it was the same day. We know the explosion and Marika's escape happened the same day. But what possible connection could Stanislas' disappearance way up in Ohio have to do with all of this?

While he waited for Sergeant Weaver to return from Gary, the sheriff went to the record room and located the file about the explosion of the moonshine still. He wasn't sure what he was looking for but there must be something he had missed and something which tied all this together.

He took the file and opened it up on the table in the room. He pored over the details. He made note of the exact date the explosion occurred. Then he read the list of articles taken from the scene. There was one delivery truck—blue-green. And then he noticed a second vehicle listed. A 1935 Model T Ford with an Ohio license plate NO 879. He pulled the sheet of paper out of his breast pocket and made a note of the vehicle information. *That's something to ask Mrs. Stanislas, he thought. There must have been someone else with Angelo when that still blew up. Did he escape? Why did he leave his car? Was it damaged in the explosion?* He looked at the notes about the vehicles in the file. The only thing about vehicle condition was a note the truck was rusty and muddy. Presumably it was in running condition. Why not take the car and get away?

I did not see the remains of two people there. We found only one head and torso and the arms and legs of one body. I need to go back there again and check it out. I can't believe I missed all these details.

He put the file back and hurried back to his office. He looked at his watch. It was 12:30. He dialed the county auto lot. When a voice answered, the sheriff said, "Hey George, Sheriff Chatham here, how long do we keep cars in the lot after they are brought in?"

George responded, "Well, sir, we generally keep them for a year or so, if we have room."

The sheriff continued, "How long would it take you to check to see if you still have a 1935 Model T Ford Ohio License NO879?"

George answered, "Oh, Sheriff, I know we still got that one. I've got my eye on it. If it goes up for sale, I'm gonna try to get it for myself. It's a nice car. Course sitting out here on the lot don't help its condition. So, soon as I get some space in the barn, that car is coming in."

The sheriff said "Thanks, George. Don't get rid of it quite yet. I need to look it over."

"Right boss" was the reply the sheriff heard as he hung up the receiver.

New piece of the puzzle he thought. If I were a gambler, I'd bet that car belonged to Stanislas—Ohio license and all. Lena said they had a car when they lived in Gary. What was he doing with Angelo and how could he have not known about the cabin? And Marika? Those thoughts sent shivers down his spine. What kind of father could do that? Maybe Stanislas and Angelo were birds of a feather. And where did he go? Since the car was still there, how did he get away? I don't want Marika to know her father was so close and never came to rescue her. It would break her heart. So, I won't mention this in front of Lena. I'll tell Sgt. Weaver later.

He walked out of the courthouse into the parking lot just as Sergeant Weaver pulled in. He got into the back seat and they were on their way to Mohegan.

Ronnie Ball was having a cup of coffee when his wife walked into the kitchen. He looked up, "Where are the kids?" he asked.

"They're happy playing together right now. At least for a little while" she responded.

"Come sit down for a minute, honey, I have something I need to tell you." When she was seated, he began, "I need to tell you I was the one who found the girl in the cabin and let her go. When Zoe had been with us a couple or three months, one day I was watching the two of them sleeping. And I got to thinking about this whole situation. How could a baby—a newborn baby—be jest layin' in the woods like that? There had to be a woman somewheres close. We didn't see anything the day we found Zoe but they had to be somebody up there somewhere close to where we found her. As you know, she was brand new. So, I drove up to the spot where I remembered finding her. I parked my car on a hill and walked into the thickest part of the woods. Lo and behold, I found this old rickety cabin. I tried to open the door but it was bolted. It was then I heard screamin' and hollerin'. I kept tryin' and finally knocked the door down. I couldn't believe my eyes. The place was an awful mess and it stunk to high heaven and there was this girl in a cage. She was locked in this little skinny cage. She showed me where the key was and I let her out. She looked and acted like a wild animal. She run out of that cage, grabbed some stuff hangin' on a peg and ran. I don't reckon I ever seen a human bein' run so fast. I yelled at her to stop as loud as I could and said I would help her but she jest kept on a-runnin'. When I couldn't see her no more, they was this big explosion on the mountain somewhere behind the cabin. I was scared about the explosion so I run to the car and took off."

Then he continued, "Forgive me for not tellin' you sooner. It was too hard to think about. I never saw where she went—I looked along the road on the way home. She had to hide somewhere in the woods around there. I never knowed what happened to her till she showed up at the pot-luck on Easter Sunday. It's the girl who's stayin' with the Wertz family."

Audrey Ball, who had sat staring into her coffee the whole time Ronnie was talking, looked up. She said, "You did the right thing, dear. I can't imagine what she went through or who locked her up. Whoever it was who locked her up prob'ly took the baby away. I mean almost before it was separated from the womb. That makes my blood boil. I wonder if she ever even seen it. It's a wonder she didn't bleed to death or die of infection in that place."

Ronnie said, "Audrey, do you see God's hand in all of this? I can't help but think it was God who protected that little thing in the woods. We heared the cry—that little cry could've blended in with all the bird chirpin' and the wind in the leaves. But we heared it. I reckon it was God callin' me to that little girl." Tears were beginning to flow down his cheeks, as he said, "And about goin' back out there and findin' that cabin. When I had the thought to go, it was like somebody was pushin' me to go see. I couldn't not go. Does that make sense? I think it was God's hand of protection over that baby and the girl. And he used me! Does that make it a miracle?"

Audrey smiled and reached for her husband's hand. "Well, I reckon it does, you're my miracle worker."

Then she continued, "You know at the pot-luck supper when she picked up Zoe, there seemed to be a connection between them. I don't rightly know if I believe in that "in-womb connection stuff" I've been readin' about—but I did notice Zoe calmed down just as soon as she picked her up. Do you think babies know their birth mothers by the heart beat or something like that? I've thought about it a lot. The baby listens to the heartbeat of the mother for 9 months so why wouldn't there be a connection? Why wouldn't that heartbeat soothe a restless child? And Zoe looked at her face like she was studying it—strange. And she curled up and went to sleep just that easy. She don't use-ly do that. I can always get David to settle down real quick but with Zoe, it takes a while."

Ronnie said, "That's interestin', honey. But one thing I noticed at the supper was how excited Zoe got when you brought her back to sit by her brother. Those two are really close."

Then with a laugh Audrey said, "What do you 'spect, they're twins?"

"But seriously" Ronnie said "She will be informed of Zoe's situation. Up to now, she thinks her baby died. I wouldn't be surprised if the sheriff tells her today. We are going to have to let her go, I think. It's gonna break my heart and David will be lost."

"I know", Audrey said, "remember what you said a little bit ago. She's in God's hands. We are just the servants. We have trusted God so far and He never let us down. We will just go on trusting Him and enjoying our family. When the time comes to make decisions, I know He will make a way."

"I married a wise woman", Ronnie said as he put his arm around her.

"This wise woman hears something in the other room that sounds like it needs some Mother's wisdom" she said as she went to check on the twins.

When Sgt. Weaver parked in front of the Wertz house, Aggie and Marika were working in the garden patch. When Aggie noticed the car by the house, she and Marika came to greet the visitors. Within a matter of minutes they were all seated around the table in the Wertz' kitchen.

The sheriff began by saying through the interpreter he had news for her that was very exciting.

Lena began to talk with Marika by telling her she had good news.

"We have found your baby alive." The sheriff had expected a shout of joy or at least a "whoopee", but none was forthcoming. Marika simply said, "Wiem.(I know) It's the baby girl the Balls have. Her name is Zoe and she's beautiful. But I don't know how she got to them. Can you tell me?"

Lena said to the sheriff, "She knew about the baby. She wants to know how she got to the Balls. Do you want to tell her and I'll translate."

The sheriff hesitated then said, "Tell her Ronnie Ball found the baby in the woods not too far from the cabin. She was wrapped in a piece of the blanket off the bed. She had just been born—the cord was still attached. Mr. Ball wrapped her in his jacket and took her home. Mrs. Ball tied off the cord. She nursed her along with her little boy, who is 2 months older than Zoe. They are excellent parents and your baby could not—I repeat—could not have been in better hands. They treated her like their own child and they love her. They want to keep her and raise her as a twin to their little boy, David."

As memories came flooding, it was like she was reliving the feeling of despair and hopelessness of that day. She struggled with each word, "I could hear my baby crying. I tried to get up and go find it but Angelo knocked me back down." It seemed each new thought was more difficult to express. "I could hear the crying—crying—crying and then no crying. I thought the baby died wherever it was—or got too weak to cry anymore. I must have passed out because the next thing I remember was waking up in the cage. I could barely move and I was still bleeding. I was hurting but I was okay." Then she smiled and said, "When I couldn't do anything, God took care of my baby and put her in the arms of a loving mother."

Her body began to shake. She took a deep breath. Her voice was becoming softer and softer. "God knew I wasn't fit to be a mother—I should have gone and found my baby. Lena, I bet you would have found your baby. You wouldn't have left her in the woods. When I didn't hear her crying no more must be when he found her and took her away. Thank God she didn't die. But I am ashamed I didn't go find her. I should have found her." Her voice was barely above a whisper as she kept repeating, "I should have found her. I should have found her." She put her head on the table and sobbed violently. "Why didn't I find her?"

Lena relayed Marika's words to the sheriff and Sgt. Weaver, who wrote in the case journal. No one said anything for a few minutes.

Sgt. Weaver said, "Lena, ask her what she thinks would have happened if she had been able to find her baby in the woods."

Lena said, "That's a good question, Sergeant". When Lena relayed the question to Marika, she had a startled look on her face. "I never thought of that." She said, "I think we probably would have both died." Then she looked at Aggie and said, "God always knows best, doesn't He?"

Aggie shook her head and said, "You are wise beyond your years, my dear."

The sheriff wanted to give Marika a few minutes to regain her composure so he asked Aggie if she had anything to drink. She offered them tea or coffee. When they all had a cup in front of them, the sheriff instructed Lena to tell Marika her mother and brothers had been found in Ohio.

When Marika heard the news, she was noticeably excited. Then she asked, "Tata?"

When Lena told her only her mother and brothers had been located, she said. "I'm glad he's not with them. When I see them again, my Tata won't be there—he can't beat me. I know he thinks I ran away. He knew I wanted to get away from him. But Mama will believe me—I didn't run away. Angelo stole me while I was asleep."

After a brief pause, Marika said, "I would never run away and leave my Mama. Jakub and me wanted to protect Mama. Tata got mad when he was drunk. Jakub and me was afraid of him when he got drunk. Since he wasn't working in the mines, he got drunk a lot. Where did he go? Do you know what happened to him? Why isn't he with Mama and my brothers?"

Lena looked at the sheriff and shrugged her shoulders. "What did happen to him, Sir?"

The sheriff responded, "The lady in Ohio didn't know where he went. She just said about 3 months ago, he left them. That was about the same time the moonshine still blew up."

When Marika heard the phrase 'moonshine still blew up', she said in English, "Ronnie Bell let me out of cage. KABOOM!" She pointed behind her.

Then the sheriff said, "Ask her if she would like to go see her Mama and brothers?'

Marika said, "Oh, could I? My heart aches to see my Mama and brothers."

The sheriff said, "We are working to get you over to Ohio. Your Mama and Jakub are working on a dairy farm in Ohio. They have a cottage there so they have a place to work and to live. It would probably take about 10 hours to drive it. The lady on the phone was excited there could be a reunion. We'll work it out."

The sheriff told Marika he would arrange for her to see an attorney to work out the details concerning the baby when she was ready. Does she know what her plans are at this time?

Marika told the sheriff she still had to think about it for a while. She said through her interpreter, "It won't be many days but right now, I just have to think and pray about it."

When John came home from work that evening, he had a passenger in his truck. When Marika saw Joe get out of the truck, she ran to greet him.

Marika exclaimed, "This is my perfect day! My baby is alive, I know where my Mama is and now Joe is back! What more can I ask for—my prayers have been answered."

She said all that in Polish so no one was 100% sure what she said. While they couldn't understand her words, they could understand her body language. She communicated the fact she was indeed excited and hilariously happy.

Joe put down his suitcase to greet his Mom and Daniel, who had come in from the garden and were cleaning up at the well.

Joe looked at his Mom and said, "What's goin' on here? Have we hit the jackpot or something?"

Aggie explained to Joe it had been an exceptionally good day for Marika. "She had some good news today. They have located her mother and brothers. I reckon they don't know where her father is, though. He left the family over in Ohio about 3 months ago.

"Do you know where in Ohio?" he asked.

Aggie replied, "The sheriff said the name of the town. It's a small town—not like Cleveland or Akron or any place you ever heared of. He's workin' on a way to get Marika over there to see them."

When they were alone in the house, Aggie said to Joe, "Joseph, they's somethin' else she found out today. This can change her life, too. Her baby is alive. She has all this time thought the baby died in the woods. Not only is the baby alive but she has seen her, held her and knows the people who are taking care of her."

"Wow" said Joe, "That's a lot to take in at one time. Let me get this right—the baby is alive—a little girl? Where is she?"

"She's just on the other side of Mohegan camp. She is with Ronnie and Audrey Ball. Ronnie found her in the woods right after she was born and took her home. They've been treating her like their own little girl. They want to keep her and adopt her."

Joe ran his fingers through his hair, he looked at his mom like he had been hit by a lightning bolt. "That means she has a dilemma, doesn't it? She has a decision to make. Does she feel like she can take care of a baby? How would she support a child? She doesn't have a home or a job. It is awful hard to be a single mother."

Joe's thoughts ran wild, *a lot has happened since I've been gone. I wish I had been here when all this happened. I'm sure it has been hard on her. The swing of emotions from joy and sorrow is always difficult—even exhausting--the joy of discovery and the sorrow of separation. Why do I have this protective attitude toward her? There's this sense that we are connected somehow. I'm the one she chose to take to the cabin. She wanted me to share what she had experienced. She wanted me to understand. Why me? What is the bond we have? Today when she ran out to meet me, I wanted to take her in my arms. Why didn't I? She obviously was glad to see me. I just realized she was the one I wanted to see. I wanted to know she was alright. How does she feel about me? Does she look to me to support her emotionally or physically—or both? I wish I could just sit down with her and discuss it. This language thing is a problem. I have to figure out a way to communicate with her. I want to help her as she makes this important decision about the baby. When she decides about the baby, will she care what I think? Will she want to please me with her decision? How can I tell her if she decides to leave the baby with the Ball family, that it's okay with me? And on the other hand, if she decides to keep the baby, how will I feel about being a father? Where did that come from? I haven't even thought about marriage and yet when I'm thinking about her future, I'm including myself. I need to talk to myself more often—I always learn something about myself—she is my future. Should I ask her to marry me before she makes her decision or should I wait? Would it make a difference? This is hard—there are so many things to consider.*

Joe said, "Mom, I wonder if I could take her over to Ohio. I would like to meet her mother and brothers. I just need a vehicle to drive. I think I'll talk to the sheriff about it. It's gonna be a couple of days before I can go. I reckon Alvin needs my help."

Alvin was busy with the details of getting his business going. He had visited the management of each of the various coal mines in the area and pointed out the need to begin cleanup now. He presented an optimistic attitude about the mines opening up soon. He talked about the situation in Europe and how they were going to need to import coal to make armaments and airplanes. The deal he offered was his company would clean up the area around the tipple yards for $500 dollars plus all the salvage they could find, including coal. He and his brothers had started cleaning out the area around the tipple at Capels two weeks ago. It was a big job to gather and then sort through all the different materials they picked up. They scraped up the stray piles of coal left along the rail line and piled it on the outside of the fence. Jim made a sign that read: FREE COAL—YOU HAUL IT AWAY. People needed coal to heat their homes and for their cook stoves. The coal pile disappeared overnight.

Alvin's goal was when the mines started up again, the company could come right back to work without any advance cleanup or set up. It could save them money in the long run. He wanted to build a reputation for a high standard of service, by so doing, he could develop a clientele. With a fleet of trucks, he could haul coal during the week and do cleanup work on Saturdays. He could visualize how this could become a lucrative business. Is this what Doc meant by strategizing?

Joe joined the crew the first evening after he arrived back home. Since it was Friday, they loaded the truck with steel scrap they had amassed during the week. They also had boxes of scrap copper wire and a few batteries. A pretty decent haul, he thought. He would take it up to Matlock's Scrap Yard in Welch on Saturday morning. They would probably have enough time to take a second load. Things were going well.

Before he had spoken to a single coal company representative, Alvin had set up a budget for his business. If things progressed according to his plan, he would soon be able to buy his own truck and start paying his brothers and Dad. The first twenty dollars he made would go back to Doc Bondy plus of course the one dollar interest. He had inspired him to strategize.

The Wertz men came home tired every night. There wasn't much conversation as they cleaned up and got ready for bed. John was thankful for the chance to work with his sons, but he knew he could not keep up this schedule long term. He hoped when the Davy sector work was done, he could quit the WPA and work full time for Alvin. If there was some way Alvin could turn this cleanup business into a full time business after the mines went back, he would never step foot in a coal mine again. Even if he took a pay cut, he would do it. He and Aggie had been through deep waters before, with God's help, they could do it again, if necessary.

John had observed that Alvin knew how to talk to people. He could convince them they needed the service he could provide for them. He showed them on paper how it would save them money in the long run—especially if they had to pay union wages to get the cleanup done. He must have got that from Aggie. She could be very convincing when she had a mind to.

Alvin had surprised him. That medicine Doc Bondy gave him really worked. He seemed strong as a horse out there working. There was a lot of shoveling and lifting. It was strenuous but they were making progress.

As soon as they finished loading the scrap out, the lot at Capels would be shipshape and they would move down to Twin Branch.

What he missed about the new schedule was having Bible time with the family after supper. Aggie had been good about having supper ready as soon as he got home so they could eat and get to work. She had bath water ready when they got home just after dark. She was a real trooper. He had to figure out a way to work this out. Helping Alvin get his business going was important but not as important as staying close to God and leading his family to know God's Word.

The sheriff had arranged for Lena to meet Marika when she went to see the attorney to discuss the future of her baby. Marika was happy she could express herself freely but also she could have complete understanding of what the attorney said. She was glad for Doctor Bondy's support. He had arranged this Saturday meeting with the attorney.

As she rode with the doctor to the appointment, she thought, *I don't know what I'm going to do. I know how I feel but I have to consider the circumstances, too. What is best for Zoe? When Angelo left her in the woods, he meant for her to die or some animal to get her. But God sent a loving father to find her and take her to his home. What Angelo meant for evil, God has used for good in the life of that discarded baby. She has a wonderful stable loving family. Would it be fair to remove her from that situation? If I removed her and had her with me, where would I take her? The Wertz family has been so good to me. They have treated me like their own daughter. Is it fair for me to expect them to take care of Zoe, too? If I had to take care of a baby, I couldn't help around the place like I do now. Ooooh! What am I going to do? Is it possible to be broken in two and go in two directions? Would it be easier if I didn't know exactly where she was, what she looked like—if I hadn't held her? I want to be sure I think it through because I am going to have to live the rest of my life, knowing who she is and where she is. But they could move away and take my little girl and I might never see her again. Oh, Lord, help me. What is God's view of this? Does the fact I birthed her mean she has to always be with me? What was it that John said? 'We can only make decisions based on what we know today. God alone knows the future and He holds tomorrow. We trust Him for the future results of the decisions we make today. We walk by faith and not by sight.' John is so wise. He has become like a father to me. I am glad my Tata is not here—he would just get drunk and be angry. I can't deal with this in anger. I can't deal with this in fear. I must deal with it in faith. I don't know if that makes it harder or easier. I just know I'm tied in a knot. I need to untie the knot but I don't know where to start. Okay, number one, the decision must not be about me. I must, therefore, make the decision on my own. I don't ever want to have someone to blame if I later regret my decision. I will take full responsibility for my actions. Number 2, I must consider Zoe—what is my best estimation of the best thing for her—right now and for the future? I want her to know Jesus when she is still young—the Balls will make sure she hears the gospel. Number 3, would the circumstances of her conception and delivery be remembered each time she didn't please me? How would I treat her in comparison to other children I might have later? As she grows would I expect too much or perhaps expect not enough of her? Ooooh! I would want her to grow up and be like Audrey Ball—she is a fine woman. I would want her character to be molded by that family—not my family. They might have more children and that would be a loving environment for her. On the other hand, I have nothing to offer her except my love. If I give her up, Lord, I give her to You. Lord, help me make the decision and trust You with the results.*

Her reverie was broken when the doctor pulled into a parking spot and turned off the engine. He came around and opened the passenger door for her. "Thank you", she said.

Lena had already arrived and was waiting in the hallway outside the attorney's office. When they entered they were greeted by Ben Sizemore. He invited them into his office and closed the door. Doc explained that Lena was there to interpret the conversation.

The entire situation was explained to the attorney. When it was done, Marika said, through Lena. "Sir, I have to decide if I want to claim Zoe as my daughter or leave her where she is. If I leave her, I will sign papers so the Balls can get her a birth certificate naming them as her parents so they can adopt her. I have given this a lot of thought and prayer but I have not yet made the decision. I am leaning in one direction, but every time I think about it, I am overwhelmed with emotion. I want to take emotion out of it and make the decision based on what is right for Zoe."

The attorney stopped her and asked, "What legal claim do you have to the baby? How can you prove she is biologically your daughter?"

Dr. Bondy spoke up and said, "Her claim would be based on circumstantial evidence. She was in a cabin less than 100 yds from where the baby was found. When I examined her, it was obvious to me that she had given birth recently. We cannot use blood typing for evidence--it is not reliable for establishing biological lineage. I have the blanket off the bed where the child in question was presumably born. It has a large piece that was cut out of it. I believe that missing piece represents the blanket the baby was wrapped in when found in the woods. I think finding the piece that the child was wrapped in is the crucial piece to tie the baby to the birth bed. Mrs. Ball said she got rid of it."

Then he continued, "Would the court give credence to circumstantial evidence? I've seen the baby twice in my office. She has Marika's coloring of hair and eyes—and I might add—shape of face. The Balls are both blue eyed and light hair. She looks like she belongs to Marika. Is physical familial resemblance ever considered as evidence of parentage?"

The attorney answered, "That's a good question. I have researched similar cases and found that the results vary. It more or less depends upon how the judge interprets 'welfare of the minor child'.

Marika asked, "Sir, what is the best way to continue with this case?"

The attorney looked at Marika for a minute and then spoke to Lena. "I think you will have to wait until the Ball's petition the court for permanent guardianship and adoption. Part of that process would be to issue a birth certificate. If you wanted to challenge it, you could present your claims to the court at that time. The downside of this is they may wait for a long time to proceed since it is my understanding Mr. Ball is not employed at this time. They would be responsible for attorney fees and court costs. If you want to pursue this case and try to gain custody yourself, we could petition the court on your behalf."

Marika looked puzzled as Lena explained what the attorney had just said. She blurted out, "I have decided, I want to make sure she can stay with the Ball family. I think God placed her there. Angelo put her out but Ronnie Ball took her in. What was meant for evil God intended for good—the good of my baby girl. How can I go against God?" She began to cry softly. "This was not easy. But I want what is best for Zoe. I don't want her to go to anybody else but the Balls. I know they will love her and take care of her. I want them to be able to raise her but if they change their minds, I want her. I don't want her going to an orphanage. If I thought for a minute she would not be taken care of as an infant and throughout her life, I would fight like a tiger momma for her. But I am at peace with the decision to leave her where she is."

It was clear everyone in the room empathized with Marika as Lena interpreted her words. Even Doc Bondy wiped his eyes. The attorney looked at Marika and said, "Since you have made your decision, I will draw up papers, submit them to the court and we will see to it your wishes are carried out. I will make sure the Ball family is notified of your decision. It will be a big relief for them, I'm sure. However, I want you to understand when you relinquish parental rights, you will have no further say in the life situation for this child. If the Balls decide they are not able to provide for her, they will have the right to determine where she lives and with whom she lives. You are giving up all rights."

Marika smiled when Lena told her what the attorney had said. Marika asked for the Wertz family to not be informed of her decision. She didn't want them to worry about it. She would tell them in her time. Then she rose to leave, extended her hand to the attorney and said, "Thank you, Ben Sizemore. I like you."

Doctor Bondy found it difficult not to smile at such simplicity of heart and expression. He was proud of her. He thought, *she is a very loving person—selfless love. She will go far with a heart like that.* He wished he could tell her how much he admired her for her decision. Maybe someday he would have the opportunity.

On Monday morning, Joseph hitched a ride to Welch. He dropped in at the sheriff's office. He learned the sheriff was out of the office. He met with Chief Deputy Dalton. After he explained the situation, Joe asked if there was a vehicle he could use to take Marika to see her mother and brothers. He showed his driver's license and assured the deputy he had never had an accident and he was an experienced driver of many different kinds of vehicles.

The deputy assured Joe he would check with the sheriff and let him know. Joe realized it was the best result he could hope for today. As he prepared to leave, he shook hands with the deputy and turned to go. When he opened the office door, he came face to face with Sheriff Chatham.

"Joe" the sheriff said. "When did you get home?"

Joe said, "a couple days ago. It must have been the same day you were there. When I got home Marika was rejoicing over learning her mother and brothers had been located in Ohio."

Then he continued, "she really wants to go see them and I would like to take her. But I have no vehicle. I came today to ask if there is a vehicle I could use to drive her over there."

The sheriff picked up the phone, and then he said, "George, how's your inventory of vehicles that are not being used? By law, we can use impounded vehicles. I need one that has been cleared for release either because the case is closed or it has been in inventory for over 2 years."

George said, "Well sir, I have at least three I can think of right now. If you want to come over I'll show you what is available."

"Okay, George, I'll see you in about 10 minutes."

When Joe saw the three cars, he chose the Model T Ford without knowing it had belonged to Joseph Stanislas.

The sheriff took him aside and said, "Joe, you need to know this car belonged to Marika's father. It has been in the police garage since the explosion. We found it at the still after the explosion along with the vehicle that belonged to Angelo. Are you sure you want to take that one?"

Joe was shocked by the news. "What was the Stanislas car doing at the still? Was Joseph there? What was his association with Angelo? Did he know Marika was held in a cabin not ½ mile away?"

The sheriff answered, "I really can't say for sure exactly what it was but there seems to have been some connection between Joseph Stanislas and Angelo. To make the mystery deeper, we do not have a clue where Joseph is and why he abandoned his car at the exploded still. From what we have learned from Marika, her father was cruel and mean when he drank. And he drank a lot. We are assuming moonshine was the connection between the two men—but we don't know for sure. Under the circumstances, I think you should choose a different car. That one might stir up bad memories for Marika."

Joe thoughtfully replied, "I think you're right, Sir. This should be a happy time for Marika and her mom. I don't want to bring up any questions I can't answer —because I have a lot of those myself."

After looking at the other two cars, Joe chose a 1936 Ford Sedan. This should be comfortable, he thought.

The sheriff said, "Okay, Joe. If you will follow me to the courthouse, I have some paperwork we have to take care of. We want to make sure you are properly insured for this vehicle. I'll see you back at the office."

He thanked the sheriff and took the keys. "I'll follow you."

Joe's mind was spinning with 'what ifs' as he drove to the courthouse. *What if Marika's own father was involved in her abduction? Didn't the deputy say the sheriff was suspicious of the situation from the start? Could he have traded Marika for moonshine? That's a horrible thought! I don't want to think that about her father-- but his car being found close to the still sure is troubling—and it shows a connection. That is where he came when he left Ohio—why? What if they have been in business together— bootlegging? Could he have just happened to be there as a customer at the time the whole thing blew up? Did they know each other in Gary? What if he were a customer, how many times had he visited the still to get moonshine while Marika was in the cage so close?* His thoughts were interrupted when he arrived at the courthouse.

As Joe followed the sheriff into the courthouse, he said, "I've got to thank you for all your help. She drives like a dream. I'm going to need information on where I'm headed. Mom says she ain't ever heared of the place where her Momma is. Do you have any maps? Let's get all this straightened out."

When all the papers were signed and Joe had mapped out the route to his destination in Ohio, the sheriff accompanied Joe to the parking lot.

"I appreciate all you have done for Marika" Joe said to the sheriff. "I sure am thankful for the loan of the car. I will do my best to bring it back in good shape."

"You saved me sending one of the deputies—and I can't spare any right now."

Joe started the car and with a wave of the hand was off to Mohegan to pickup his girl.

As Joe pulled his borrowed car into home, everyone seemed to be working. He walked around the house and marveled at the beauty of the gardens his mother had created—there were flowering bushes and plants everywhere. He sat down on the bench he and his brothers had made two years ago as a Mother's Day present for Aggie. *Sits alright, he thought.*

After a few minutes, he was aware of company. He turned and saw Marika approaching. He stood and invited her to join him. She sat down and said to him, "Talk, Joe?"

Before he could answer, she said, "Baby to Ronnie and Audrey Ball. Momma and Tata." Then making the motion of writing, she said, "Sign"

Joe didn't know how to respond to this news. It was obvious she had wanted him to know and she wanted to be the one to tell him.

He turned to face her and held her shoulders so she had to look him in the eye. He asked, "Marika happy?"

With tears streaming down her face, she shook her head in response. He put his arm around her and drew her close to him. She laid her head on his shoulder and sobbed.

After a few moments, Marika stood up and said, "Okay, Joe. Marika cry no more." Then pointing to him, she said, "You, tell Aggie and John. Okay?"

When they walked around the house and Marika saw the strange car, she looked at him with a question in her eyes.

Joe said simply, "Ohio?" She leaped into his arms but before he could fully embrace her, she was running to check out the car. *I guess you could say that she is excited. I hope this trip is a happy time for her. She deserves it, he thought.*

After the Wertz family had eaten supper that evening, just before the men hurried off to work, Joe said, "Marika wanted me to tell you she made a decision about the baby. She signed papers so that Ronnie and Audrey Ball can adopt Zoe as their daughter. She told me herself so I got the bare essentials of the situation."

Aggie said, "Doc took her to the attorney. I'll ask him for the details. He told me he was willing to help her whatever she decided. He just wanted to make sure it was her decision."

Then Joe said, "I guess y'all have seen the car sittin' out there. I borrowed it from the county to take Marika over to Ohio. I plan to leave as soon as she is ready. I think the sooner she can take care of these things, the sooner she can get back to normal in her life." *I wonder what normal is for her.*

As he prepared to leave, John said, "That's good, son, she needs to put the trouble behind her. We can all deal better with trouble when it's behind us."

"Now, that there was downright wise, I reckon" said Aggie to her husband as she kissed him before he walked out the door.

The Everlasting Arms

CHAPTER NINE

Reunion

It was late in the day when Joe drove into the small town of Sarahsville, Ohio. He stopped to fill up the gas tank at the Sinclair filling station in the village. He asked the young man who pumped the gas if he knew where the Hicks Dairy was located.

"Sure thing, sir" he said. "You must be new around these parts. I noticed the West Virginia plates on the car. Well sir, what you do to get over to Hicks place is go east on this road until you come to the second 4-way stop. You're gonna want to turn north there and just drive till you see it on the left. You can't miss it.".

Joe smiled and said, "I appreciate the information. I reckon I'm facing east since the sun is behind me and north would be left. You've gotta understand on mountain roads you can go all four directions in a few miles. We jest say over yonder or up that holler."

He continued "These straight roads and intersections are a pleasure for the driver." *Then he thought, but your arms don't get much exercise. A driver could get bored and nod off. But on the other hand, you have a chance to look at the countryside.*

He leaned in the car and asked Marika,"hungry?

She replied, "Momma cook for us."

Joe followed the directions he had received at the filling station. The rolling hills of eastern Ohio were in full early summer array. The hay fields were lush and looked like velvet in the late afternoon sun. Most of the corn was about ankle-high. *Beautiful, he thought. Mom would be in awe of this farmland. Mom has a little patch of ground. There are farms here as far as you can see in every direction.*

After driving for about 15 minutes, he spied a large black and white sign 'HICKS DAIRY' on the left side of the road. The property was surrounded by white board fencing along the road. As he pulled through the open gate, he was impressed with how neat and clean everything looked. There didn't seem to be one blade of grass out of place. *Quite different from the coalfields he thought.* Marika was excited as she pointed to the cows coming in from the fields.

"Gettin' close to milkin' time, I reckon", Joe said.

"Oh, look, Joe. Sign black and white. Cows black and white. Funny."

"Flowers! Beautiful!" Marika exclaimed. "Aggie been here?" she said with a giggle.

Joe smiled and said, "Uh-huh." Seeing her so excited made him happy.

From the entrance gate, one could see a series of buildings in the distance on the right. They were obviously barns for milking. There were grain bins and several tanks attached to the barns. These buildings were clearly meant for employees only since there was another gate that blocked entrance to that section of the farm.

All the buildings were painted white with black trim. *I guess they have a black and white thing going here—even the cows got involved.* Against the crisp green of the farmland and the surrounding countryside, Joe thought it made a beautiful picture, indeed. *Lovely, he thought. It's a far cry from McDowell County.*

Near the entrance gate on the opposite side of the drive from the residence was a building marked OFFICE. Joe stopped the car in the parking area just a few feet from the door. As he got out of the car, a man came out of the door, followed closely by a woman. Paul and Holly Hicks greeted Joe as if he were a long-lost relative and pulled Marika from the car to greet her, too.

Holly said to Joe and Marika, "Please don't be disappointed when you see your Momma. She has had a terrible time since she lost you. She is very thin and has been in kind of depression since they came here. Your father left—I don't know exactly why. He said she blamed him for your disappearance. She doesn't know where he went. Since she speaks so little English, she hasn't made friends here. I think your coming is just what the doctor ordered. I hope seeing you will cause her to perk up."

Then Holly continued, "we have 10 cottages on the farm for employees to live in. To get to them, you follow this road to the left and they are about ½ mile beyond that cornfield" she said as she pointed to the south.

"There are only 5 of the cottages occupied at this time. Since they have so much to catch up on, we thought Marika and Susanna would be comfortable staying together in the cottage the family occupies now. The cottage next door will be a good place for you, Joe. Jakub and Anatol will bunk with you. I hope that is okay."

Joe said "that sounds perfect to me. I don't need much. I'm used to roughin' it. I want to get to know Marika's brothers, too."

"Okay, then off you go" said Paul Hicks. "It's the fifth cottage on the right."

Joe's heart beat faster as he rounded the bend and saw the two rows of small white cottages, with black trim of course. When he stopped in front of the fifth one on the right, he looked at Marika. She looked like he felt. She looked at him and said, "Joe, pray."

Joe took her hand and began to pray, "Lord, You know this has been a long journey for Marika to come to this place this day. I pray You would give her courage to face this situation. I pray for a spirit of forgiveness and compassion would guide both Marika and her mother. Let love rule and all be forgiven and forgotten. I love her, Lord and my heart's desire is she make peace with her past so she can look to the future. Amen."

Marika looked at Joe and said, "You love me, Joe?"

Joe smiled and said "Oh, yeah. I've been meaning to tell you."

Marika threw her head back and laughed. As she hopped out of the car and bounded up to the door of the cottage, *she thought, Joe, you finally figured it out.*

When the door opened, Marika was in the arms of her Momma. A little boy about 4 years old came up and hugged her around the legs. "Marika?" he asked. Then he said, "my sister."

Joe stood and watched the reunion with pleasure. They lapsed into Polish in the blink of an eye and he was lost to the secrets they shared in those first few moments together. Her mother was holding Marika and crying and the little boy was jumping up and down. Joe wondered where the older brother was. He assumed he was working.

After the first welcome, Marika turned toward Joe and motioned for him to join them. He felt like a fifth wheel but he joined the happy group and closed the door behind him. Marika said to her mother, "This is Joseph—my Joe—he loves me." Then she said in Polish, "he don't know it yet but he is going to marry me someday." They both laughed.

Joe said, "Come on, Marika, no secrets." She winked at him.

Joe looked around the cottage. It was very nice for a worker's cottage. There was a small kitchen and living room with a sofa and chair and a bunkbed in the corner. There was just enough room for a table between the kitchen and the living room. In the back there was a bedroom and a bathroom with a flush toilet and bathtub. *Wow, thought Joe, this is nice. A little small but I sure like the flush toilet and bathtub.*

Jakub came in shortly after they arrived. Marika hugged him then held him back at arms length and said in English, "Little brother not little. He's a man." He laughed and said in English, "I could say the same for my sister. You've grown up, too."

Susanna said, "my children learn the English. I happy."

Marika was right, her Momma had cooked a big Polish supper for them. When they sat down to eat the meal. Marika said, "Joe, you pray?"

They all bowed their heads. This was something Marika had never experienced until she went to live with the Wertz family. Now, she wanted prayer at meals—it was right to be thankful.

Joe prayed, "Dear Lord, Today we have so much to be thankful for. We are thankful for Marika being able to see her family again. We thank You for allowing us to be here and for safe traveling to this place. We thank you for protecting Marika and bringing her back to her family. We are so blessed. Thank you for providing this home and work for Susanna, Jakub and Anatol. We pray for Joseph, wherever he is. Thank you for this wonderful meal set before us and give us pleasure in enjoying it together. Amen.

He prays like his daddy, Marika thought. I love that.

After the meal was finished, Jakub said to Joe, "Let me show you around the place."

As they prepared to leave, Jakub said to Anatol, "Hey Nat, you want to go with us. We're going to ride in Joe's car."

Anatol came running to join the big boys. Joe said, "Thanks, Jakub, this will give the ladies a chance to talk privately. Marika has so much to share with her mother. She has been on a long, painful journey but she's in a good place now. I'll tell you later what I know. I don't know everything but I know enough to tell you that your sister is a fighter— she's tough and she's got a stubborn streak that kept her going when a lot of people would have given up and died."

Jakub was telling Joe where to make turns as they made their way around the farm. "This over here is where they make cottage cheese. Hicks Dairy has their own label on cottage cheese, sour cream and buttermilk. They also market the standard homogenized milk products with the Hicks label. We just service the area from Akron south to Gallipolis and west over to Chilicothe. That's about as far as we can go without big refrigerated rigs. They are so expensive and this is a small operation. But the working conditions are good and the Hicks are good people to work for. They figured out a way for me to work and go to school. I go to high school for 4 hours a day and work 6 hours. After I do my homework at night—that's my life. I don't know how my Tata found this place but it has been good for us. I never figured out why he left. And we don't know where he went."

Joe said,"I might be able to help you on that, he said. I don't know where he is but I know where his car is. It's in the police impoundment in Welch West Virginia. I know the sheriff had it hauled away from the site of a moonshine still that blew up. There was one man killed in the explosion. They found his truck and your father's car but they only found one body. They think your father was there when the thing blew up but they never found any remains so they reckoned he was still alive. Thing is nobody has reported seeing him around McDowell County. The sheriff don't know what happened to him. If you need a car for the family, you might be able to get his car to use. I saw it. It's still in good shape."

Jakub said, "It don't surprise me none about him being at a moonshine still. Tata liked his likker and he was mean when he got drunk. Mystery—I mean about the car. I'll talk to Momma and see if she wants the car. Sometimes I think a car would be nice. I know how to drive. I drive all the farm vehicles but I'm too young to get a permit. And Momma don't drive a car. Do you think Marika would like to have it? Would we want a car that belonged to him? I think it would be hard for Momma to have that car around. Better since he left. Momma is happy Marika found."

Then he continued, "Mrs. Hicks is real nice. She takes Momma to the grocery store in town. When she bakes bread, she always bakes an extra loaf for us. The same with cakes and pies. Our place is small but all in all, I like it a lot better than Gary—at least what I remember of it. The main thing I remember is when Marika disappeared. Momma and Tata fought over that all the time. He said Marika run off with somebody. Momma said Marika would never run off. I knew she would never run off because she wanted to protect Momma. We was afraid Tata was goin' kill her—he got so mad. After Marika was gone, he would say mean things just to hurt Momma. He would say 'yeah, she done run off with Angelo.' Momma would scream and say she never run off with nobody. Somebody come and took her while she was sleepin'. Do you know who Angelo was?"

Joe was surprised to hear Angelo's name come up in conversation. He wanted to be careful how he answered Jakub. "I have heard of Angelo Purilli. He was the man who got blown up in the moonshine still explosion. Your Tata must have known him if his car was at the scene. How do you reckon he knew him? Is that where he got his moonshine? Was he just a customer or was he more? I know that Angelo lived in a tumble down log cabin not too far from the still. I wonder if your father ever went to the cabin. What did you hear?"

Jakub responded, "That's the only time I remember hearing about Angelo. Since his car was there, Tata did know where Angelo lived. If he thought Angelo had Marika, why didn't he go get her? Did my Tata know where she was all the time? Why wouldn't he go get her?"

"This is something I have wondered about myself, Jakub. I will let Marika tell you about what happened. I've just tried to answer your questions."

Jakub said, "Well, tell me how you know her. It looks like she is fond of you. What's your connection in all this?"

"I've got to hand it to you, Jakub. You don't beat around the bush. That's the way a man handles things. He just comes right out and asks. I like that about you. I've got two versions of the story—the long one and the short one. Which one you want?"

Jakub grinned and said, "I'll take the short one for now."

Joe said, "Okay, Jakub, just the facts. When Marika escaped from the cabin where she was held, she found her way to our house. She slept in the hay loft in our barn for a couple of months before we discovered she was there. It was during the winter and my mother saw her by our well. She left food for her and some warm clothes but they still didn't know she was sleeping in our hay loft. Anyway, my brother, Daniel, brought her into the house and my mother gave her a bath and clean clothes. She took her to the doctor. Marika has been at our house ever since. I've been working with CCC so I was gone when all this was happening. When I came home, Marika just seemed to trust me. She took me to the cabin where she came from—I was the first person she showed. Since she didn't talk English, we had a hard time communicating with her at first. It's a lot better now that she knows some English. That's the short version of the story."

When the fellows left, Marika and her mom busied themselves

cleaning up after supper. The kitchen was just big enough for the two of them. Marika said, "Momma, I like this place. It's just what you need. And the Hicks are real nice people."

Her mother said, "Yes, they are very nice. But I am not going to spend our time talking about the Hicks. I want to know about you. What happened at Gary when you disappeared?"

Marika responded, "You mean you want to know what happened to me?"

"Yes, of course I want to know. I go to bed and get up and you were gone. Where did you go?"

"Well Momma, I did not go anywhere on my own or by myself. I was sleeping in the bedroom with Jakub. I woke up when somebody clamped a hand over my mouth. I tried to bite the hand but I couldn't. I tried to scream but I couldn't . He carried me out of the house like I was a sack of flour. He threw me into his truck and took off. He drove real fast. When I screamed, he stuck a nasty tasting rag in my mouth. I was so scared I just rolled up in a ball and cried. I cried for you or Tata to come find me. When I looked at him, I noticed the size of his hands—they were huge. I was so scared and so cold. Momma, so cold." She began to weep in remembering the ordeal.

"He drove for a while, we went through Welch I think. When he stopped, he pulled me out of the truck and took me into a dirty cabin in the woods. This is the worst part, Momma, he put me in a cage. It was a metal cage that was too skinny to lie down. I could stand up or squat but I couldn't stretch my legs out to sit. He locked me in a cage like an animal. He let me out when he wanted me to do something for him. And then he put me back in the cage. Every time he left, I was put in the cage. Sometimes he would be gone for a couple of days. If I heard a noise outside, I would scream and yell as loud as I could. But nobody ever came to let me out."

When she got to this part, she put her face in her hands. It was as if she wanted to block out the memory forever. She continued to speak, "one day, I thought I heard Tata's voice outside. At first, I thought I was imagining things. The voice was talking about moonshine. The more it spoke, the more convinced I was that it was my Tata. I began to scream, 'Tata, it's Marika! Tata, it's Marika!'. I kept shouting it till I couldn't yell anymore. I could hear two voices talking and laughing outside the cabin so I know they could hear me. Why didn't he come? Why didn't he come?" That day I realized that my Tata did not love me. In fact, I think he hated me. If he cared at all, he would have come. I wish I knew for sure if it was my Tata that I heard. But then I think, any person would try to find who was screaming. My Tata is not a good person. Wouldn't you try to find out who was screaming so desperately? But my mind was so confused at the time, I could have dreamed it or imagined it. I'm not sure it was real."

When Marika finished she looked at her mother who was clutching her arms around her body. She was trembling and moaning. Marika reached for her mother and said, "Momma, I don't want you to be sad. I want us to be happy now that we're together again." Susanna looked at her daughter with a look that can only be described as desperation. "Who was it? Do you know who took you?"

Marika said, "It was a monster named Angelo Purilli."

Her mother fainted onto the couch.

Marika was trying to rouse her mother when the boys came back. "Does she do this very often, Jakub?" she shouted.

"No, never" was his response.

"Do you think we should take her to the hospital? Or to see a doctor?" Joe asked. "I wish Doc Bondy was here. He would know what to do."

While they were deciding what to do, Susanna came to. "I'm so desperately sorry. I cannot express how sorry I am. I thought it might have been Angelo—he was always so brutish. But Yosef said no it wasn't Angelo. You had run away. Why did I believe him? I knew I sinned before God—that's one reason why I kept going to confession every week. I didn't think God would forgive me. I want God to forgive me. And Marika can you ever forgive me?"

Marika sat beside her mother on the couch and held her. She said, "John taught me a Bible verse: It's Ephesians 4:32: Be ye kind one to another, tenderhearted, forgiving one another even as God, for Christ's sake hath forgiven you."

"Who is John?"

Marika spoke up, "He's Joe's father and he is a man of God. He teaches us the Bible. When we talk about our sins, he says all of our sins are forgiven when we trust in Christ. When we believe in Jesus Christ as Savior, all our sins are forgiven. He didn't just forgive the little sins, but the big sins, too. How many is all?" she asked, looking toward Susanna.

Susanna said, "I guess all means everyone of them. You mean if I believe Jesus died on the cross and rose again. If I trust that he did it for me, all my sins are forgiven?"

Marika asked, "Why do you need to go to confession? All your sins are already forgiven."

Susanna looked puzzled, "If I don't need to make confession, what do I have to do?"

"Oh, Momma, you have to believe—have faith in what Jesus did when He died on the cross and rose from the dead. What else do you have to do?"

Marika paused and then smiled and said, "Nothing in English. Za nic in Polish."

Joe caught on to what they were saying and said, "Whatever language you say it in, Jesus did it all. Everything that was necessary to take our sin, He did it."

Then Joe said, "Susanna, can you accept the fact that Marika forgives you and that Jesus forgives you too?"

Looking at Marika, who repeated Joe's question, she said, "Oh my darling daughter, I am so relieved. I looked forward to this moment and I dreaded it at the same time. I thank God you have come back to us."

Marika looked at her mother and in a very serious tone of voice, said, "Momma, I've come back—that is true. But I'm not the same Marika who was stolen from her bed in Gary West Virginia. I have been through a horrible time that is almost too terrible to talk about. Joe knows some of it but not even he knows it all. I have been to the edge of hell and back again. I have come near death but God brought me through. Even through all the torture and pain, I have known I was being held by the Everlasting Arms. Somehow, I knew God would bring me through—that He would keep me alive for His glory. Therefore, as tough as it got, I never gave up hope and never quit trying to get out of the cage. And that's enough for tonight. I think we should save some of this for tomorrow, don't you?"

Then she said, "Hey Joe, let's go walk."

"Sounds like a good idea." He said as he reached for her hand.

When they got outside, Joe said, "have I told you how very proud I am of you." She said, "yes, but say it again."

The next morning, while Susanna and Jakub went to work, Joe and Marika took Anatol, who was a very mature almost five year old into the town for breakfast. They found a little café whose sign caught their attention. DINGLE'S DINER HOMECOOKING

As they ate their bacon and eggs, Anatol informed them he would be going to English school in September when summer was over. He was excited to begin to learn to read in English. This was an advantage his sister and brother had never had. Marika smiled, he was so cute when he talked about his plans.

She thought, I hope your plans are never interrupted by evil, my little brother. I, too, wanted to learn English but Tata said, "Polish good for you. You not forget homeland." How could I forget something I never knew? I don't remember Poland. If I had grandparents, I didn't know them. I was only 1 year old when they came to America. If I ever had any pleasant childhood memories, they have been wiped away by the horrors of the recent years. If I am going to be whole and happy again, I must create some wonderful, happy memories. Is that what the Wertz family is trying to help me do? Are all the future happy memories that will sustain me to be made with Joe? I have many questions to answer. I have much to forget. I must make a life for myself that is not continually haunted by Angelo and Tata before I can begin to move forward.

She shook her head as if to shake her thoughts away and return to the moment. As they left the diner, Marika asked Anatol, "Anatol, what do you do everyday while Momma is at work?"

He replied, "Aw, Sis, call me Nat. Anatol seems too grown up a name for a boy who is five years old."

Marika smiled, *he's a lot older than five in his mind and experience*, she thought.

He continued, "I go to the nursery where the kids of the workers stay. But, don't you think I'm too old for a nursery? I'll be glad when school starts so I can get out of the nursery. The good part is there are two other boys my age. They don't like the nursery either. We play together so it's not too bad."

Marika responded, "Nat—you know that name suits you. I like it. AND you don't have to go to the nursery today. Joe and I are going to be here. So what would you like to do today?"

When Susanna arrived home from work, she discovered Joe and Marika had prepared supper for the family. "I could get used to this, dear hearts" she exclaimed. "What's for supper?"

Joe replied, "We fixed the Aggie Wertz special fried chicken, mashed potatoes with gravy. Marika made a custard pie."

Susanna said, "Wow, that sounds great."

After they had finished supper, the boys decided to go next door and play some games. Nat wanted to teach them a card game he learned from his friend, Nolan. Joe winked at Marika as they went out the door.

Marika knew she had to tell her Momma about Zoe. This was going to be hard to do but it had to be done.

She began, "Momma, there is something very important that I must tell you. It's part of the reason I came to Ohio right now."

"What's that, dear?" her mother asked.

"I really don't know where to start. I told you about the cabin and the cage. Well, when Angelo took me out of the cage, he would put me on the bed and hurt me. He really hurt me. Many times—almost every day."

From Susanna's expression Marika knew her mother understood. Susanna stood and began to pace the floor as Marika talked.

"I began to get fat. I didn't know what was happening to me, at first. Then one day, I felt something move inside me and I knew. I had a baby inside me. You told me about how babies are born so I knew what to expect."

"Where is the baby?" she asked.

"I'm getting to that part" Marika said. She continued, "You told me how babies were born but you didn't tell me it hurt so bad. I begged him to take me out of the cage so I could get the baby out. He put me on the bed. When I pushed and pushed, I finally saw a little dark head between my legs. I fell back against the bed and he grabbed the baby. He took out his knife and I thought he was going to kill the baby right then. But instead, he pulled up the blanket that was on the bed and cut out a big piece of it. He wrapped the baby in that piece of blanket and took it out of the cabin. When he came back in, he didn't have the baby. I tried to get up to go find the baby but he pushed me back down. I must have passed out for a minute or two. When I woke up, I could hear the baby crying. It cried and cried and then it didn't cry anymore. I didn't know what he did with the baby –I mean, I didn't know where he put it. I didn't even get a chance to look at it. I didn't know if it was a boy or a girl. When I couldn't hear it crying anymore, I thought it had died or some wild animal had got it. I passed out and when I woke up, I was back in the cage."

All the while Marika was talking, Susanna had paced and moaned. But Marika kept talking—she had to get it out. Her Momma needed to know about Zoe.

Marika said, "That's not all."

Her mother said, "Go ahead, get it all out. I need to know."

Marika described in detail how she was rescued from the cage and ran away from the cabin. She told about the explosion and hiding in a cave overnight.

She stopped talking and looked at her mother. She was still pacing and was ashen. Marika thought she was going to pass out again, so she stopped talking.

"Are you alright, Momma?"

Her mother replied, "Of course, I'm not alright. How can I listen to this and be alright? There must have been some way we could have found you. If you thought you heard your Tata's voice, you probably did. He bought moonshine from Angelo. For a while before we left Gary, he and Angelo sold moonshine out of our house while we were at church on Sunday. I didn't like it but we needed the money."

After she paused for a moment, she said, "I don't know why he didn't come to check when he heard you scream.Wouldn't you go to see where screams were coming from? If you could hear voices outside, you know they could hear you screaming. If I had known, I would have found a way to get to you. How could Yosef have heard you scream and then buy his moonshine like nothing was wrong? Was he as much of a monster as Angelo? What kind of man is so hard-hearted?"

Marika said, "Can you listen to more? It gets better, I promise."

Susanna said, "Okay, I would like to hear something good."

Marika continued by describing her walk along the railroad tracks and hiding in the hay loft of a barn. She said, "When I climbed the ladder to the hay loft, I was ready to collapse. It was cold—winter time. I found some horse blankets. So I made me a bed between the hay bales and stretched out and slept most of the day. It was so good to stretch out my legs after being in that cage so long."

After looking at her mother to see if she was okay. Marika continued, making it as upbeat and positive as possible. She didn't think her Momma could take much more.

"When it started to get dark, I went down from the loft and found a well. I needed a drink. I couldn't remember the last time I had a drink or eaten anything. There was a house close to the well. I found a bucket with a dipper and got a good drink of water. That water tasted so good but not as good as the taste of freedom I felt at that moment. I was free from Angelo. Somehow, I knew if I stayed close to this family I would be alright. I was so dirty, I just covered up with the black clothes Angelo had in the cabin so no one would see how dirty I was. When it got warm enough, I planned to wash myself in the river. Well, when I was going back to the barn—it was after dark-- as I walked back by the house, I smelled food. I looked and found a box of food on the porch of the house. I didn't know who it was meant for but at that moment it was mine. I took it and ran to the barn. I was famished. I ate every bite in that box. It was the best thing I ever tasted. When I came in with the food, I gained some friends. There were 5 or 6 barn cats that joined me in the loft that night and every night I spent there. God knew I needed some heaters to keep warm so He sent me some cats. They were a blessing and entertainment."

When Marika looked at her mother, she said, "Momma, I think this is enough for tonight. We have four more days to talk about all this. I just want you to know I have been through some awful stuff but God was with me and I'm doin' good now. I am happy and I am looking to where God will lead me in the future. I want you to be happy for me."

Mother and daughter tearfully embraced. The moment was shattered when the door flew open and Nat ran in. "I beat 'em! I beat the big boys in a kid's game."

Joe looked at Marika and said, "Who wants to go for a drive to the ice cream shop?"

As they all piled in the car, Marika caught Joe's eye, she mouthed the words, "I love you, Joe." Joe looked like he had won the jackpot.

The next day, Paul Hicks took Marika and Joe on a tour of the farm. Joe was impressed with the milking machines and the chillers that kept the milk cold. It was a highly technical operation. Just as soon as the morning milking was finished, Jakub cleaned the milking barn. First with a small inloader and then he washed down the barn with disinfectant. By the time he was finished, it was as clean as any home kitchen. Then he set up for the next milking by cleaning and sanitizing all the milking machines. Mr. Hicks was very pleased with Jakub's work. "When that boy is finished with high school, I would like to send him to agricultural college. We need somebody who is so diligent to take over this farm some day. I really like his work ethic. He is bright and he likes to work—that's a rare combination. He has a sense of responsibility that is unusual in one so young."

When the tour was over, Joe thanked Mr. Hicks. "I am really

impressed by your operation, Sir. I don't know how Joseph Stanislas found you out here in this little town, but I'm glad he did. This is an ideal situation for them. I appreciate your interest in young Jakub, too. I couldn't imagine a better place for them. Thank you so much. You and your wife have been so kind to them."

Then he asked Joe, "Has anybody heard from Joseph? He left so suddenly. He was an anguished man—you know, like there was something eating him up on the inside. He seemed angry all the time but the anger really came out when he started drinking. I would never tell his daughter this but there were several times we came very close to calling the police. He really got violent when he was drunk. Honestly, I think this family is better without him."

Joe replied, "I haven't heard a word about him. Neither has Susanna or Marika. So we don't know where he went either."

Marika said, "Thanks for the tour, Mr. Hicks. Thanks for all you are doing for my family—appreciate it.

Since Nat wanted to go to the nursery today to see his friend Nolan, Joe and Marika had some time to do some sightseeing around the area. "This is pretty country." Joe observed. Marika agreed but she seemed deep in thought.

"What's goin' on in that pretty head?" he asked.

"Well, Joe, I've been thinkin' maybe I ought to stay here in Ohio with Momma. I could see if Mr. Hicks needs somebody else to work here. If he could give me a job, I could save some money and pay your family back. Your family wouldn't have to take care of me anymore. What do you think?"

"I think that idea stinks. I can't leave you here. My Mom would disown me if I came back without you. What would we do without you?"

"I know, Joe, this is hard for me, too. I have such mixed emotions-- I love your family and they seem more like my family than my family. That sounded silly didn't it? I would miss you all so much—specially you and Aggie—and John—and Daniel. Oh Shucks, I'd miss you all. And Louanna is goin' have her baby anyday now. I hope she waits til we get back. I can't wait to get back to see everybody. But then I think it might be good for the Ball family if they didn't see me at church every week. I wouldn't blame them for wanting to separate Zoe from me. The temptation for me to watch her too close would be so strong. It's easier if I don't see her. I want to hold her and love her. Do you understand, Joe?"

Joe pulled over and stopped the car, "Sure, I can understand how you feel. I honestly can. And I think you make a lot of sense. I think your Momma needs you—but we need you, too. We're connected to each other—I'm not sure exactly how that happened so fast but you are a part of us. But at the same time you are a part of this family, too. I can see why you're torn between the two."

After a few moments, Joe said, "Okay, how does this sound? We go talk to Mr. Hicks and see if he has a job for you. Another thought is you need to get your high school diploma. Do you have any interest in going to school? You could go to school with Jakub in the fall when school starts. The language might be a problem—I don't know. What do you think?"

Marika sat quietly for a few minutes and then said, "I'd like to talk to Mr. Hicks about a job. About school, I don't really want to go to regular school. The thing I need is to learn to read English and write English. I'm gettin' so I can talk English pretty good, but it looks so funny when I see it in writing. It really is different from Polish. I need to go to school with Nat—now wouldn't that be funny?" She laughed, "I'd have a hard time fittin' in the 1st grade chairs." They both laughed.

Joe said, "Why don't we talk to Mr. and Mrs. Hicks about that. They may have some ideas."

As they drove toward the next town, Joe thought, *I am enabling her to live apart from me. I don't want us to go separate ways. I want her with me. Mom has grown so attached to her—she considers her a daughter. Marika is making perfect sense about a job. She sees a chance to be independent and at the same time help her mother. I admire that in her—she needs to spread her wings and develop her talents and see who she really is. She is strong but she understands her own vulnerability where Zoe is concerned. She wants what is best for that little girl. I have to remember so much development of becoming who you are happens between 12 and 15 years of age. That was the time Marika spent locked up in a cage as slave to a cruel master. She has that horror to put behind her and make up for those lost years. Boy, I didn't expect this. Okay Joe, man up. You may have to let her go so she can find her way. I'll just pray she finds her way back to me.*

Within about a half hour drive, they came into a picturesque little town. Marika oohed and aahed at the attractive shops which lined the streets. They found a quaint little inn at the edge of town and stopped there for lunch. *Joe thought, this may be the nearest thing to a real date I will ever have with my favorite girl. I want us to enjoy this day together.*

Ronnie Ball walked over to the main building at Mohegan Coal Company to see if anything was posted on the company bulletin board. He, of course, was curious about any news of the mine reopening. While he was there, he picked up the mail. Among the letters was an official looking letter from Benjamin Sizemore, Attorney at Law.

What in the world is this, he thought? I'll wait till I get home to open it. I want Audrey to see it.

When he got home, Audrey was bathing the children. When she finished, she put David down and he took a few tottering steps toward his father. "Look, Audrey, he's starting to walk."

Audrey said, "Zoe won't be far behind. It will be fun when they're both underfoot. I can't wait."

Ronnie opened the letter he just received. He read it aloud.

Dear Mr. and Mrs. Ball,

This letter is to inform you Marika Stanislas has relinquished all claims to parental rights and privileges concerning the minor child herein identified as Zoe Grace Ball. Miss Stanislas understands with this declaration she gives up the right of being named as parent on a birth certificate or any other legal documents pertaining to said minor child. Miss Stanislas' name will not be attached in any way to the record of the birth of said minor child. She believes God has placed this child in the Ball family and she does not wish to undertake a challenge of that designation at this time or any time in the future.

She wants it understood she has made this decision of her own free will without coercion from any outside source. She takes full responsibility for said decision.

Miss Stanislas extends her deeply felt appreciation to you and for you. She wishes you the very best in the future as you raise said minor child with your other child(ren). She assures you of continuing prayers and kindest regards.

Enclosed with this letter is the signed and witnessed document that sets forth the conditions described in paragraph one of this letter.

This declaration has been made with the understanding Ronnie and Audrey Ball wish to retain custody of said minor child and proceed toward legal adoption. If you wish to challenge the provisions of the attached documents, please advise this office as soon as possible.

If you should have any questions concerning this transaction, please contact me at my office in Welch.

Sincerely,

Benjamin Sizemore, Attorney at Law.

Exclosures: Signed and dated Documents of relinquishment of parental rights.

Stunned, Ronnie and Audrey just sat and looked at each other. "Is it as simple as that?" he said.

Audrey said, "I told you God would work it out. She saw that when she couldn't get to the baby, God put the baby where He wanted it. Then He caused her to see that. She is an amazing young lady. And I might say she is unselfish—I am not sure that I could do that—I mean be so selfless. Doc Bondy must have helped her get the attorney and all, don't you think?"

"I will talk to Doc Bondy to help us do what we need to do to finalize everything. We do need a birth certificate for her."

As they watched the children playing together on the floor, Audrey said, "Ain't God good!"

When Joe and Marika met with Mr. and Mrs. Hicks, they were both offered employment at Hicks Dairy. Marika would start in the cottage cheese plant with her mother. They wanted her to learn all the aspects of their business in the hopes she could help Mrs. Hicks in the office. Holly Hicks was excited about Marika learning the language and spoke about all the possibilities for her.

Marika's face told the story. She wanted to stay and work at the dairy. "I know it will be hard to leave Aggie and your family but I think this is a great opportunity for me to learn what I need to know. I've missed so much and I need to find out who I really am. I want to like myself again. And I need to reconnect with Momma and my brothers."

She looked at Joe and said, "You understand, don't you, Joe?"

He replied, "I understand completely."

Joe told Paul Hicks, "Mr. Hicks, I really appreciate the job offer. At this time, I have to go back to West Virginia. My brother has just started a new business and he is counting on me to help him. We are all pitching in—including my father. We're hoping Alvin's—that's my brother—business will grow so our Dad won't have to go back in the mines when they open again. Coal mining is a killer job."

"We are sure going to miss Marika. She is a hard worker and I know she will do a good job for you. She is very bright and exceptionally creative. She has been through an awful lot personally but she still maintains an upbeat look on life. I think she will add a lot to your company morale and productivity. As hard as it is for me to leave her here, I think it's probably the best thing for her right now."

When the day came for Joe to leave, Marika walked to the car with him. She looked like she was going to cry.

She said, "It's hard to say goodbye, Joe. I don't want you to go."

He said, "Marika, I think you know I love you. Every minute I am with you is every minute I want to be with you more. My heart tells me we belong together and I pray someday you will be my wife. For right now, I think you have made a wise choice. You need to work through a lot of things. You have demons from the past that must be done away with. This is something only you can do with God's help. Do you have a Polish Bible?"

Marika shook her head. "Then have Jakub read to you from the Bible. Mom learned the Bible by hearing it—you can, too. That is until you learn to read English—and I know you will. I have confidence in you."

Marika looked at him with tears running down her face. "I love you, Joe."

He took her in his arms and kissed her gently. She put her hand to her mouth and said, "My first kiss, Joe." She was smiling through her tears.

He pulled her close and said, "Well, let me give you the second one."

He got in the car quickly and drove away. That was the picture of his girl he wanted to remember—freshly kissed and smiling through her tears.

When Joe got home to Mohegan, he was missing Marika already. Aggie and John were excited because Louanna had her baby. It was a boy with curly blond hair. "Curliest hair I ever seen on a baby" Aggie said.

"What's his name?" Joe asked.

"They wanted to name him after the grandfathers but change the names a little bit. So they named him Johnson for your father John and Drew for Andrew, Reggie's father. So his name is Johnson Drew Lovins. Pretty dignified name, if I have to say so myself." She laughed.

John spoke up and said, "That's what they say. But I reckon they got the name off the baby powder can—you know, Johnson and Johnson Baby Powder."

Then, as if she had just noticed her absence, Maggie said, "Where's Marika?"

Joe replied, "She stayed in Ohio with her mother and brothers. She got a job at the dairy. They are some really nice folks. And Mom, they have these little white cottages—they have flush toilets and refrigerators. That's what we've got to get you—a refrigerator."

Aggie asked, "Is that the same thing as a Kelvinator? Louanna's in-laws just got one of them. She says it is wonderful for keeping milk fresh and vegetables and things. It has a little section at the top where you can make ice cubes. You wouldn't have to mess with big blocks of ice and drain the ice box. I reckon that would be nice."

Then Aggie laughed and said, "I reckon I'll put that on my wish list right after flush toilets."

Aggie poured a cup of tea and sat down at the table. "Do you want somethin' to eat, son? We got some ham left from supper."

Joe replied, "No, thanks Mom, I ain't hungry. I think I'll have a cup of tea and turn in. That's a long drive. You want a cup, Dad?"

As Joe shared with his parents the events of the past week in Ohio, they, too, agreed it was the best thing for Marika to stay in Ohio for now. Finally Joe said, "I know one thing, I want to marry her. I love her—she's in my heart. I think she feels the same way about me right now. I don't know if that will change—we will see. I know she needs time—she has demons she needs to get rid of. She can only do that with God's help. I miss her already. She brings joy to my heart. I want to see her face when I wake up in the morning and the last thing before I fall asleep at night. But I need to give her time to want that too. I pray God she will. That's all I'm gonna say about it."

"I guess I'll take my old bed back since she won't be needin' it." He picked up his suitcase and went to the bedroom.

When he lay down in the bed that night, he thought. *This bed smells good—smells like Marika.*

Louanna was enjoying being a mother. Reggie was off on another assignment so she was lonely. Taking care of Johnny helped her not to miss Reggie so much. Her in-laws were so proud of their first grandchild—they thought they had invented grand-parenthood.

When Pop Lovins went to the Post Office, he came home with a package for Louanna. "It's from Marika" she said. When she opened it she found a little boys outfit complete with stockings and cap. "Look," she said, "A cap just like Reggie wears. This is so sweet. I really wanted her to be here when the baby came. This gift shows that she wants to stay connected to the family."

Louanna thought, *I should dress him in it and take a picture. Mama Lovins has a camera. We could take several pictures. One for Marika, one for Mom and Daddy, one for Mama and Pop Lovins, one for me. That's what I'll do. We don't want to lose touch with her. I think Joe has his eye on her.*

When Joe got home the next day, he found a letter from Marika laying on the table. He decided to wait before he opened it.

While he was waiting for his father to come home, Joe said, "Dad should be home pretty soon. How much longer does he figure on the "outhouse project"? I don't like him working on two jobs."

Aggie said, "Me, either, it's too much on him."

Then Joe added, "I'm thinking about buying a car. I wanted to talk to Dad about it. I want to be able to go to Ohio to see Marika once in a while. He could use it, too. It would be like a family car. I'll talk to him on the way down to Twin Branch."

While he waited, he opened Marika's letter.

June 30, 1937

Dear Joe,

Holly is writing this for me so I can't say anything real personal. If I could write it myself, I could say anything I wanted to but that will have to wait until I see you. We are all okay. Momma is feeling better I think—at least she acts like it. Last night I told her all about Zoe and how Ronnie Ball found her in the woods and took her home. I told her I decided to leave Zoe with the Balls and let them raise her as their daughter. I told her I signed papers for them to adopt her, too. At first she thought you had talked me into it. But I told her it was my decision—nobody else could make it for me. She was sad about it and at first did not understand how I could do that. I told her that it was not about me and what I wanted but it was about what was best for the baby now and for her future. I know that Ronnie and Audrey are wonderful parents and they will love her as much as I could. They have a good marriage and a happy home for her to grow up in. I also told her I was totally at peace with the decision.

I wanted to explain to you why I didn't include you in the decision about Zoe. If I had asked you, I knew you would answer the way you thought I wanted you to answer. I had to do it on my own. I never wanted to look at someone else and say, "You made me do that. I didn't want to but you told me to." I never wanted it to be a wedge between us. I know in weak moments, it is easy to look for someone to blame for decisions. I may some day in some way regret the decision that I made concerning Zoe. But I can say in my heart without any regret today I did what was best for that little girl. That was my only motivation and desire. I hope you understand.

Nat talks about Joe all the time. You made an impression on him. He is real excited about going to school in the Fall. Holly found me a tutor for English. She don't know a lot of Polish, but she is helping me with English. One of these days—I hope it won't be long—I will write a letter to you all by myself. That's the main reason I want to learn English. I miss you Joe. The time we had together when you were here was so special. I hope you still feel the same way you did then.

Love,

Marika

September 2, 1937

Dear Marika,

We are all okay here. Louanna was thrilled with the things you sent for the baby. That was really nice of you. Don't spend all your money. Make sure you save some of it.

Alvin's business is growing. He bought a used truck so we can work on two different sites at one time. He plans to buy as many trucks as he can. When the mines open up, he plans to truck coal from the small independent mines to the rail siding. He's lining up contracts now. He is a really good business man. He has a lot of ideas about how to make money. Alvin's plan is somebody else doing all the hard work and he is the arranger and manager. Pretty smart, huh? We're hoping Daddy won't have to go back to the mines. He and Mom want to move out of Mohegan to Davy or Hemphill as soon as they can afford it.

Oh, Alvin bought Mom a Kelvinator. It's a refrigerator like you have in the cottage. She loves it. Now she's wantin' to get flush toilets. I guess she'll be wantin' a telephone before long. It would be nice to have a telephone so I could talk to you. I miss you like crazy.

It's late and I have a long day tomorrow. I wish I could kiss you goodnight. Could you use some of your money and get a picture taken of yourself and send it to me? I would love to look at your sweet face before I go to sleep and when I get up in the morning.

Love,

Joe

Dec 21, 1937

Dear Joe,

It's almost Christmas time. The village is decorated for Christmas. Everything is so festive. I wish I could be with you for Christmas. I am writing this letter myself. The English tutor told me I'm doing good. She says that I caught on to English real quick. I wanted to say things to you that I didn't want anybody else to know. There are special things you say to the one you love that are private—just between the two of you. I wanted to tell you I am thinking about marrying you—you may not be thinking of marrying me but I'm willing to wait till you do.

When I'm thinking of marriage, the thought of intimacy comes to my mind. You know my painful history, of course. You know what was forced upon me—and you realize I carried and delivered a baby. All of this was done in the most brutal and cruel way. There is not a part of what I experienced that does not create sheer terror in me when I am forced to remember it. This experience has colored my thinking about intimacy in marriage. I am asking God to deliver me from the dread and horror that I feel even at the thought of it. I want to think about intimacy in marriage as being sweet and tender like your kiss. I think, with God's help, I will get there. I think about your tenderness when you kissed me by the car. When I kissed you back, I wanted to go with you so I could experience that over and over again. I remember that kiss just before I close my eyes at night. You are my Joe. Please pray for me. The experience in the cabin has deeply scarred me—only God can heal those wounds.

Mama told me something tonight that shocked me. She told me Joseph Stanislas is not my father. When she was 18 she married Albin Szlatchte in Poland. He was 20 years old and a mathematician. He was going to be a professor at the University of Warsaw. When I was 6 months old, he was killed in a car accident outside Warsaw. My momma had me but did not have any means of support for us. She met Yosef Stanislas, who had immigration papers to come to the United States. He could bring a family with him. He asked Momma if she wanted to go with him and she did. That's how we got to the U. S. Yosef is not my real father. He and Momma were never married but they had Jakub and Anatol together. I couldn't believe it when I heard that my real father's name was Szlatchte. When I was confused and didn't know who I was, I remember sitting by the well—right there next to Aggie and John's house. I was trying to remember who I was. I could remember Marika but the rest wouldn't come to me. I would say to myself, Marika who? Then I remembered my

Momma told me that I had a noble name. Szlatchte means noble in Polish. So I said to myself, "I am Marika Szlatchte. That's my name." How could I have remembered the name of someone that I never remember meeting? God gave me a name to keep me going. He gave me the name of my father so that I would know I was somebody and I was loved. Ain't God good!

Oh, Joe, I miss you. I wish I could talk to you about all of this and not have to write it in a letter. Good night, Sweet Joe.

Love,

Marika

P. S. Did you get the picture? That's your Christmas Present.

January 1, 1938

Dear Marika,

It's a new year. It's a day when you are supposed to make resolutions or promises to yourself to do things or not do other things. I only have one resolution. I resolve to tell you that I love you every chance I get. I hope you feel the same. I love you.

When I left you in Ohio last summer, I wondered if you would meet someone else and forget about me. I don't have much to offer you. I am a laborer who works for his brother. Alvin pays me decent money but I will never be rich. When he gets a few more men to work for him, I plan to come and get you. I wonder what your plans are. Do you want to stay in Ohio? Do you want to live in West Virginia? Think about it. I hope to come and visit you this summer. We'll talk about it then. I love you. I don't know how much longer I can wait to see you. I think about you all the time. I love your quirky sense of humor and how you laugh and how you walk and how you wiggle your nose. Oh heck, I could spend all day thinking about all the ways I love you. I love you.

Here's a bit of news from Mohegan. Ronnie and Audrey Ball moved out of Mohegan. Ronnie said he couldn't make it any longer without work. They went to live with Audrey's parents over in Premier. That's a coal camp between Welch and Roderfield on U. S. 52. It's not too far away but it's far enough that you wouldn't be seeing them all the time. Just thought you'd want to know.

I wanted to tell you that we bought a car. It's not new. It belonged to Louanna's neighbor. He needed the money. It's a Ford coupe and it's in good shape. So I use the car, so does Alvin and of course my parents use the car, too. They took a trip to Tennessee to see my little sister. I bet you didn't know about her. Her name is Louise and she lives with our aunt and uncle in Bristol. She's probably close to Jakub's age. Oh, by the way, I love you.

Happy New Year. I resolve to make plans for us to be together always. I love you.

Just trying to keep my New Year's Resolution. Ha! I love you

In case I forgot to say it: I LOVE YOU!

Love

Joe

P. S. Love the picture! Love you more!

April 29, 1938

Dear Joe,

Today is my 17ᵗʰ birthday. My momma says I can get married when I'm 18. I'm no great mathematician but I think that is one year. Can you wait for me, Joe? If you can't, I'll understand. If you can't, I will probably never marry anybody. You are the only tender heart that could make me forget all the brutality and cruelty in my past. When I am with you I can forget all that hurt and pain. I can lose myself in your sweet tenderness and it's wonderful. I don't want to wait another year—it will be one really loooooooooooooong year. I wish today was our wedding day. I want to be with you. I never thought that I would be able to say that God has healed me mind, body and spirit. I am free to love you Joe. God has set me free from the past pain. I am liberated. This next year will be spent in drawing closer to God through the Word and preparing myself to be your wife. Please let me know if that's not your plan, too. That is except the wife part—prepare to be a husband—Marika's husband. You will need special grace from God to be Marika's husband—so pray hard, My Joe.

Holly just promoted me to the main office. She said that I'm a natural accountant—she says that I keep track of everything—like how much we got and how much it costs and things like that. I'm learning about all the accounts. The barn manager gives me production figures for all the animals and I keep track of that. Soon I'll be keeping all the books for Hicks Dairy. It pays a lot more than making cottage cheese. I'm saving money for us to buy a house when we get married. That's my wedding present to you. Did I tell you that I love you? I do—I do—that's what we'll be saying in about a year—I hope.

Happy Birthday to me!

Love

Marika

P. S. I found a Bible verse for us: Psalm 37:4-5: Delight thyself also in the Lord: and he shall give thee the desires of thine heart. Commit thy way unto the Lord; trust also in him; and he shall bring it to pass.

July 4, 1938

Dear Marika

I want to come to see you in August. Do you think that would be okay? I would probably stay about three or four days. Would you ask Holly if there is a cottage available? I want to spend as much time with you as possible. Do you think you could take at least one day off? I will try to come on the weekend so you would already have time off. Let me know when I can come—the dates. Alvin said anytime would be okay with him. I have the car to drive. I've got the car, I've got the girl and I just need the date.

Mom said to tell you hello. We had little Johnny's 1 year birthday party yesterday. He's sure a cute little guy. He's outgrown the outfit you sent but he loves the hat. He wears it all the time—like his Daddy. He looks more like the Lovins family with the curly hair—it's blond but he has brown eyes. All the Wertz's are blond with blue-gray eyes. Louanna loves being a mother and she is good at it. She wants to have another baby—I don't know what Reggie thinks.

Alvin's business is growing. There's a lot of buzz about the mines opening. He doesn't need me now. There are plenty of qualified truck drivers around McDowell County. The best part of all is that Alvin can give Dad a full time job. He won't have to go back to the mines. He and Mom are happy about that. They'll probably move out of Mohegan soon. So, that frees me up to live where we choose.

I can't wait to see you. Can I kiss you again? Surely after I drive so far just to see you, you will kiss me again. I know you said you were going to wait till we got married to kiss me again. Warning: I'm going to try real hard to change your mind. I love you!

Love

Joe

When Joe went to visit Marika in August, he carried with him an engagement ring he hoped to put on Marika's hand. He wanted to set a date for their wedding and make plans about where they would live. Joe was not opposed to living in Ohio. In fact, he found the idea of living in that beautiful area of Ohio quite appealing. He was going to leave it totally up to Marika. He had assurance of a job in either location. Mr. Hicks could use his experience with machinery and construction in a lot of ways around the Dairy. But if Marika wanted to live in West Virginia, he always had a driving job with Alvin.

Joe had learned during the past two years that his place was with Marika. He felt pretty sure that she saw things the same way. The purpose of this trip was to find out and chart a course for the future.

The Everlasting Arms

CHAPTER TEN

At the Altar

April 29, 1939 was a day Marika had long dreamed of. When she was a little girl, she dreamed of being married on a beautiful spring day. She dreamed of a handsome though faceless groom who would be waiting for her at the altar. But the reality of this day was far from the dream. She would be walking down the aisle on the arm of John Wertz not her Tata. Her sweet Mama was there to see her dressed in her own lacy white gown and veil she had carried with her from Poland. Lilacs picked from the garden, not roses, filled vases all around the small church and scented the air with fragrance. The grand reception at the stately church hall was replaced by cake and fruit punch in the Wertz' dining room. Nothing was as she dreamed but everything was perfect because she was marrying Joseph Wertz—her Joe.

The little church was filled with friends and family. Aggie sat with her mother, Susanna, on the front row. Her brothers served as ushers. Doctor Bondy sat with Jim and Daniel near her mother. Uncle Jessie and Aunt Hattie sat behind the mothers. The Ball family was there with the twins, Zoe and David. The whole Mc Grady family sat on the bride's side of the church. Paul and Holly Hicks had made the trip from Ohio. Sheriff Chatham and Deputy Weaver were there along with Lena and Rudy Babinski. The whole Lovins family was there with Louanna's friend

Lucy, who had given Marika clothing. Other friends came to celebrate with the Wertz family. All in all, it was a festive day in Mohegan.

As she stood in the back of the church waiting for the music to begin, *her thoughts took her to places she did not want to go today. That is all behind me, she thought. I haven't thought of that horror for months. Oh, Lord, fill my soul with thoughts of your mercy and goodness to me and Joe. Help me to bring all those evil thoughts into captivity in obedience to Christ. Help me to lay aside the spirt of fear and grab hold of the spirit of love, and power and a sound mind. Prepare my heart to be his wife—the helper he needs today and for each day the rest of our lives together. Thank you for the good man You have brought into my life. I dedicate myself to make this marriage everything You desire it to be.*

Louanna came up beside her and whispered, "Are you ready?"

She smiled and whispered, "I'm ready."

Louanna looked beautiful in her light blue dress. Marika had chosen the color and Louanna had chosen the style. She walked down the aisle and took her place in the front of the church opposite Joe and the best man, Alvin.

When the wedding march began, Marika took the arm of John Wertz and began the journey toward her future.

Joe couldn't take his eyes off her as she made her way toward him. *He was sure he had never seen anything so beautiful. Oh, Lord, what have I ever done to deserve this wonderful amazing woman becoming my wife? Thank You for bringing her into my life. I pray I will be the husband she needs to fulfill her life. I dedicate myself this day to make this marriage everything that You desire it to be. Help us grow together in Your ways as we love each other according to Your design.*

When they joined hands at the altar, Marika's hands were shaking and then she realized Joe's hands were shaking, too. They looked at each other and smiled. "This is our day," he whispered. She nodded.

When the marriage vows were spoken by the Pastor and it was Marika's turn to say, "I do" she said, "I do. But I want to say something else, too."

The Pastor seemed surprised but nodded in approval. She began, "This is the happiest day of my life. The Wertz family took me in when

I was the most unloveable young girl you can imagine—lost in a world of fear and confusion. They loved me like I was their long lost sister— even though they couldn't understand one word I said. They showed me Jesus Christ in ways that surpassed language. They made me part of their family—no questions asked. As a result, I came to believe in Jesus Christ as my Savior. Today is joyous not only because Joe wants to marry me but also because today I officially become a Wertz."

The audience applauded.

When Joe's turn came, he answered, "I do." He paused, then added, "But I don't want to be outdone by my soon-to-be wife. I would like to say I have waited two long years for this day. I had to wait for her to grow up. And God knows it was worth the wait. When I first met her, she spoke no English but she won my heart from the first smile. I think that I am the most blessed man in the world today to be marrying this amazing, courageous, loving and clever young lady. I want to pray right now over our marriage. Dear Lord, thank You for the mercy and grace that You have shown to Marika and me. We are incredibly blessed this day to stand before You and all these friends and pledge our love for each other. We dedicate our marriage to You as we declare our love for one another. Amen."

A hush fell over the audience. There was the sense that this was a sacred moment. The couple exchanged rings and then the Pastor said, "I now pronounce you husband and wife. You may kiss the bride."

Joe took Marika in his arms and kissed her very tenderly. The congregation aahed.

Then the Pastor said, "I would like to introduce Mr. and Mrs. Joseph Wertz."

As they left the church, both Joe and Marika tried to hold back the laughter. When they got outside, they looked at each other and burst into laughter as they embraced on the church porch.

After attending the wedding, on the drive back to Welch, Sergeant Weaver said to Sheriff Chatham, "Do you think we could stop by Peter's

Branch on the way? I have never seen the cabin we have discussed so much. And I would like to look at the site of the explosion. I think it would help me close this case in my mind."

The sheriff said, "Sure, that sounds like a good idea for me, too. With the wedding today and Marika's decision about the baby, I feel like this case is closed. Do you realize we've been involved in this case for almost 5 years? Five years and there is still one nagging detail we have no explanation for. Where is Joseph Stanislas? If he were at the still, why didn't we find a body? I am certain he was there because his car was there. Why did he leave the car? If there was a third person there, who was it? Is it possible that Joseph left the site of the still with that third person before the explosion? That's the one thing I would like to have an explanation for. It's been over two years now and no one has reported seeing him or hearing from him."

When they came to the cabin, the sheriff was surprised to see weeds and small saplings had grown up between the floor boards on the porch. The door stood open just like the last time he was there. When they walked in the door, a couple of raccoons scampered around their legs and out the door. Their appearance also disturbed a nest of doves living in the rafters. "Welcome to the wildlife sanctuary!" the Sergeant said with a chuckle.

The sheriff pointed out the cage which was still there as well as the bed. "This is it, Sgt. Weaver. This is where Marika was held for over two years. She was only 12 1/2 years old when she was put in that thing. I shutter to think of what she endured in this place at the hands of that evil man. But I will say it smells better than it did the first day I was here."

"I've seen enough. I think I might be sick if I don't get out of here" the Sergeant said.

The sheriff responded, "When the Wertz brothers brought me here the first time, I did get sick. I lost my breakfast out there in the woods. Are you ready to walk up the hill to the still?"

When they approached the site of the still explosion, the sheriff remarked, "It's been about two years since I was last here. It's so grown over now it's hard to see what happened—or even imagine it. For your information, the coroner gathered all the body parts we could find. Angelo Purilli was blown to smithereens. I'm glad we finally got the FBI confirmation on the fingerprints."

The sheriff walked around the still while Sergeant Weaver walked further up the hill along the perimeter of the clearing that surrounded the location of the still. As she walked, she looked into the woods. She wasn't looking for anything in particular but she spotted something blue on the floor of the woods. She decided to check it out and discovered that it was a blue jacket. When she lifted the jacket, a partial skeleton was revealed. Upon further investigation, other fabric pieces were removed to disclose a fairly complete human skeleton."

She walked out of the woods and called the sheriff to have a look. She reached into the pocket of the jacket in her hand and pulled out a wallet. The wallet held a driver's license and identification for Joseph Stanislas. Tucked into the pocket was a piece of paper that had been folded. It was damp and falling apart. Without mentioning it to the Sheriff, the Sergeant put it in her pocket.

"This is the final piece of the puzzle" the sheriff said. "Now, Marika can be at peace. She has a new husband who adores her and her future looks bright."

On the way back to Welch, the sheriff said, "Am I glad you suggested we stop there! I guess we didn't think to look in the woods for bodies. I don't know what the coroner can tell us about the circumstances of the death from the skeleton but I am more than ready to put this case to rest. What do you think? I would guess he was injured and stunned and then ran to try to get away from the explosion and died there from his injuries—possibly from inhalation of the flames and smoke."

When they returned to headquarters, Sgt. Mary Weaver took the piece of paper from her pocket. As she unfolded it, the moist paper came apart in her hands. She carefully pulled the pieces apart and placed them on her desk and then reassembled them much like one works a jigsaw puzzle. She was shocked to see:

DOOR UNLOCKED J.

She thought, I don't want to think about what this note means. I'm so afraid that it means what I think it means. This is a secret that will stay with me. It never needs to be revealed. She wadded the moist paper in her hand and tossed it in the waste basket under her desk.

Shortly, the sheriff came out of his office. "I'm headin' home".

She said, "I'm glad this case has been solved. From the day the Wertz brothers came, there has been a sadness that has sort of hovered over the whole thing, for me. Today showed me how their faith in God pulled her through something so horrendous it is hard to imagine. As I watched that couple today, there was pure joy in that place. I wanted to jump up and sing Amazing Grace. That's what I thought of when they were taking their vows. There was a sense of real victory over life's hardest struggle. Today was a triumph for them and for both families."

The Sheriff said, "I hate to say this, but I don't think there will be a lot of tears shed for Joseph Stanislas when they get the news, do you?

Before she could answer, he added, "I guess that means we can release that fine automobile that has been sitting in the county garage for over two years. I think that would be an excellent wedding present for Marika and Joe, don't you?"

When all the guests had left the reception, Joe said to Marika, "I have a surprise for you. I had some help from our brothers and Louanna. We all wanted to surprise you. I am going to blindfold you. So you just relax and when it's the right time, I'll remove your blindfold."

After her blindfold was in place, Joe said, "Are you sure you can't see?"

"Come on, Joe, I can't see a thing and besides it's getting dark." Joe picked her up and carried her to the barn. Then he said, "now, put your arms around my neck and hold tight. This next part may jostle you around a little." He walked carefully up the ramp that the boys had built to replace the ladder to the hay loft. When he sat her down, she commented, "This smells like the barn. What are you doing, Joe?"

Joe said, "Okay, let's take off the blindfold." When he removed the blindfold, she could hardly believe her eyes. White sheets had been draped around the perimeter of the hay loft enclosing the whole area into a private room. In the middle of the room was a bed built from the hay bales and cushioned with layers of quilts and padding and then covered with sheets and piles of pillows. The bed was covered with a brand new quilt with a heart in the center. Within the heart was embroidered

Joe and Marika
April 29, 1939

Hanging from a nail to one side she saw the gown she had chosen for her wedding night.

As Joe lit the lanterns that hung from the rafters, Marika said, "I can't believe you thought of this. It is magical."

Joe said, "This is the place where we found you—I wanted it to be the place where we discover each other."

Then he continued, "Louanna has put everything she thought you would need over in that corner. I'm going to go get another surprise and I'll be back soon."

In a matter of moments, Joe returned with a tray containing two pieces of wedding cake, a pitcher of punch and two of the fanciest glasses in Mohegan.

He took one look at his bride and set the tray on the hay bale prepared for it. "You—you take my breath away. I am speechless" he said.

He took her in his arms and looked in her eyes. There was no sign of fear or anxiety. That was the look he had longed to see. "Happy?" he asked,

"Happy!" she said.

God continues to work out His perfect plan through times of adversity and times of prosperity.

Underneath are the Everlasting Arms

The Everlasting Arms

AFTERWORD

In the story you have just read, you have seen the tragic life of a young woman set before you. Most of the hardships in her life were not of her own making. In every sense of the word, she was a victim. She was the victim of her father, who used his daughter for his own purposes. She was the victim of a pedophile who kidnapped and abused her. She was the victim of repeated rape which resulted in pregnancy. Her baby was stolen from her at birth. One can hardly imagine a young girl more tragically victimized than Marika in this story.

When you were reading the story, did you rejoice with Marika when she identified her child and had hopes for a happy reunion of birth mother with her baby? Were you disappointed when she chose to leave Zoe with the Ball family? If you were, though I have no statistics to prove my point, I suspect you would be among the majority of readers. Mothers belong with their babies—babies belong with their mothers. Although she never got a good look at the child she bore, having no knowledge of its gender, she grieved when she thought the child had died. There was a longing within Marika for that baby, even though the circumstances of conception and birth of the child were no doubt painful in every imaginable way.

When I began to write this story, I had in mind she would find her baby and marry her prince in the end. But as the story unfolded and the characters developed, I found myself wrapped up in Marika's decision.

One might say I got personally involved with the character. Would she claim the child? Should she leave the child with the Ball's? I at first thought I would have Marika fight for parental rights for Zoe, using the blanket fragment to connect the infant with her and the cabin. Then I thought it would be better for Zoe to stay with the Ball family where she had been loved from birth. Out of his compassion, Ronnie Ball sought to help her, Marika ran away because of fear. Would fear be a good place for Marika to begin her effort to gain custody of the infant? During the process of deciding which way to take the character of Marika in this story, I thought at length about the heart-wrenching decision that Marika made. While working Marika through her decisions, I came to appreciate afresh the two young women who, many years ago, made the same decision Marika made. Those decisions, which were selfless and made out of love and concern for the child, enabled me to become a mother. Motherhood has been the greatest joy and blessing of my life. God's ways are indeed above our ways and His thoughts are higher than our thoughts.

Marika found herself in a situation where she could not provide for her child—either materially or emotionally. It wasn't because she had no desire or love for the child. Just the opposite, she desired a loving family and a stable home for her daughter because she loved her. When she chose to leave Zoe in a loving home with a "twin brother", she did it out of deep love for her birth-child and at a depth of personal sacrifice only those who have faced similar circumstances can understand. Although she had never had the chance to bond with her baby, she was a true mother when she made her decisions. Mothers are the most unselfish individuals in any society. When Marika performed this selfless act for her daughter—it was a step of faith for her. God had interceded to protect her child from birth. She trusted Him for the future— she had already seen her child resting in the Everlasting Arms.

Beverly G. Urps Scellato
Mother's Day, 2020